CHILDREN'S GAMES IN THE
NEW MEDIA AGE

D1522070

Ashgate Studies in Childhood, 1700 to the Present

Series Editor: Claudia Nelson, Texas A&M University, USA

This series recognizes and supports innovative work on the child and on literature for children and adolescents that informs teaching and engages with current and emerging debates in the field. Proposals are welcome for interdisciplinary and comparative studies by humanities scholars working in a variety of fields, including literature; book history, periodicals history, and print culture and the sociology of texts; theater, film, musicology, and performance studies; history, including the history of education; gender studies; art history and visual culture; cultural studies; and religion.

Topics might include, among other possibilities, how concepts and representations of the child have changed in response to adult concerns; postcolonial and transnational perspectives; "domestic imperialism" and the acculturation of the young within and across class and ethnic lines; the commercialization of childhood and children's bodies; views of young people as consumers and/or originators of culture; the child and religious discourse; children's and adolescents' self-representations; and adults' recollections of childhood.

Also in the series

The Making of Modern Children's Literature in Britain
Publishing and Criticism in the 1960s and 1970s
Lucy Pearson

Young People and the Shaping of Public Space in Melbourne, 1870–1914
Simon Sleight

Representations of China in British Children's Fiction, 1851-1911
Shih-Wen Chen

Contemporary Adolescent Literature and Culture
The Emergent Adult
Edited by Mary Hilton and Maria Nikolajeva

Children's Games in the New Media Age

Childlore, Media and the Playground

Edited by

ANDREW BURN
Institute of Education, University of London, UK

AND

CHRIS RICHARDS
Institute of Education, University of London, UK

ASHGATE

Library
Quest University Canada
3200 University Boulevard
Squamish, BC V8B 0N8

© Andrew Burn, Chris Richards and the contributors 2014

All rights reserved. No part of this publication may be reproduced, stored in a retrieval system or transmitted in any form or by any means, electronic, mechanical, photocopying, recording or otherwise without the prior permission of the publisher.

Andrew Burn and Chris Richards have asserted their right under the Copyright, Designs and Patents Act, 1988, to be identified as the editors of this work.

Published by
Ashgate Publishing Limited
Wey Court East
Union Road
Farnham
Surrey, GU9 7PT
England

Ashgate Publishing Company
110 Cherry Street
Suite 3-1
Burlington, VT 05401-3818
USA

www.ashgate.com

British Library Cataloguing in Publication Data
A catalogue record for this book is available from the British Library

The Library of Congress has cataloged the printed edition as follows:
Children's games in the new media age: childlore, media and the playground / edited by
    Andrew Nicholas Burn and Christopher Owen Richards.
    pages cm. — (Ashgate studies in childhood, 1700 to the present)
    Includes index.
    ISBN 978-1-4094-5024-5 (hardcover: alk. paper) — ISBN 978-1-4094-5025-2
(pbk: alk. paper) — ISBN 978-1-4094-5026-9 (cbook) — ISBN 978-1-4724-0146-5 (epub)
    1. Games. 2. Games and technology. I. Burn, Andrew Nicholas. II. Richards, Christopher
Owen.
    GV1203.C344 2014
    790.1'922—dc23

                                                                2013029927

ISBN: 9781409450245 (hbk)
ISBN: 9781409450252 (pbk)
ISBN: 9781409450269 (ebk – PDF)
ISBN: 9781409450269 (ebk – ePUB)

Printed in the United Kingdom by Henry Ling Limited,
at the Dorset Press, Dorchester, DT1 1HD

This book is dedicated to Iona Opie, without whose work our project would have been impossible.

Contents

List of Figures and Tables   *ix*
Notes on the Editors and Contributors   *xi*
Acknowledgements   *xiii*

1   Children's Playground Games in the New Media Age   1
    Andrew Burn

2   The Opie Recordings: What's Left to be Heard?   31
    Laura Jopson, Andrew Burn, Jonathan Robinson

3   'That's how the whole hand-clap thing passes on': Online/Offline
    Transmission and Multimodal Variation in a Children's Clapping
    Game   53
    Julia C. Bishop

4   Rough Play, Play Fighting and Surveillance: School Playgrounds as
    Sites of Dissonance, Controversy and Fun   85
    Chris Richards

5   The Relationship between Online and Offline Play: Friendship and
    Exclusion   109
    Jackie Marsh

6   Remixing Children's Cultures: Media-Referenced Play on the
    Playground   133
    Rebekah Willett

7   The Game Catcher: A Computer Game and Research Tool for
    Embodied Movement   153
    Grethe Mitchell

8   Co-Curating Children's Play Cultures   187
    John Potter

Postscript: The People in the Playground   207
    Chris Richards and Andrew Burn

Index   *215*

List of Figures and Tables

Figures

1.1   Children playing a ring game "Rosy apples, lemon & a pear",
        Leyland gas works, Lancashire, Oct 1967. Photograph by
        Fr. Damian Webb. Copyright courtesy of the Pitt Rivers
        Museum [2003.88.2594]   5

1.2   The children's home page of the Playtimes site - Design by
        Bjorn Rune Lie   6

2.1   Four versions of 'Under the Bram Bush'. Transcription by Julia
        Bishop.   44

3.1   Media sources influencing the learning of clapping games at
        Monteney schoolSchool   59

3.2   Transmission of 'Eeny Meeny Dessameeny' at Monteney School,
        2006–2010   64

3.3   'Eeny Meeny Dessameeny' as sung by Meredith and Sally
        (v01636)   77

4.1   The author, circa 1956   87

5.1   Per cent frequency of Internet use (n=173)   110

5.2   Offline friendships in Class 4   116

5.3   Online friendships in Class 4   117

7.1   Individual hand orientations for clapping games.   166

7.2   Trace visualisation using the Kinect for the full body skeleton and
        Wiimotes for hand orientation   171

7.3   Children's drawings of suggested additional games   173

7.4   Testing the full body multiplayer version of the *Game Catcher*.
        Photograph by Chris Richards.   175

7.5   A selection of children's comments and suggestions after
        user-testing the *Game Catcher*   177

8.1   The Kids' Zone interface from the Playtimes pages on the site,
       by Danish artist Bjorn Rune Lie (2011)   191

8.2   'Games from now and then'   193

8.3   Some favourite games suggested for the web page by one of the
       children in the project   195

8.4   Proposed waiting game for visitors to the site   196

8.5   Games of the past and present   197

8.6   Skipping games as drawn for the animated sequences   200

8.7   Conker game drawn for the animated sequences   201

8.8   Sailor on the sea drawn for the animated sequences   202

Tables

3.1   Comparison of movement patterns in 'Eeny Meeny Dessameeny'
       performances   74

3.2   Musical features of 'Eeny Meeny Dessameeny' performances
       compared   79

5.1   Children's favourite Internet sites   111

6.1   Practices of media-referenced play   137

Notes on the Editors and Contributors

Andrew Burn is Professor of Media Education at the Institute of Education, University of London, and co-director of the DARE centre (Digital | Arts | Research | Education). He has researched and published widely in the fields of media literacy, young people's production of moving image media and computer games and multimodal semiotics. He previously taught English, Drama and Media in schools in the UK. His most recent book is *Making New Media: Creative Production and Digital Literacies* (2009). He was Principal Investigator for 'Children's Playground Games and Songs in the New Media Age'.

Chris Richards, now retired, was a Senior Lecturer in the Department of Culture, Communication and Media at the Institute of Education, University of London, and an ethnographer for the Playground Games project. He co-authored *Children, Media and Playground Cultures: Ethnographic Studies of School Playtimes* (with Willett, Marsh, Burn and Bishop, 2013). He is the author of *Young People, Popular Culture and Education* (2011), *Forever Young: Essays on Young Adult Fictions* (2008) and *Teen Spirits: Music and Identity in Media Education* (1998).

Julia C. Bishop is a researcher at the University of Sheffield and the University of Aberdeen, specialising in traditional music and children's folklore from historical and contemporary ethnographic perspectives. She leads the team working on a multi-volume critical edition of the James Madison Carpenter Collection of folk song and drama and is a past editor of *Folk Music Journal*. Her publications include *Play Today in the Primary School Playground* (co-edited with Mavis Curtis, 2001), *Inclusion of Disabled Children in Primary School Playgrounds* (co-authored with Helen Woolley, Jane Ginsborg, Mavis Curtis and Marc Armitage, 2005) and *The New Penguin Book of English Folk Songs* (co-edited with Steve Roud, 2012).

Laura Jopson was researcher for the Children's Playground Games project at the British Library, where she was responsible for annotating the digitised recordings in the Opie Collection and the creation of the project's website 'Playtimes' (http://www.playtimes.bl.uk). She previously undertook an MA at the University of Oxford, where she researched children's culture in relation to the Opie archive at the Bodleian for her dissertation.

Jackie Marsh is Professor of Education at the University of Sheffield. Her research focuses on the role and nature of popular culture, media, new technologies in literacy education and children's out-of-school literacy practices. Recent publications include: *Handbook of Early Childhood Literacy,* 2nd edition (co-edited with Larson, 2012), *Children's Virtual Play Worlds: Culture, Learning and*

Participation (co-edited with Burke, in press) and *Virtual Literacies: Interactive Spaces for Children and Young People* (co-edited with Merchant, Gillen and Davies, 2012). She is an editor of the *Journal of Early Childhood Literacy* (Sage).

Grethe Mitchell is Reader in Digital and New Media at the University of Lincoln. Her research interests include movement capture and embodied interaction and she has written widely on videogames. As part of the project, she led the development of *The Game Catcher* – an innovative computer game which also acts as a motion capture research tool for recording, visualising and analysing movement – and made *Ipidipidation My Generation*, a documentary film about children's contemporary playground games. She is editor of *The Theory, Practice and Art of Movement Capture*. Newcastle Upon Tyne: Cambridge Scholars Publishing (forthcoming 2014) and co-edited *Videogames and Art.* Chicago: University of Chicago Press (with Andy Clarke, 2nd edition, 2013).

John Potter is a Senior Lecturer in Education and New Media in the Department of Culture, Communication and Media, Institute of Education, University of London. His research interests include digital video production by young learners; cultural practices and new literacies: memory, self-representation and curatorship; media education: investigating ICT, creative activity and learner agency. He is the author of *Digital Media and Learner Identity: The New Curatorship*, published by Palgrave Macmillan in 2012.

Jonathan Robinson is Lead Curator of Sociolinguistics and Education at the British Library. He is responsible for the Library's collection of sound recordings of vernacular speech and his research focuses primarily on English accents and dialects. Jonnie selects content for the Library's online dialect archive at http://sounds.bl.uk/ and created *Sounds Familiar*, an educational website that explores and celebrates regional speech in the UK. He curated the BL exhibition, *Evolving English: One Language, Many Voices* and is currently working on *Voices of the UK*, a project to establish a searchable online dataset of British regional speech.

Rebekah Willett is an Assistant Professor of Library and Information Studies at the University of Wisconsin-Madison. She has conducted research on children's media cultures, focusing on issues of gender, play, literacy and learning. Her publications include work on playground games, amateur camcorder cultures, young people's online activities and children's story writing. Her publications include *Children, Media and Playground Cultures: Ethnographic Studies of School Playtimes* (co-authored with Richards, Marsh, Burn and Bishop, 2013), *Home Truths? Video Production and Domestic Life* (co-authored with Buckingham and Pini, 2010), *Play, Creativity and Digital Technologies* (co-edited with Robinson and Marsh, 2008) and *Video Practices: Media Technology and Amateur Creativity* (co-edited with Buckingham, 2009).

Acknowledgements

We are indebted to the children and staff of Monteney and Christopher Hatton Primary Schools, whose support over the two years of working together provided us with our research data and a lot of fun – even on the coldest days. We would like to acknowledge the dedication of the children's panel at Monteney and the student councils at Christopher Hatton and the coordinating staff members, Nicola Shipman and Peter Winter (Monteney), Clare McBride and Gwen Lee (Christopher Hatton).

We would like to thank the British Library for their dedication to the archiving of children's cultural materials, for hosting our children's panels and the dissemination event; and Anna Lobbenberg for her scrupulous work in creating a rich and interactive website to support the wider public profile of the project. Data from both of the schools involved in the project are held in the British Library archive and are cited with the prefixes MP and CH in this book. We are also indebted to the Pitt Rivers Museum, Oxford, for their collaboration and help with the Damian Webb collection; and to the Bodleian Library, Oxford for their assistance with the Opie manuscript archive.

We would like to thank the UK's Arts and Humanities Research Council which funded this project as part of the *Beyond Text* programme; and Professor Evelyn Welch, Director of *Beyond Text*, and Ruth Hogarth, *Beyond Text* administrator, both of whom personally supported the project throughout.

We are indebted to the advisory group who contributed substantially to the project, especially: Michael Rosen, Liz Grugeon, David Grugeon, Dan Jones, Malcolm Taylor, Peter Blatchford, Roger Walshe, Seth Giddings, Clive Hurst, John Potter, Lucy Green and Tim Shortis. We are also grateful for the extensive support of Steve Roud and Kathy Marsh, whose wealth of expertise informed our research incalculably.

Chapter 1

Children's Playground Games in the New Media Age

Andrew Burn

Introduction: Childhood, Childlore and the Media

> The generally-held opinion, both inside and outside academic circles, was that children no longer cherished their traditional lore. We were told that the young had lost the power of entertaining themselves; that the cinema, the wireless, and television had become the focus of their attention; and that we had started our investigation fifty years too late. (Opie and Opie, 1959: v)

This book emerges from a project[1] centrally concerned with the relationship between children's traditional play cultures and their media-based play, an issue addressed by the British folklorists Iona and Peter Opie over 50 years ago. We explored this relationship in a variety of ways, described in this chapter and more fully in the chapters that follow. Briefly, we pursued five activities. We digitised, catalogued and selectively analysed the sound recordings of Iona and Peter Opie in the British Library Sound Archive – recordings of children's playground and street games from the 1970s and 80s. We conducted a two-year ethnographic study of play and games in two primary school playgrounds in the UK, one in London, one in Sheffield. We developed a website at the British Library (www.bl.uk/playtimes), which presents examples of games over the last century, including selections from both the Opie archive and our own study. We made a documentary film of the games played in these two playgrounds. Finally, we developed a proof-of-concept prototype motion tracking research tool and computer game adaptation which both captures children's physical play and allows them to play against the computer.

The intention was to build on the pioneering work of the Opies, and re-present their audio recordings for new and old audiences; and to extend and add to the body of work they and others have accumulated over the last 60 years or so. The project carried the study of oral transmission into the cultural moment of the digital age, where the fluidity, performativity and inventiveness of playground games, the computer game console and the participatory internet co-exist and interpenetrate.

---

[1]   The project was funded by the UK's Arts and Humanities Research Council under the Beyond Text programme. It was entitled 'Children's Playground Games and Songs in the New Media Age', and ran from April 2009 to May 2011.

This chapter will briefly consider the history of popular and academic perceptions of children's games, songs and rhymes, in relation to changing constructions of childhood and of the agency of children. It will then describe the research project before moving on to propose three broad categories to help identify what might be specific to children's games in the age of new media.

In the academic field, children's folklore has been an object of study for over 150 years, with researchers recognising playground games and songs as important cultural texts. Early collections enact a desire to preserve and protect traditional rhymes and games (Halliwell 1849; Gomme 1894/8), while more recent ones emphasise the inventiveness and richness of an oral tradition sustained by children alone (Opie and Opie, 1959, 1969, 1985).

A notable theme of this research is what the Opies call the 'wear and repair during transmission' (1959). Studies note the interplay between historical continuities and the continual change, evident in playground responses to contemporary cultural preoccupations. Children's games reflect 'continuity and change, stability and variation, dynamism and conservatism' (Bishop and Curtis, 2001: 10). We explored these paradoxes of oral culture, setting them against analogous forms of preservation and rapid change in the new media of the digital age.

Children's playground games have been investigated from various perspectives: as forms of identity and socialisation (James, 1993); as linguistic patterns (Crystal, 1998); as informal literacies (Grugeon, 1988); as musical and compositional practice (Marsh, 2008); as forms of creative learning (Bishop and Curtis, 2001) and, of course, as play (Sutton-Smith, 1995; 2001). However, our team was multi-disciplinary, including specialisms in folklore and ethnomusicology, media and cultural studies, software design, history and sociolinguistics. This gave us the opportunity to conduct a conversation about the phenomena of play from several different perspectives, applying different analytical and theoretical approaches. While we cannot pretend to have produced an ideal inter-disciplinary synthesis, we can at least claim to have made a sustained effort to attend to the many different aspects of playground culture that we found, in ways unconfined by any one of these disciplines.

Although many collections record the integration of popular cultural references (pop songs, advertising jingles, theme tunes, soap operas and other genres) into games and songs, the evolving relation of play to the media cultures of contemporary childhood has remained under-researched, though there has been a long-standing critique of the infiltration of popular and commercial culture into children's play (Elkind, 2006; Postman, 1983). However, the Opies found productive connections between play and the practices of children's media culture and, more recently, Marsh (2001) and Bishop et al (2006) have also emphasised the importance of media cultures to children's play. Our research develops this theme, finding evidence of a rich expansion of pretend play drawing on the landscape of both old and new media, including dramatic games which incorporate the structures, imagery and rule-systems of computer games.

The Work of the Project

The project had five major outcomes, which are represented in various ways across the chapters of this book.

The British Library Digital Archive

The digital archive includes *The Opie Collection of Children's Games and Songs,* now fully annotated and catalogued, and available as streamed audio to researchers worldwide at www.bl.uk/sounds. This collection of recordings contains a good deal of material never published before, revealing some new themes: the more extreme scatological and taboo-breaching songs and rhymes the Opies collected; the wide range of variations on 'classic' singing games and many examples of the media influences that informed the culture of play. These new themes form the subject of Chapter 2, in which Jopson, Burn and Robinson explore the significance of selected unpublished material in the archive.

We also added a wide variety of material from the ethnographic studies conducted during the project, which documented playground games in two playgrounds, in the UK cities of Sheffield and London. This material represents a sustained ethnographic investigation of playground play, including new games, songs and rhymes and the wider contexts of play.

We extended the archive beyond our original plans; contact with other researchers in this field became a very productive aspect of the project. Kathryn Marsh, of the Sydney Conservatorium of Music, and author of *The Musical Playground* (Marsh, 2008) visited the UK to give a seminar and act as discussant for our Interim Conference at the London Knowledge Lab. She subsequently generously donated her substantial collection of games and songs, from several different countries (including the UK), to our archive. Taken as a whole, then, this archive exceeded our original aims, promising to become an important international resource for future researchers. It combines historical depth, from the 1970s to the present day, with international reach, including games from Australia, the UK, America and Scandinavia.

The Ethnographic Study

The ethnographic studies were conducted over the two years of the project (April 2009 to May 2011) in our two partner primary schools. Monteney Primary School in Sheffield serves a working class community in the north west of the city and there are extensive grounds surrounding the school building. It had 450 pupils. Its most recent Ofsted[2] report noted that the school: '... is in an area of significant social and economic deprivation with above average levels of free school meals. The percentage of pupils with learning difficulties and/or disabilities is above average.

---

[2] Ofsted (Office for Standards in Education) is the independent inspection service for schools in England, reporting directly to Parliament.

Most pupils are from white British backgrounds and very few speak English as an additional language' (Ofsted, 2007). Christopher Hatton Primary School is on the edge of the Clerkenwell district of London, serving a multiethnic community. During the project, the school was attended by 220 children, of whom about 40 per cent were entitled to free school meals. There were at least 20 'minority ethnic groups', and about 68 per cent of the children were listed as coming from families in which the first language was not English. Indeed there were so many different languages among the school population that, on the whole, English prevailed as the common language in the playground. Nevertheless, there were occasional instances of younger children using Bengali and, from discussions with children themselves, it was apparent that, often, their home language was a significant and continuing aspect of their self-identities. For some, linguistic identifications were also entwined with refugee status (about 26 per cent of the school population).

The ethnographic research recorded many instances of games, songs and rhymes recognisable as latter-day versions of the Opie 'repertoire', demonstrating continuity as well as change. Versions of many of the clapping games published in *The Singing Game* were found, as well as examples of counting-out rhymes, skipping games, chasing games and ball games. At the same time, it was clear that some genres had diminished: hopscotch, conkers and French skipping, for example (though reports of hopscotch were documented on the Sheffield playground). But we also found many new instances of play, in particular a rich variety of play informed by children's media cultures (computer games, reality TV, pop songs, musicals and films) and pretend play enacting scenarios which often intermingled domestic and fantasy settings: families, superheroes, fairies, witches and zombies. The relationship between playground play and children's media cultures is explored in Chapter 5, in which Jackie Marsh considers the connection between children's online and offline play; and Chapter 6, in which Rebekah Willett analyses the forms and functions of media references in playground games. Where possible, we also considered the wider social and institutional framing of play enacted, and regulated, in closely supervised school playgrounds. There was evidence, for example, that some forms of play – those regarded as rough or as resembling real world violence – were the focus of considerable adult anxiety and concern. These enduring, but also heightened, adult misgivings are discussed by Chris Richards in Chapter 4.

We conducted surveys of the children in the two schools, partly to get a sense of the favourite games of *all* the children (rather than just the ones who were filmed or interviewed); and partly to get a picture of the media cultures that lie beyond the playground, in children's media consumption at home. Julia Bishop and Jackie Marsh, in Sheffield, and Chris Richards and Rebekah Willett, in London, also worked with panels of children representing all the ages and classes in each school. The intention was to work with the children as researchers, giving them Flip video cameras to record their own play and interview their fellow students. This approach acknowledged children as social actors able to play an active role in projects relating to their cultural worlds (James and Prout, 1990). The videos collected by the children added substantially to those made by the researchers.

Fig. 1.1   Children playing a ring game "Rosy apples, lemon & a pear", Leyland gas works, Lancashire, Oct 1967. Photograph by Fr. Damian Webb. Copyright and courtesy Pitt Rivers Museum [2003.88.2594]

The Website: Playtimes: A Century of Children's Playground Games and Rhymes

The website was intended to display selections from the Opie archive alongside samples of play video-recorded in the two schools, in order to represent the historical changes and continuities evident across the Opie collection and today's playgrounds. In the event, we discovered new material which significantly enhanced the content of the website, such as archive film from the British Film Institute, expanding the historical scope of the site to the century indicated in its title. Most importantly, we collaborated with the Bodleian Libraries University of Oxford, to whom the Opies donated their manuscript archive; and the Pitt Rivers museum, University of Oxford, which holds an important collection of the photographer Father Damian Webb. The Bodleian collection provided valuable examples of written accounts of games sent by children and teachers to the Opies; while the Damian Webb collection provided examples of high-quality audio recordings from the mid-twentieth century, as well as strikingly beautiful black-and-white photographs of children at play (Figure 1.1).

The design of the website proved to be an innovative form of library exhibition, especially in terms of the extensive consultation carried out with children in our partner schools (Figure 1.2). We held workshops with the panels of children in the schools and involved them in three ways: as researchers, designers and curators.

Fig. 1.2   The children's home page of the Playtimes site – Design by Bjorn Rune Lie

They added significantly to the research and collection of their own games, making their own videos and interviews. They contributed concept drawings for the visual design and navigational structure of the website. They produced animations introducing the nine categories of play in the children's route through the site, serving as a form of curatorial interpretation (Potter, 2009). The nature of these forms of research, (re)presentation and interpretation are considered by John Potter in Chapter 8, employing the metaphor of curation to theorise the voice of the child in these processes.

The Game Catcher Prototype

The *Game Catcher* adapts the motion sensitive videogame controllers of the Nintendo Wii and Microsoft Kinect to create an application which allows the recording, playback, archiving and analysis of playground games in 3D. Chapter 7, by Grethe Mitchell, considers the relationship between playground games and the movement-based games of platforms such as Wii and Kinect, both in terms of their ludic structures and in terms of their location in children's cultural lives.

The *Game Catcher* had two main aims. One was to develop a proof of concept of a system which would provide researchers in the arts and humanities with new and improved ways of archiving and analysing movement-based activities. The archiving of playground games currently relies upon video (or previously, as in the Opie and Webb collections, upon audio recording supplemented by still photographs). These provide an incomplete record – even video only records the events from a single viewpoint and can therefore leave details obscured or off-screen. The *Game Catcher* avoids these shortcomings by recording the position in 3D space of every major joint of the body. By recording the raw movement data and attaching it to a three-dimensional model or figure, the movement can be animated and viewed from any angle in 'real time' and at various frame-speeds. In addition, other alternative forms of visualisation – for instance tracing the path taken by the hands throughout the entire game – also become possible.

In parallel with this, the *Game Catcher* had a second aim, which was to develop a new and innovative type of computer game. This exercise was partly intended as a form of cultural intervention. We have seen how, in popular discourse, 'traditional' games and songs are often opposed to electronic or computer games which are seen to embody suspect, sedentary forms of play. By developing a computer game version of a playground clapping game, we were able to explore the tensions between these fields, as well as the areas for overlap and both actual and potential synergies. Clapping games were chosen because they contain fast movement within a constrained physical space, thereby offering a suitable level of technical challenge.

There was also some evidence in the ethnographic studies that experiences of computer games migrated into physical games on the playground. The *Game Catcher* reverses this process, asking what it would be like for physical games to become computer games. Although children's media play is often seen as distinct from and even antagonistic to what are perceived as more traditional forms of play. These traditional forms are in many ways similar to the way in which play is structured in computer games. They are routinised, formulaic, rule-governed, finely balanced between accessibility and challenge and often incorporate narrative elements.

The children's panels were involved in testing prototype versions, experimenting with different kinds of movements both related to games and to other forms such as dance; and making suggestions for further development of the prototype. The *Game Catcher* was developed with open source software and is written in the programming language Processing.

The Documentary Film

The documentary film *Ipi-dipi-dation, My Generation,* made by Grethe Mitchell, draws on ethnographic and observational methods and provides a detailed overview of playground culture and the diversity of play in the two primary school playgrounds in London and Sheffield. In doing so it follows in the tradition of filmic and photographic records of children's games, such as *The Dusty Bluebells*, the 1971 film of Belfast children's street games by David Hammond; *The Singing Street* (Norton Park Group, Edinburgh, 1951) and *One Potato, Two Potato* (Leslie Daiken, 1957). The film, like the rest of our project, updates the picture, showing how children draw both on the long historical tradition of games passed from child to child, generation to generation; and also on the resources of their own contemporary media cultures. The film was shot and edited to give children's voices the dominant role in describing and interpreting their play.

The making of the documentary was influenced by ethnographic and anthropological film practices and the work of film makers like Frederick Wiseman, in which the structure and narrative of the film emerge from the recorded material, rather than filming with a preconceived idea of storyline or result. The capture of activities of play was therefore mainly observational although a deliberate choice was also made not to hide the presence of the film-maker, whose voice can sometimes be heard in the film. In keeping with the observational nature of the film and with the aim of communicating the ephemeral and sometimes chaotic nature of play, activities were filmed as they occurred, without staging. The film-maker was also keen to avoid the idealisation of children's play. Rather than using an adult voiceover, for instance, the documentary includes interviews with the children themselves (filmed over the course of two years) to provide commentary and interpretation, acknowledging that children can speak reflectively about their play.

In the language of film and the moving image, camera placement and height is meaningful. Conventionally, looking down onto someone from a higher position indicates a relationship of power. In filming the documentary, careful attention was paid to the implications of camera positioning so that, in terms of height and position, the subjects of the documentary (the children) would be viewed as 'on the same level' as the audience. This reduces the unequal power relations often encountered in the representation of children, and again positions children as valid interlocutors of their own experience and culture.

The Changing Landscape of Play

Our exploration of the Opie Collection produced two important benefits. Firstly, it revealed, in detail, what it was like for Iona Opie and her colleagues to research children's games during the 1970s and 80s. It confirmed the status of the work as substantial ethnography, as a contribution to the landscape of childhood studies as it is today, and as a body of data even more wide-ranging than the Opies' publications might suggest.

Secondly, it provided insights into the social and cultural lives of children over these decades. While we have not conducted a formal comparative study, our project had to consider histories of play in relation to the evidence of the Opie archive and of our own data. Such a history might look at how contemporary childhoods differ from the decades when the Opies conducted their research. Family structures are more dynamic, technological advances have transformed communicative practices between family members and peers, children are the focus for more intense market research and a clearer target for the activities of commercial companies than in previous generations (Buckingham, 2000; 2011; Holland, 2004; Pugh, 2009). The boundaries between various phases of childhood and adulthood are more diffuse, an example being the market category 'tweenhood', which shifts the boundary between early childhood and youth (Willett, 2006). One might assume that children are also much stronger social agents, with greater control over aspects of their lives than in previous generations; and in some ways, this is the case (James, Jenks and Prout, 1998). Children have access to more choices in relation to leisure activities, subject to socio-economic status, and some technologies afford them greater independence from adults than in previous eras.

Nonetheless, there are aspects of childhood which have become more constrained since the mid-twentieth century. Recent decades have seen the increased institutionalisation of the child, through standardised approaches to education and the extension of the welfare state into previously marginal areas of childcare and health, with the result that there is both increased provision in these areas for families living in areas of low socio-economic status, in addition to increased surveillance from a range of professionals (Rose, 1989/1999). Children are the focus of much greater efforts to control their access to environments outside the home, with many parents and carers reluctant to allow children to play freely on the street or in community areas (Gill, 2007; Guldberg, 2009). These dichotomies and contradictions framed the work of our study and informed our understanding of how contemporary childhoods are literally played out in the spaces of school grounds.

In terms of perceptions of children's play, the cultures of the playground and the street have always been objects of adult concern. Ever since children's games, songs, rhymes, rituals and objects of play were first documented in the mid-nineteenth century, there have been concerns over their vulnerability to a succession of perceived threats. Campaigners for children's singing games in the latter half of the nineteenth century and the early twentieth century sought to document and reintroduce traditional games into schools, fearful that the twin dangers of industrialisation and urbanisation were killing them off (Roud, 2010). Research since then has established beyond doubt, however, that this culture is much more robust than is often supposed; and the work of the Opies has been, perhaps, the most visible effort in making the case for this persistence of cultural tradition.

Nevertheless, in spite of the research evidence to the contrary, perceptions of disappearing play continue. In April 2006, the UK tabloid newspaper *The Daily Express* carried the headline 'Skipping? Hopscotch? Games are a mystery to the iPod generation'. The article continued to report a poll of 2,000 parents and families conducted by the Sainsbury's supermarket chain which claimed that traditional games had entirely disappeared and children now ate crisps, played with technological gadgets and hung around shops. This perception can be seen as part of a wider popular anxiety about 'toxic childhood', which connects worries about health, sexuality and socialisation with obvious scapegoats, in particular changing cultures and technologies of media production and consumption (Palmer, 2007).

A central theme in the anxiety about childhood play is the question of children's agency. Successive social constructions of childhood imagine children as vulnerable, whether from a position of innocence or original sin (James, Jenks and Prout, 1998; Buckingham, 2000). Romantic fantasies of childhood attribute a greater degree of agency, as in Rousseau's or Blake's child-figures. But not until quite recently have researchers sought empirical evidence for childhood as a powerful cultural phenomenon, its rules, social practices and culture to a large degree created by children. The Opies themselves were early advocates of this view, perceiving the childlore of street and playground as a kind of folk art, and insisting on the self-sufficiency of children's culture, deriving their argument from their own detailed studies of play and games which anticipated the ethnographic approaches of later scholars (see Chapter 2; Goodwin, 2006). These arguments are reviewed in the new sociology of childhood. James, Jenks and Prout, for example, subsume the Opies' argument within an anthropological approach they term *the tribal child*, and which they set against other approaches, most conspicuously against a developmental approach which appears irreconcilable with that of the Opies; and indeed, scholars in the field of folklore studies have continued to resist the developmental model (Bishop and Curtis, 2000; Sutton-Smith, 2001).

In relation to our central research question, the Opie collection offers confirmation that children at that time happily integrated knowledge, references and performances from their media cultures into the vernacular culture of the playground, street and council estate (see Chapter 2). Popular media acts such as The Bay City Rollers, Gary Glitter, Lena Zavaroni and Abba jostle with the mutations of older popular cultures long since incorporated into the oral tradition inherited by these children: folksong, nursery rhyme, Christmas carols, music-hall and film sound-track. More generally, there is evidence of less-regulated play, such as the street play in Chelsea, where transgressive forms of banter and rhyme challenge conventional norms of social behaviour. Also evident, however, are the beginnings of more structured play provision, such as the play-workers interviewed in Stepney Green, who describe how they seek to re-introduce rhymes from their own childhood memories into the play of the children in their charge, something we also found in the two playgrounds we researched in this project.

There is also some record of the cultural effects of mobile populations: of children who move school to find that their version of a song or game is not accepted by the new school; of children in the American school in London who have brought new versions of well-known classics from Massachusetts (see Chapter 2 for more detail). But these are less extreme forms of mobility than those experienced by the children in more recent studies, including our own, with complex mixes of ethnic groups in London; or that Marsh found among Punjabi girls in the Midlands, playing clapping games to songs from Hindi films (Marsh, 2010). In this respect, cultural influences can be expected to have widened dramatically since the waves of economic and refugee migration in the first decade of the twenty-first century. Oddly, however, two factors conspire against such variety being universally apparent. One is the balance of languages and ethnicities in the playground: where there is no dominant language or ethnic group, English remains the lingua franca, as was the case in both playgrounds we studied. The other is the inclination of migrant children to adopt the cultural styles of the host community, or indeed the global media cultures which can be possessed by all in common, as a recent study of migrant children's cultural expression showed across several European states (de Block et al, 2005).

While children – then and now – might be differentiated by ethnicity and language, they are also clearly differentiated by social class. While the Opies do not develop a political theory of social class in relation to play cultures, their writing contains a distinct discourse of class culture and their efforts to 'become familiar with the argot which the kids still speak in London's alleyways and tenement courts' (1959: v). Similarly, in their choice of a sample they intended to be 'representative of the child population as a whole', they firmly state that it does not include 'the lore current among children in the private, fee-charging establishments' (1959: vii). Clearly they worked hard to explore the public playgrounds of streets and council estates, just as Damian Webb did in his photographic and audio recording of play in Wigan and Salford. Their keen awareness of social distinction, especially in urban contexts, infuses their commentary; and a number of the recordings suggest where the resistance of working-class children to regulatory regimes is most marked: through transgressive forms of language and embodied play at odds with the schooling that attempts to shape them, socially, morally and even physically. Chapter 2 discusses the more extreme forms of scatological and sexual reference and performance by children in a Chelsea housing estate and recalls Stallybrass and White's (1986) account of how the body of the working-class child was forced to conform to bourgeois ideals of cleanliness and propriety in the nineteenth-century city (1986: 144).

In some respects, then, the cultural constraints of social class might be seen as more marked at the time of the Opies' research, and the efforts of play to assert a defiantly different narrative and posture more evident. Certainly, in 2009–11 in the two schools in Sheffield and London, we did not find such distinctively transgressive forms of language and play.

However, there is some evidence in our study that children enjoyed certain freedoms in the mid-twentieth century that have declined significantly in the early twenty-first century. In particular, changes in the social spaces of play are observed historically in Richards's chapter in this volume. Through a process of critical memory, he recalls his own play as a boy in the 1950s and early 1960s and explores the meanings of 'play fighting' and of 'rough play' through to the carefully regulated playgrounds he studied in this project. A conspicuous difference between our observation of playgrounds and the material in the Opie collection is that we focused on school playgrounds while the Opies' work includes material recorded in public playgrounds and housing estates. While we did not seek out play in other areas, the evidence seems to be that street play has declined considerably, and playgrounds, whether school or public, have increased in importance as sites for play. In general, then, sites for play over the last century have become increasingly urban, constrained, planned, regulated and overseen. The general motive for this is the protection of children, firstly, and the designed provision for play, secondly. These seem to be self-evidently good things: and indeed it is true that the playgrounds we observed were more imaginatively planned spaces for play than the bare tarmac playgrounds observed by the Opies. The paradox, however, is that children's imaginative play often thrives in unpromising contexts, in hidden nooks and crannies, in secret codes and languages. Too much planning, provision, regulation, oversight may constrain rather than enable play.

The other great growth site for play, which we have surveyed but not observed directly, is the bedroom. Children's media cultures are considerably richer than they were when the Opies' research was conducted, and our survey of the children in the two schools reveals extensive access to television, DVDs, radio, communication technologies, a variety of computer game consoles and, increasingly, mobile phones. By contrast, street play has clearly declined under the pressure of adult anxiety about a variety of perceived and actual dangers and adult-targeted pranks like Knock-Down Ginger (Opie and Opie, 1959: 378) have given way to more highly-regulated and media-derived annual rituals such as Trick-or-Treating (Roud, 2010).

The histories of childhood and play considered so far extend over decades and generations, revealing changes in childhood as a *permanent segment of society* as opposed to changes in childhood as a *generational unit*, inhabited temporarily by individuals (Qvortrup, 2009). Studies like ours are always caught between these larger patterns of social change, and the smaller temporal sequences that make up the experiences of individual children. Both of these patterns inform the play which we might be tempted to see as rooted purely in the contemporary moment.

For one thing, this moment is thick with historical resonances. Bourdieu's concept of habitus, described by him as 'embodied history, internalized as second nature and so forgotten as history ... the active present of the whole past of which it is the product' (1990: 56), offers one way in which we might seek to understand the meeting of social structures and physical play.

Habitus as forgotten history has strong resonances for the observations made in our ethnographic research. The frequent disclaimers by children of any history of the game and song texts; unselfconscious moves from one enthusiasm, craze, even friendship group to the next; the rapid explosions of particular games and their equally rapid disappearance – all these might be interpreted through Bourdieu's view of habitus as a relation between the past conditions which generated sets of dispositions and the present conditions in which those dispositions are a resource for social action.

Both these observations of day-to-day change in the playground and Bourdieu's idea of 'embodied history' allow for what we can call micro-histories. The salient periods of time here are not, then (or not only) those of the social histories noted above, applied to mass populations and dealing in decades and centuries. Rather, they attend to the temporalities of childhood, a phrase borrowed from James, Jenks and Prout, who consider how childhood is defined and structured in certain ways by time (1998: Chapter 4). They point to the definition of childhood as a stage in the life course, and as a generational category. They explore ways in which the time of children is structured institutionally, in families, schools and hospitals, for example. Finally, they consider how time is experienced by children themselves, a theme which has arisen many times in our research, from observed instances of play as ways of dealing with the temporal constraints of the school day, to children's perceptions of time and history. In addition to James, Jenks and Prout's temporalities, we can add those documented by scholars of childlore. The Opies constructed a 'Children's Calendar', showing how different times of the year, festivals and holidays were occasion for specific rituals, games and customs (Opie and Opie, 1959); while Roud develops the same structure with more recent examples (Roud, 2010). The chapters of this book, then, can often be seen to attend to the temporalities of childhood, while also at times invoking the larger historical backdrop in which they are embedded.

Finally, we need to consider how the voice of the child may be represented in society, and more particularly for our purpose in the institutions that oversee the conditions of and provision for play. Schools are arguably more visibly attentive to the voices and opinions of children than in the 1970s, as a general effect of the UN Convention on the Rights of the Child, with initiatives in research and practice framed around notions of 'pupil voice' (Fielding, 2009; Potter, 2012). Our project sought to engage with this developing attention to children's agency as researchers, designers and curators, as described in the previous section.

The next section will move on to offer three categories which identify specific features of children's games in relation to new media, while also indicating how they connect with older practices in children's play and media cultures.

Cultural Rehearsal

The Collins dictionary has two meanings for rehearsal. The first is 'a session of practising a play, concert, speech etc, in preparation for public performance'; the second is 'the act of going through or recounting; recital'.

These meanings capture something of the ambiguity of children's perennial recycling, remaking, repetition and revision of games, songs and rhymes. They capture first of all the iterative nature of cultural expressions which settle over time in particular texts, structures, formulae. The process of recounting, reciting, repeating, in all cultural forms, involves building on old resources, and introducing new elements. This dialectic relation between sedimentation and innovation is familiar in the philosophy of language. Merleau-Ponty, for example, develops an extensive argument that sedimented forms of language become an essential element of lived language: the repositories and residues of sedimented language become the context for creativity in speaking and expressing (Bourgeois, 2002: 370). In this respect, 'rehearsal' allows for an engagement with the textual phenomena of variation across time and space which are a central focus in folklore studies, as Honko's notions of 'thick corpus' and 'organic variation' exemplify (Honko, 2000). These aspects of our project are explored by Bishop (Chapter 3) and Jopson et al (Chapter 2) in this volume.

The landscape of play charted by our project displays the dialectic of sedimentation and innovation in the play spaces of childhood more broadly than in a textual corpus, however. It is a landscape in which jacks, marbles and catapults have given way to the equally rich possibilities of MP3 players, game consoles and light sabres. Meanwhile, certain structures, objects and practices remain resilient and accommodating to changing uses: hula-hoops, skipping-ropes, Tig, kiss-chase, clapping.

A longer perspective viewing the larger histories of play suggests that these shifts accompany larger social movements, in particular the changes from agrarian to industrial capitalism between the eighteenth and twentieth centuries. Iona Opie notes this in *The Singing Game*, arguing that 'Cecil Sharp and his followers were perhaps being optimistic if they thought to revive … games whose *raison d'être* had largely disappeared' (1985: 25). In our research, there is a sense that the rhymes and rituals left over from a lost agrarian working-class culture no longer mean anything to the children of the twenty-first century urban class; and many of the forms documented in *The Singing Game*, such as variants of the longways sets and circles of country dance, were not to be found on our playgrounds. Rather, the significant narratives and images for the children in our study were those of contemporary media – superheroes, pop stars, the commandoes, assassins, mages and football managers of computer games – but also the fantasy figures of folklore which survive in fairy tales and children's literature (witches, zombies, princesses, ghosts, talking animals). Indeed, as Willett argues (Chapter 6), these two categories of contemporary media and folkloric residue, are often hard to distinguish from one another, and mingle freely in children's improvised scenario in what she terms 'ambiguously-referenced' play.

One way to think about this is in terms of what Raymond Williams called 'residual' culture. He distinguished this from the purely archaic:

> By 'residual' I mean something different from the archaic ... Any culture includes available elements of its past, but their place in the contemporary cultural process is profoundly variable ... The residual, by definition, has been effectively formed in the past, but it is still active in the cultural process ... (Williams, 1977: 122)

Similarly, James, Jenks and Prout give a good idea of what it might mean for the residual to be 'still active in the cultural process':

> It is culture as contextualised action, not ossified cultural forms (jokes, games and childhood lore) which passes between generations of children in defiance of what children 'should' or 'ought' to know. (1998: 89)

This tension between residual culture and contextual practice has always been a visible paradox at the heart of children's play, leading the Opies, for example, to characterise children as conservative guardians of tradition on the one hand and creative folk artists on the other. Our own project has produced countless examples of this tension: children in the Opie collection who introduce television's *The Saint* into the well-worn clapping game 'When Susie was a Baby'; or in the playgrounds we researched, who merge the Dementors of the Harry Potter stories with Tig, and replace older media icons like Elvis Presley with current figures like Tracey Beaker.

Rehearsal, then, suggests the recounting of something old but also the invention of something new. It also necessitates repetition, as we have noted, and as Widdowson argues in his account of the linguistic and poetic aspects of playground games (2001). This is not always a condition of playground games – some can be invented for the moment and never played again – but it is the usual condition. Like any system of communication and any system of ritual, familiarity comes from frequent repetition so that the participants can recognise and engage with the structures; though repetition always also brings change and variation: it is always reliant on difference, as Deleuze observed (1994). This idea brings together a number of themes relevant to our project. Performances based on fairly close imitation of media sources are a staple of playground culture, as the Opies observed, and as Willett discusses in relation to performances of pop songs (Chapter 6); though she also argues that it is more common for such performances to hybridise sources and produce something new, as in the performance of 'Single Ladies' by a group of girls who borrow both from a Beyoncé original and from a version of the song in the film *Alvin and the Chipmunks*.

Repetition and variation is also a familiar idea in folklore studies, where the oral transmission of material is both assumed and constantly analysed. Marsh, for example, applies the theory of oral formulaic composition (Parry, 1930; Lord, 1960) to children's musical games; while what Ong called the 'psycho-dynamics' of oral narrative are evident in the stories and dramatic scenarios we documented (Ong, 1982). It is also true that the easily-recognised character types and action sequences Ong finds in oral tradition can be seen in the popular fictions of contemporary media: comic-books, manga and animé, film and television drama, computer games. While these are (relatively) new forms of media, then, they share deep structures with the most archaic of narratives (Burn and Schott, 2004). It is unsurprising, then, that the superheroes, zombies, martial artists and monsters of films, games and comics should mingle so freely with folkloric figures such as witches, princesses, fairies and ghosts.

Bishop (Chapter 3) analyses how one clapping song is transmitted between friends on the playground, and how this process involves the learning of and perfecting of skills, in particular physical skills of clapping and mimetic performance. However, while recognising the familiar processes of oral transmission, Bishop's study suggests a new kind of rehearsal. The girls she studies originally derived this game not from the conventional folkloric process, but from YouTube. The age of new media, in this specific context, performs a similar function to oral transmission. But it also changes the process. Firstly, the emphasis shifts from local to global transmission (though the new game is then localised through a series of further transformations). Secondly, in principle many different versions can co-exist, and be compared and drawn on, whereas local, face-to-face transmission would typically only offer a few variations over a longer period of time. Indeed, as one recording in the Opie collection shows, the arrival of a different version of a game with a new pupil could arouse hostility and rejection (see Chapter 2). Thirdly, rather counter-intuitively, online resources can provide older material as a form of popular archive. Elsewhere, we have discussed the case of a group of girls drawing for dance inspiration on Michael Jackson videos, for example (Burn, 2012).

These examples also demonstrate that the process of cultural rehearsal is not simply a question of linguistic or even musical transmission. These two communicative modes have received most attention in published collections of children's games, with the mode of language taking the lion's share. Jopson et al (Chapter 2) argue that though this is also true of the Opies' published work, the recordings reveal a broader attention to physical movement in play. The rich video data of our project makes it impossible to ignore the fact that the performative practices of the playground are made up as much of music, physical movement, gestural repertoires and the imaginative use of found physical objects and environments as they are of language: they are, in fact, *multimodal* (Kress and van Leeuwen, 2000). Needless to say, scholars of playground culture have long been aware of this: Julia Bishop and Mavis Curtis's book includes studies of the cultural geography of the playground (Armitage, 2001); the patterns of clapping repertoires and of musical variation (Arleo, 2001); and the physical structures of hopscotch (Lichman, 2001). A methodological challenge for our project, then, was to analyse the games we found across all the modes of signification they employ.

Finally, rehearsal involves the tension between private practice and public performance. The question of audience is oddly problematic in this landscape of play. In the case of clapping games, there appears to be no audience (and yet performance of the difficult skill of hand-clapping is constantly being judged by fellow participants). Elsewhere, routines may oscillate between private and public. A dance routine combining cheerleading with other sources switched between an inward-facing circle of three girls and an outward-facing line – a movement between what Turino calls *presentational performance* and *participatory performance* (Turino: 23–65). But in the age of new media, performances may be captured. The girls in Bishop's study (Chapter 3) talk of putting their version on YouTube; while children we gave cameras to captured examples of their friends' games. Electronic media allows for the capture, representation and distribution of play culture globally, and the significant number of clapping games, from the US especially, to be found on YouTube is evidence enough of this.

However, the ability to rehearse material through the digital moving image can also be seen as a kind of interpretive form of display and exhibition, akin to the processes of curation in museums and galleries. As Potter argues (Chapter 8), this concept can be applied to the ways in which young people archive visual representations of their lives in photograph and film through social media sites, selecting, combining, interpreting and displaying narratives of self and society. In our own project, these processes became a more literal act of curation. Here, as we have described above, children from our partner schools represented categories of play through animation and voiceover commentary, developing their tacit knowledge (Polanyi, 1966/1983) of their own play cultures through researching families and histories. We will return to this example in the third part of this section.

The idea of cultural rehearsal, then, allows for continuity between the folkloric processes of oral transmission, sedimentation and innovation, and those enabled by digital media and participatory online practices. As Henry Jenkins argues:

> Now, the rise of participatory culture represents the reassertion of the practices and logics of folk culture in the face of a hundred years of mass culture. We now have greater capacity to create again and we are forming communities around the practices of cultural production and circulation. (Jenkins, 2010)

The combinatory ingenuity of the generations documented by the Opies is expanded by the mash-up practices of contemporary media cultures; the face-to-face repetition of rhyme, melody and choreographed movement expands into global, online repetition; the living archive of older siblings, cousins and parents is complemented by the digital archive. Folklore goes online, as Blank demonstrates (2009); but by the same token, online culture acquires the improvisatory, protean character of folklore, as Walter Ong's notion of secondary orality suggested (1982).

Ludic Bricolage

Levi-Strauss's concept of bricolage is familiar in anthropology, and is an apt metaphor for the persistent collecting and re-working of fragments of language, music, movement, mime and artefact that has always characterised children's play. It is also familiar in media theory, and has been used in Cultural Studies to describe, again, the collection of cultural resources from a variety of sources, and the re-assignation of meanings to them, as in Hebdige's classic account of the spectacular new signifieds attached to domestic items like safety-pins in the punk aesthetic (1979).

There are innumerable examples of bricolage in the Opies' work: of children shoehorning pop stars into hymns, cartoon characters into skipping chants, TV adverts into folksongs. We found plenty more in our playgrounds: Harry Potter Tig, zombies and superheroes in family games, characters from children's books in clapping games. Many of these combinatory processes consist of what Bishop et al called *onomastic allusion*, names of favourite media characters inserted into formulaic lines of song and rhyme on a slot-and-fill basis (Bishop et al, 2006). More broadly, Willett considers in Chapter 6 how resources from media culture are integrated into children's games as 're-mixes' (Ito, 2008). In some cases these practices exemplify Bishop et al's category of *syncretism*, where larger segments of language, music or action from media sources are integrated into an established game (Bishop et al, 2006).

What we mean by *ludic bricolage* is more specific, however. It refers to the adoption and transformation of game structures: to the more rule-governed forms of play that Caillois terms *ludus*, as distinct from the looser play he calls *paidea* (Caillois, 1958/2001). In physical games these would be not only physical structures like chequer-boards and goalposts, but also the rule-systems which determine them. In computer games they would be the game engine, the programmed foundation which determines what is possible in the game, and specifies the rules which govern a player's progression through the game (Aarseth, 1997). This idea adds, to the familiar notion of children as *players* of games, a conception of children as *designers* and *mediators* of games. In some respects this is not a new idea: recent accounts of the cultures of play have also emphasised a creative function, suggesting that children in certain ways creatively produce their own culture. Corsaro, for example, makes this argument, emphasising however that this creativity is not an expression of the complete cultural autonomy of childhood, but rather that the resources for such creativity are adapted from adult culture (2009: 301).

In positioning children as authors of their own games, however, we are making a more specific argument than a general claim about creativity. Analogies for the process we propose are figures such as the game designer, who plans the levels, missions, rewards and other structures of a game to achieve a satisfying experience of play; or the Dungeon-Master, who keeps the rule-book in the table-top game Dungeons and Dragons, and arbitrates the play. In computer game versions of role-playing games, the role of the Dungeon-Master is effectively taken by the game-engine, which rolls the (virtual) dice, effects the rules and steers the play (Burn and Carr, 2006).

Three examples will give some idea of the variety of forms such structural borrowing and adaptation could take. The first is 'imaginary tennis' (our name), seen on the London playground. Here, the structure of tennis is borrowed, but played with an imaginary ball. At first glance this seems to be simply a form of what Bishop et al, referring to media sources, call *mimesis* (2006); and it does have mimetic qualities. However it also borrows and necessarily adapts the *rule-system* of tennis. Because it cannot replicate rules fulfilled by physical phenomena (balls going out of court), it has to replace them with rules based on mutual consent that an imaginary event has in fact occurred. Where the consent breaks down, the game ceases to function. The same dilemma was seen on the Sheffield playground where a boy recounted the problem of children who refused to 'die' when 'shot' in a playground adaptation of the computer game *Call of Duty: Modern Warfare 2*.

A second example is a group of 6-year-old girls playing a game using hula-hoops. The hoops were laid out on the playground, and the game involved trying not to be inside a hoop when touched by the 'on' player. This adapts the basic rules of Tig, of course. However, when interviewed, the girls excitedly said that there was a ghost on the next level, and it became clear that the rules of the game were being invented, adapted and tested as they played. As well as introducing representational material, like ghosts (and later zombies) into the game, this introduced a structure of rules, consequences and levels clearly derived from computer games, in which the girls featured not only as *players* but as *designers* of the game.

A third example is of a boy playing with a piece of wood. At one moment he uses it as a gun; at other times it transforms into a guitar. Sources for these adaptive practices are not known; but we can speculate about the possibility of games like the *Guitar Hero* and *Call of Duty* franchises (the latter very widely referenced on both playgrounds). However, while the mimetic practice is interesting in itself, the example of ludic bricolage here is the combination of these generic practices with a new set of rules. What governs when it is a gun, and when a guitar? The answer, interestingly, may lie at least partly outside the game. In this playground, imitation guns and references to guns are forbidden. It seems possible, then, that at least part of what determines the metamorphosis is whether adults are watching: the regulatory regime which governs all play in this space.

This particular instance challenges the theory of the 'magic circle' coined by Huizinga (1938/1955) and adopted by game theorists to describe the sealed nature of the game-world and its immunity from real-world consequences (e.g. Salen and Zimmerman, 2004). In this case, however, the very rules of this simple game derive from the real-world consequences of defying the gun ban imposed by teachers and play workers (see Richards, 2013a, in Willett et al). The 'magic circle', then, is a more permeable barrier than was once thought, as recent game research has argued (e.g. Taylor, 2006).

Ludic bricolage, then, covers the creation of 'game-engines' on the playground: adapting rule-systems from all kinds of games, from tennis to shoot-em-ups, from Tig to adventure games, from level-editing to adult regulation. It covers the wide variety of adapted rule-systems we saw, from the stealth structures of action adventure games, adapted to render the player supposedly invisible to opponents like (real) play-workers or (imaginary) sharks, to the rules governing character-changing in a game based on *Star Wars*, described by Richards in Chapter 4. It recognises children as players, of course; but also as mediators, referees and designers of their own games. And finally, it recognises that computer games, while they share many features of older, even archaic, forms of play, have distinctive structures which are being imaginatively exploited and adapted in the physical play of twenty-first century childhood.

Heterotopian Games

The notion of the heterotopia is borrowed from Foucault's influential essay (1984). Foucault presents the heterotopia as a contrast to the utopia: where utopias are ideal unreal spaces, heterotopias are liminal spaces which mirror, contest and invert various sites in the real world.

This metaphor has been used to think about virtual worlds and game-worlds. McNamee uses it to consider videogame worlds as spaces of escape and resistance for children (2000). Boellstorff uses it to reflect on the nature of virtuality in his ethnography of Second Life (2008). Dixon uses it to characterise children's play in virtual worlds, formulating the phrase 'heterotopic play' (2004), and presenting videogame worlds as spaces for social interaction that escape to some degree adult regulation. While she considers the game space in relation to the physical spaces of play available to the boys she is studying, she does not consider traffic between the virtual space and the real space: rather, her point is to emphasise how heavily-regulated parks and playgrounds are by comparison with the virtual worlds of *Grand Theft Auto* and *Pikmin*. However, she does consider ways in which the imaginary worlds constructed by children in physical spaces resemble those inhabited in game-worlds (2004: 92–3).

We are indebted to these accounts, on which we can build to reflect on the forms of play we observed. The point of the heterotopia metaphor for us is more specific, and twofold. Firstly, it can be used to describe both the imaginary worlds of physical play and of computer games, as Dixon suggests, but also the shuttling of specific structures and representational devices *between* them. Where once children had only the imaginary world built in a corner of the playground, an attic or a back alley, they now have the playgrounds of shooting, adventure and strategy games. Unsurprisingly, they draw on the resources of the latter to populate the worlds of the former. Boys on both playgrounds gave examples of how they adapted scenarios and structures from the shooting game franchise *Call of Duty*, describing sequences of dramatic play using characters from the game, snatches of dialogue borrowed from game sequences, imaginary weapons based on those available in the game, stealth tactics (going unseen by the enemy) and systems for experiencing game-death (Burn, 2013).

These kinds of play scenario were adapted from various games, sometimes specific, sometimes generic, sometimes directly attributable to a computer game origin, sometimes intermingled with fairytale sources or other media references (see Willett, Chapter 6). The point of the heterotopia metaphor is to recognise that one kind of virtual world is being translated, effectively, into another, as Marsh argues in this volume (Chapter 5). As with all translations, something is lost – though something is also gained. What is lost is the programmed certainty of the game engine. If an enemy is shot in the game, the programmed entities of ammunition and levels of vulnerability produce a reliable, predictable outcome. In the playground, if the enemy simply refuses to dies, as one boy ruefully noted, not a lot can be done about it. Similarly, the elaborate visual detail – the representational guise of the game – has to be imagined: the desert sands, commando outfits, weapons and explosions all exist only as a shared imaginative construct in the minds of the players. However, they gain in expressive range: the physical gestures, movements, facial expressions and linguistic resources at their disposal are not limited in the way that they are by the media databases on which the game must rely. The two heterotopian spaces are differently multimodal, equipped with different semiotic resources.

Perhaps, then, we need to imagine the heterotopia as a twofold space: the connected spaces of virtual and physical play, between which the images, narratives and ludic structures of games can flow. An immediate objection might be anticipated: the flow can only go one way; and this is certainly true of *Call of Duty* and any game in which the player can make no creative intervention to change the game permanently (though the same would not be true of other games where the player's role can be to build, such as *The Sims*, whose family-building process strongly resembles the sociodramatic family games of the playground).

However, in what appears to be a very different approach, part of our project involved the design of a prototype computer game that allowed children to 'record' their game, and play 'against' their recording, using a specially devised motion tracking system and the movement-based game platforms of the Nintendo Wii and Microsoft Kinect (described earlier).

This strand of the project, exploring the relation between embodied play and the virtual embodiment made possible by advances such as the Wii and Microsoft's Kinect, is described by Mitchell in Chapter 7. One set of user-tests, conducted in London, showed a range of comments by the students experimenting with an early version of the prototype. One type of comment relates to the scoring system introduced by the prototype: the game involves trying to clap the player's hand (holding a Wii-mote) against a virtual hand on the screen, with a point scored for each hit. One child's comments related this to the scoring systems used in commercial Wii games; while the attempts of several children to achieve high scores suggested a particular pleasure of this ludic function. One girl from the London school found satisfaction in two quite different ways: she discovered that minimal movements gained more hits and thus higher scores (just as minimal movements in Wii sports games are more effective than fully mimetic moves); while at other times, she used the Wii-motes to execute dance-like movements with her hands which gained no reward within the game but produced its own aesthetic pleasure. The evidence here seemed to suggest, then, that transplanting a traditional playground game such as a clapping game to a computer game environment, and hybridising it with other ludic functions such as scoring, produced certain kinds of pleasurable play and a different set of cultural associations; while adaptive, improvisatory, open play also seemed a possible way forward.

In a later session of user-testing and participatory design in Sheffield, this time based on a more advanced prototype using a mix of Wii and Kinect technologies, children were asked to provide comments on post-it notes for the improvement of the game. Ideas produced here reflected to some degree the children's gaming experiences, but also their awareness of the possibilities of this kind of kinesic environment. They suggested particular activities, including sport, wrestling (field notes record a media-inspired interest in wrestling at the Sheffield school), fighting games and karate; and the inclusion of different characters, such as pets and 'creatures'.

This experiment, then, forms another example of the heterotopian game: where the physical play in one world produces a virtual equivalent on the other side of the screen. And because it can be recorded, exported, replayed elsewhere by different children, the virtual version enjoys the generic benefits of new media: portability, global reach, digital iteration; in fact, the features of 'cultural rehearsal' described above.

As well as providing a metaphor for imaginary worlds, Foucault's heterotopia includes a set of specific applications to the dramatic content of playground games. He gives examples of the liminal spaces in real societies that exemplify the heterotopia, including cemeteries, brothels, ships, prisons and barracks. These seem to be particularly adult places, remote from the preoccupations of childhood: until we realise that, as Corsaro argues (2009), the resources for children's culture are poached from adult culture; that children's play imagines adult dangers and explores them in imaginary form; and that liminality and transgression are as important in children's culture as they are in adult culture (see Richards, 2013a). In these respects, then, all of Foucault's examples have a place. Children on the London playground made ships (and planes, and assault courses) out of loose wooden structures available to them. Adaptations of Tig used imaginary prisons to confine those who were touched by the one who was on. Boys playing *Call of Duty*-style commando games echo the barracks, and the forms of agonistic play described by Richards in Chapter 4 experiment with combat-styled play likely to attract the censure of watching adults. Brothels seem both less likely and inappropriate – and indeed, we found no explicit references to sexual play in either of our playgrounds. However, as Jopson et al describe (Chapter 2), the Opies found more explicit depictions of adult sexuality in spaces less constrained by adult regulation.

Finally, Foucault has one other kind of heterotopia of relevance to our project, which he calls 'heterotopias of indefinitely accumulating time, for example museums and libraries'. He is characteristically bleak about 'the project of organizing in this way a sort of perpetual and indefinite accumulation of time in an immobile place'. We may borrow the metaphor, perhaps, in a more optimistic spirit, though it is worth noting the dangers of taking a culture whose vitality depends on restless transformation and freezing it in a library display. However, there are qualities of the British Library website of our project which attempt to contest this freezing, or in Foucault's term, immobility. This element of our project which involved panels of children as co-curators of their own games on the website can be seen as another example of heterotopian games. The physical games are captured, delimited in the frames of the sample video-sequences on the site; they are interrogated in the voiceover commentaries of the children and the drawings of the animated films they made about their own play; and the accumulation of time Foucault comments on so drily is indeed performed in the inclusion of archive examples (audio, photographic, filmic) of games across the last century (see Potter, Chapter 8).

Two points can be made about this kind of heterotopia. Firstly, it represents a coming to terms with time and history on the part of the children. The typical condition of their play with sedimented cultural resources is an unawareness of history, often accompanied by a claim to have made the game up, as researchers from the Opies onwards have noted (Bishop, Chapter 3). Games may be seen as a dimension of the child's habitus, the combination of physical play and cultural dispositions; and we have already noted above Bourdieu's concept of habitus as embodied but forgotten history (1990). In the act of curating the website, the children researched their own play and that of their parents; and this interpretative work involved a remembering of these forgotten histories. If the heterotopian space accumulates and freezes time, then, it also inverts the child's customary amnesia, provoking a remembering of history.

Secondly, this curatorial work is allied to the kind of informal practices of curation characteristic of participatory online cultures: children's photos on Flickr, their own sites on Facebook or Bebo, their avatars in *Habbo Hotel* or *Club Penguin* (see Marsh, Chapter 5; and Marsh, 2010); their videos on YouTube and here, on the British Library site, their animations, characterised by the parodic humour of child art. Potter suggests the metaphor of curation for these new assemblages of selfhood, describing the digital videos of the primary school children in his research as:

> … a new kind of literacy practice which can be metaphorically characterised as curating. The resources from which they made meaning were collected, catalogued and arranged for exhibition. These included practices which were previously unseen, acts of memory and habitualised behaviour which were not previously recorded in this way, but which were part of their everyday, lived experience. (Potter, 2009)

In this respect, the framing of games in moving image archives surrounded by spoken and written commentary is a process central both to the informal curatorship of the YouTube videos Bishop discusses in Chapter 3 as well as the more formal curatorship of the British Library website. Both arrest the flow of time, accumulate histories and construct archives, as Foucault says; but both also display dynamic movement, and invite further contributions in a dialogic offer, an affordance which Foucault could not have considered.

A final point to make about heterotopian games is again suggested by Foucault's essay. He counterposes heterotopias against utopias, transgressive reality contrasted with ideal unreality. In our study, the imaginary worlds of children's play were superimposed on the physical playground itself. In many cases, this involved an imaginary transformation of objects: tree stumps became consoles, tarmac patches became poison pits, toilet doors became magic portals (Armitage, 2001; Factor, 2004). In any case, the imaginary landscape was laid like a palimpsest over the physical terrain. This constant layering of imaginary over real raises questions about the ontologies of play and its geographies. The playgrounds are designed with the best of intentions to promote imaginative play, and can be seen as utopian spaces: adult aspirations for children's play. Despite their material nature, these aspirations represent an unreal space of play; the real game-worlds are those constructed in the shared imaginings of the children, designed, developed, tested, revised, inhabited and abandoned through the imaginative transformation of physical and ideational resources, including language, music, movement and the manipulation of objects and the built and natural environment. The utopian space is both ignored and exploited by heterotopian games; it provides raw materials, but its hopeful projection of peaceful play and rural idyll may well be rudely overwritten with the explosions of commando attack, the menacing sharks of shipwreck scenarios, and the out-of-control monsters of demonically-possessed families. A cautionary note, however, is introduced by Richards in Chapter 4, who argues that the modality of such imaginary scenarios is variable, modality[3] here referring to the degree of reality, or distance from it, maintained in the play event. The relative 'reality' status, then, of the adult-designed utopian playground and the child-authored heterotopian game will fluctuate, each moving in and out of focus, flickering into being and fading from view with changing circumstances and motivations (see also Richards, 2013b).

Conclusion: A Short Century of Play

Like Hobsbawm's 'short twentieth century' (1995), our project addresses a historically bounded segment of time, between post-war Britain and the age of the internet. The Opies remarked in *Lore and Language* that they were 'watching the rising generation, the first in the new Elizabethan age' (Opie and Opie, 1959: ix). The children we have worked with are perhaps the last generation of this age: our project finished in the year before Elizabeth II's Diamond Jubilee, though the historical markers we have identified bear less relation to successions of monarchs than to changes in the social structures of childhood and in the cultural

---

³   Modality is the term derived from linguistics and employed in Social Semiotics to denote the truth claim made by a text; in effect, its credibility (Hodge and Kress, 1988).

materials, resources and technologies it adapts to its purpose. As we look back over this period, listening to the ghostly voices of Iona Opie and the children of the 1970s in the archive, we experience a constant oscillation between identity and difference. Some of the children's observations about their play are uncannily close to those made in the playgrounds we studied; others seem remote, frozen in time. With specific reference to our research question about the relationship between children's traditional play cultures and their media cultures, part of our answer is very similar to the Opies' response: all media material is grist to the mill of play, and the children make no differentiation between its toys, stories and images and the rhymes, songs and objects of what appears to adults as a kind of folklore. Another part of our answer, however, has been to recognise the distinctive features of the new media age. While children have always practised, rehearsed and reiterated games and songs, these processes are materially altered by the mechanisms of rehearsal available in digital media and online spaces. While they have always devised their own games, building on time-honoured ludic systems, the structures of digital games offer specific features which did not exist before: levels, avatars, stealth-modes, health-points. While they have always constructed elaborate imaginary worlds and taken centre stage in them, they now have access to immersive 3D worlds made for them, and the result has been, unsurprisingly, traffic between the two kinds of virtual space. And while the social formations of early twenty-first century childhood in many respects would be utterly familiar to the Opies, in its intensely local peer cultures, its familial rituals and its school hierarchies, the forms of global communication in which old play genres find new conduits, and new play genres emerge, have shrunk space and time in the transmission of play practices, and brought together not only wildly disparate cultural resources, as children have always done, but also converging technologies of play (Jenkins, 2008).

The Singing Game begins with this evocation of a moment of play: 'On a hot summer's day in July 1974, in Coram Fields in Bloomsbury, a small cockney sang with energy and conviction a game-song she had just learnt from her cousin …' (Opie and Opie, 1988: 1). We did not find the song she sang ('There's a lady on the mountain') – like other songs and games the Opies recorded, it may have disappeared. We did find other songs and games documented in *The Singing Game*, however; and, just round the corner from Coram's Fields, in Mount Pleasant off London's Gray's Inn Road, we found a young girl who had watched Michael Jackson videos with her cousins, and adapted them into her own dance routines and in Sheffield, a small boy who had played Spiderman and Wii Golf with his relatives and shooting games with his friends, and connected them with his playground games. Though these cultural resources may seem startlingly different, and though the age of new media may have provided specific kinds of augmentation for children's play, the broad categories of play which appear are still those proposed by the great play theorists: the play-acting, games of chance, vertiginous pleasure and agonistic thrill identified by Caillois; the phantasmagoria, fate and identity play suggested by Sutton-Smith. We have not needed to invent new categories, but rather to identify different ways in which they are realised, literally played out, by children whose play spaces seem like palimpsests: documents on which the digital characters, fantasy landscapes and elaborate weaponry of computer games may have been inscribed, but through which fragments of fairytale, choosing game, clapping game and chasing game show through, much as the bricks and tarmac of Victorian school buildings show through the smart new playground's painted rivers, hills and trees. We return to the theme of time in the Postscript to this book: in the meantime, its chapters puzzle away at this conjunction of the archaic and contemporary, sedimented and innovative, embodied and technologically-mediated.

References

Aarseth E (1997) *Cybertext; Perspectives on Ergodic Literature.* Baltimore: John Hopkins University Press.

Arleo A (2001) The saga of Susie: The dynamics of an international handclapping game. In Bishop JC and Curtis M (eds) (2001) *Play Today in the Primary School Playground.* Buckingham: Open University Press.

Armitage M (2001) The ins and outs of school playground play: 'Children's use of play places. In Bishop JC and Curtis M (eds) (2001) *Play Today in the Primary School Playground.* Buckingham: Open University Press.

Barthes R (1975) *The Pleasure of the Text.* New York: Hill & Wang.

Bishop JC (2009) "Eeny Meeny Dessameeny': Continuity and Change in the 'Backstory' of a Children's Playground Rhyme'. Paper presented at Children's Playground Games in the Age of New Media Interim Conference, 25th February 2010, London Knowledge Lab, London. Available in the 'Research & workshops' area on http://projects.beyondtext.ac.uk/playgroundgames/

Bishop JC and Curtis M (eds) (2001) *Play Today in the Primary School Playground.* Buckingham: Open University Press.

Bishop JC and Curtis M with Woolley H, Armitage M and Ginsborg J (2006) Participation, popular culture and playgrounds: Children's uses of media elements in peer play at school. Paper presented at the Folklore Society Conference, *Folklore, Film and Television: Convergences in Traditional Cultures and Popular Media,* 31st March – 1st April 2006, London.

Blank TJ (2009) *Folklore and the Internet: Vernacular Expression in a Digital World.* Logan, Utah: Utah State UP.

Boellstorff T (2008) *Coming of Age in Second Life: An Anthropologist Explores the Virtually Human.* Princeton: Princeton University Press.

Bourdieu P (1990) *The Logic of Practice.* Stanford, CA: Stanford University Press.

Bourgeois P (2002) Maurice Merleau-Ponty, philosophy as phenomenology. In Tymieniecka A (ed.) *Phenomenology Worldwide.* Dordrecht: Kluwer.

Buckingham D (2000) *After the Death of Childhood: Growing up in the Age of Electronic Media.* Cambridge: Polity Press.

Buckingham D (2011) *The Material Child: Growing Up in Consumer Culture*. Cambridge: Polity.

Burn A (2007) Writing computer games: game-literacy and new-old narratives. *L1 - Educational Studies in Language and Literature* 7(4): 45–67

Burn A (2012) The case of the wildcat sailors: The hybrid lore and multimodal languages of the playground. In Darian-Smith K and Pascoe C (eds) (2012) *Children, Childhood and Cultural Heritage*. London: Routledge.

Burn A (2013) Computer games in the playground: Ludic systems, dramatised narrative and virtual embodiment. In Willett R, Richards C, Marsh J, Burn A and Bishop J, *Children, Media and Playground Cultures*. Basingstoke: Palgrave MacMillan.

Burn A and Carr D (2006) Defining game genres. In Carr D, Buckingham D, Burn A and Schott G (2006) *Computer Games: Text, Narrative, Play*. Cambridge: Polity.

Burn A and Schott G (2004) Heavy hero or digital dummy: Multimodal player-avatar relations in Final Fantasy 7. *Visual Communication* 3(2): Summer 2004.

Caillois R (1958/2001) *Man, Play and Games*. Chicago: University of Illinois Press.

Carr D, Buckingham D, Burn A and Schott G (2006) *Computer Games: Text, Narrative, Play*. Cambridge: Polity.

Corsaro W (2009) Peer cultures. In Qvortrup J, Corsaro, WA and Honig MS (eds) *The Palgrave Handbook of Childhood Studies*. London: Palgrave.

Crystal D (1998) *Language Play*. London: Penguin.

Curtis M (2001) Counting in and counting out: Who knows what in the playground. In Bishop JC and Curtis M (eds) (2001) *Play Today in the Primary School Playground*. Buckingham: Open University Press.

Deleuze G (1994) *Difference and Repetition*. London: Continuum.

de Block L, Buckingham D and Banaji S (2005) *Children in Communication about Migration* (CHICAM), Final Report of EC-funded project, at www.childrenyouthandmediacentre.co.uk; project website: www.chicam.net

Dixon S (2004) *Heterotopic Spaces of Childhood*. MA thesis: Concordia University, Montreal, Quebec.

Elkind D (2006) *The Power of Play: How Spontaneous, Imaginative Activities Lead to Happier, Healthier Children*. Da Capo Press.

Factor J (2004) Tree stumps, manhole covers and rubbish tins: The invisible play-lines of a primary school playground. *Childhood* 2: 142–54.

Fielding M (2009) Interrogating student voice: pre-occupations, purposes and possibilities. In Daniels Lauder H and Porter J (eds) *Educational Theories, Cultures and Learning: A Critical Perspective*. London, Routledge, 101–16.

Foucault M (1984) Of other spaces, heterotopias. In *Architecture, Mouvement, Continuité* 5: 46–9.

Gill T (2007) *No Fear: Growing Up in a Risk Averse Society*. London: Calouste Gulbenkian Foundation.

Gomme AB (1964 [1894/1898]) *The Traditional Games of England, Scotland and Ireland: With Tunes, Singing-Rhymes, and Methods of Playing According to the Variants Extant and Recorded in Different Parts of the Kingdom.* New York: Dover.

Goodwin MH (2006) *The Hidden Life of Girls: Games of Stance, Status, and Exclusion.* Oxford: Blackwell.

Grugeon E (1988) Underground knowledge: What the Opies missed. *English in Education* 22(2). 9–17

Guldberg H (2009) *Reclaiming Childhood: Freedom and Play in an Age of Fear.* London: Routledge.

Halliwell James Orchard (1849) *Popular Rhymes and Nursery Tales.* London: John Russell Smith.

Hebdige D (1979) *Subculture - the Meaning of Style.* London: Methuen.

Hobsbawm E (1995) *Age of Extremes: The Short Twentieth Century 1914–1991.* London: Abacus.

Hodge R and Kress G (1988) *Social Semiotics.* Cambridge: Polity.

Holland Patricia (2004) *Picturing Childhood: The Myth of the Child in Popular Imagery.* London: I.B. Tauris.

Honko L (2000) Thick corpus and organic variation: An introduction. In Honko L (ed.) *Thick Corpus, Organic Variation and Textuality in Oral Tradition.* Studia Fennica Folkloristica 7. Helsinki: Finnish Literature Society, 3–28.

Huizinga J (1938/1955) *Homo Ludens: A Study of the Play Element in Culture.* Boston: Beacon Press.

Ito M (2008) Mobilizing the imagination in everyday play: The case of Japanese media mixes. In Livingstone S and Drotner K (eds) *The International Handbook of Children, Media, and Culture.* London: Sage, 397–412.

James A (1993) *Childhood Identities: Self and Social Relationships in the Experience of the Child.* Edinburgh: Edinburgh University Press.

James A and Prout A (eds) (1990) *Constructing and Reconstructing Childhood.* Basingstoke: Falmer.

James A, Jenks C and Prout A (1998) *Theorizing Childhood.* Cambridge: Polity Press.

Jenkins H (2010) Sites of Convergence: An Interview for Brazilian Academics (Part Two). At Confessions of an Aca-Fan: the official weblog of Henry Jenkins. http://www.henryjenkins.org/convergence_culture/. Accessed 30.7.2012

Jenkins H (2008) *Convergence Culture: Where Old and New Media Collide.* New York: NYU press.

Jenkins H (2007) Confronting the Challenges of Participatory Culture: Media Education for the 21st Century. At http://digitallearning.macfound.org/atf/cf/%7B7E45C7E0-A3E0–4B89-AC9C-E807E1B0AE4E%7D/JENKINS_WHITE_PAPER.PDF. Accessed 31.7.2012

Kress G and van Leeuwen T (2000) *Multimodal Discourse: The Modes and Media of Contemporary Communication.* London: Arnold.

Lichman S (2001) From Hopscotch to Siji: Generations at play in a cross-cultural setting. In Bishop J and Curtis M (eds) (2001) *Play Today in the Primary School Playground*. Buckingham: Open University Press.

Lord AB (1960) *The Singer of Tales*. Cambridge: Harvard University Press.

Marsh J (2010) Young children's play in online virtual worlds. *Journal of Early Childhood Research* 7 (3): 1–17.

Marsh K (2001) It's not all black and white: The influence of the media, the classroom and immigrant groups on children's playground singing games. In Bishop, JC and Curtis, M (eds) (2001) *Play Today in the Primary School Playground*. Buckingham: Open University Press.

Marsh K (2008) *The Musical Playground*. Oxford: Oxford University Press.

Marsh K (2010) 'That's the way I like it': A children's guide to musical meaning, transmission and performance. Seminar at the Institute of Education, University of London, 24th February 2010.

McNamee S (2000) Heterotopia and children's lives. *Childhood* 7 (4): 479–92.

Ong W (1982) *Orality and Literacy: The Technologizing of the Word*. London: Methuen.

Opie I (1993) *The People in the Playground*. Oxford: Oxford University Press.

Opie I and Opie P (1959) *The Lore and Language of Schoolchildren*. Oxford: Oxford University Press.

Opie P and Opie I (1969/2008) *Children's Games in Street and Playground, Volume 1: Chasing, Catching, Seeking*. Edinburgh: Floris Books.

Opie I and Opie P (1985) *The Singing Game*. Oxford: Oxford University Press.

Palmer S (2007) *Toxic Childhood: How The Modern World Is Damaging Our Children And What We Can Do About It*. London: Orion.

Parry M (1930) Studies in the epic technique of oral verse-making. I: Homer and Homeric style. *Harvard Studies in Classical Philology* 41: 73–143.

Polanyi M (1966/1983) *The Tacit Dimension*. Gloucester, MA: Peter Smith.

Postman N (1983) *The Disappearance of Childhood*. London: WH Allen.

Potter J (2009) Curating the self: Media literacy and identity in digital video production by young learners. Unpublished PhD thesis: Institute of Education, University of London, London.

Potter J (2012) Learner voice and lived culture in digital media production by younger learners: Implications for pedagogy and future research. In Trifonas PP *Learning the Virtual Life: Public Pedagogy in a Digital World*. Routledge: London.

Pugh A (2009) *Longing and Belonging: Parents, Children and Consumer Culture*. Berkeley: University of California Press.

Qvortrup J (2009) Childhood as Structural Form. In Qvortrup J, Corsaro WA and Honig MS (eds) *The Palgrave Handbook of Childhood Studies*. Basingstoke: Palgrave, 21–33

Richards C (2013a) Agonistic scenarios. In *Children, Media and Playground Cultures: Ethnographic Studies of School Playtimes*, Basingstoke: Palgrave Macmillan, forthcoming.

Richards C (2013b) "If you ever see this video, we're probably dead" – a boy's own heterotopia (Notes from an inner London playground). In *Journal of Children and Media* 7(3). 383–98

Rose N (1989/1999 2nd edition) *Governing the Soul: The Shaping of the Private Self.* London: Free Association Books.

Roud S (2010) *The Lore of the Playground.* London: Random House.

Salen K and Zimmerman E (2004) *Rules of Play: Game Design Ffundamentals.* Cambridge, MA: The MIT Press.

Sutton-Smith B (1995) *Children's Folklore: Source Book.* Bloomington: Indiana University Press.

Sutton-Smith B (2001) *The Ambiguity of Play.* Boston: Harvard University Press.

Stallybrass P and White A (1986) *The Poetics and Politics of Transgression.* Ithaca, N.Y.: Cornell University Press.

Taylor TL (2006) *Play Between Worlds: Exploring Online Game Culture.* Cambridge, MA: MIT Press.

Turino T (2008) *Music as Social Life: The Politics of Participation.* Chicago: University of Chicago Press.

Widdowson J (2001) Rhythm, repetition and rhetoric: learning language in the school playground. In Bishop JC and Curtis M (eds) (2001) *Play Today in the Primary School Playground.* Buckingham: Open University Press.

Willett R (2006) Constructing the digital tween: Market discourse and girls' interests. In Mitchell C and Reid Walsh J (eds) *Seven Going on Seventeen: Tween Culture in Girlhood Studies.* 278–93. Oxford: Peter Lang.

Willett R, Richards C, Marsh J, Burn A and Bishop JC (2013) *Children, Media and Playground Cultures: Ethnographic Studies of School Playtimes.* Basingstoke: Palgrave Macmillan.

Williams R (1977) *Marxism and Literature.* Oxford: Oxford University Press.

Chapter 2
The Opie Recordings: What's Left to be Heard?

Laura Jopson, Andrew Burn, Jonathan Robinson

In 1985, Peter and Iona Opie published the third of their works relating to the play of schoolchildren: *The Singing Game*. Peter Opie had died before it could be completed. Iona Opie wrote the Preface, Introduction and what text remained to be completed[1] after the editing of the transcripts and commentary she and Peter had built up over the years. She had also organized these materials in the elaborate filing system now archived at the Bodleian Library. An ambitious exposition, their work surveyed children's singing games across the UK, including clapping games as a subset, and explored individual verbal texts, variations and histories. A landmark contribution to the subject area of children's folklore, much of the book drew on a large collection of audio recordings made mostly by Iona Opie from the late 1960s to the mid 1980s. This collection was deposited with the British Library Sound Archive in 1998 and is now entitled 'The Opie Collection of Children's Games and Songs' (BL shelfmark: C898). It has been digitised and made available by the British Library as part of the project which the present volume describes. Offering a geographically and chronologically diverse collection of songs, the collection brings to life the material that fills the pages of *The Singing Game*. The audio archive consists of 85 open-reel and cassette tapes recorded by Opie between 1969 and 1983. It is now fully catalogued and available online as streamed audio to the public at large.

However, the collection's significance lies not simply in the chance to sample the songs included in *The Singing Game*. As this chapter will show, there is still much left to be heard in the Opie collection which has never been published. Themes such as the role of play in the inclusion and exclusion of children on the playground; the role of the media in children's play; the question of transmission of games and songs and the appearance and function of scatological and transgressive songs and rhymes during playtime resonate throughout this archive of recordings.

This chapter will explore these themes in the light of recent research in childhood studies emphasising agency in children's culture (e.g. James, 2009; Qvortrup, 2009); the importance of children's media cultures in their play (e.g. Buckingham, 2000) and the form and function of children's folklore (e.g. Bishop and Curtis, 2001; Grugeon, 1988).

---

[1] She writes: 'In the event, he died before the book was finished. I wrote the Preface, Introduction, and the remainder of the text'. Letter to Julia Bishop, 2012.

The Opies' Methods

Before attending to the contents of the archive, we will consider what it reveals about the Opies' approach to research and how this has determined the shape and extent of the collection.

The Singing Game (1985), while based partly on surveys completed for *The Lore and Language of Schoolchildren* (1959), also includes a different kind of field research. The Opies conducted the surveys largely with the help of teachers. They took the form of a written questionnaire and the children wrote their replies which the teacher forwarded to the Opies (who might then correspond and ask for more details or clarifications). The fieldwork for *The Singing Game*, by contrast, involved the use of sound recording technology and Iona Opie collected much of it at first hand, travelling the country in search of her material, sometimes accompanied by fellow collectors of children's games such as Father Damian Webb and Berit Østberg. Interestingly, there is little indication from the recordings that Peter Opie accompanied Iona on these visits. On a few recordings in the archive, particularly those from the London area, Iona Opie makes reference to the fact that she is accompanied by her Norwegian friend who is presumably Berit Østberg, mentioned in the preface to *The Singing Game*. Opie explains that Østberg is also a collector of children's games and songs in Norway; little else is said about her, though we know she collected children's singing games in Trøndheim in the late sixties and early seventies. Father Damian Webb can also be heard on a set of recordings from St Benedict's Roman Catholic Primary School, Garforth, Yorkshire where he taught (C898/12). He is heard discussing with the schoolchildren their singing games and songs and commenting on these with Opie. Webb's approach to the collection of children's games was facilitated by sophisticated audio recording and photographic equipment. His substantial archives of photographs and audio recordings were given to the Pitt Rivers museum in Oxford on his death. Several of his photographs are used as illustrations in *The Singing Game*; and a selection is also used on the British Library website developed during our project. Digital copies of the sound recordings are available at the British Library as the 'Damian Webb/Pitt Rivers Museum Children's Games and Songs' (BL shelfmark: C1431).

Sometimes in the company of these colleagues, then, and sometimes alone, Iona Opie collected traditional singing games and other songs from a range of childhood haunts including school playgrounds and council estates, inner city recreational grounds and country villages, including her own village of Liss in Hampshire, which provided the material for her sustained investigation of play presented in *The People in the Playground* (Opie, 1993). The locations are widely distributed, covering the West Country, the Midlands, the Welsh borders, the North-West, Yorkshire, Scotland and various sites in London. She writes of her efforts to complete the geographical picture of children's play cultures:

> It was only when we failed to find a contact in some corner of Great Britain, or in some offshore island, that I went off on an expedition with a tape-recorder: to Cape Wrath in the left-hand top corner of Scotland, to the Land's End in

Cornwall, to the westerly tip of Wales, and to the Isle of Wight. For the last of our books on school lore, *The Singing Game*, I also made special forays into the places where the older lore flourishes best, the depths of the cities, and there I found games like "There comes a Jew a-riding" which were believed to have quite died out. (Opie, 1988).

The interviews and performances were collected on open-reel tapes and cassettes. The medium of each recording can be found by searching the British Library catalogue which provides the details. Opie writes self-deprecatingly of the technology in a personal letter:

> Peter didn't even use a typewriter, and I made the playground recordings on a 12-guinea tape-recorder from Selfridges, with 3-inch tapes – nice little machine it was. (Letter to Julia Bishop, 1 January 2011)

When meeting with the children, Opie ensured that these were not formal or prescriptive interviews, but relaxed discussions amongst small friendship groups of children as they played and sung. Often letting the children hold the microphone or experiment with the recording device, she appears a welcome member of these gangs, casually discussing with the children songs and games, boyfriends and enemies. In this sense, her research method is characteristically ethnographic, featuring what today's qualitative methodology textbooks call semi-structured interviewing techniques, focus groups and attention to discursive interplay between participants and to their cultural context. She speaks in an interview of being pleasantly surprised when *Lore and Language* was reviewed by Edmund Leach, who wrote 'the Opies have arrived as anthropologists', saying that they had never seen themselves in this way[2]. Yet clearly Iona Opie's method in her fieldwork went far beyond a narrow focus on a textual corpus, and the recordings reveal how extensive her interest was in the cultural sources and contexts of the children's play. In this respect, she was in the vanguard of contemporary developments in folklore studies, which by the 1980s had an academic presence in the UK, at Leeds, Sheffield and the School of Scottish Studies in Edinburgh. Folklore studies in the UK in the 1970s and 1980s were also influenced by the European 'folk life studies' and by 'folkloristics' in North America, as well as developments in British social anthropology. The Opies would have been aware of these developments and were attendees at the Folklore Society centenary conference in 1978 which attracted innovative researchers from Europe and North America (Newall, 1980).

The lengthy accounts she elicits of children's cultural practices also come close to the territory explored by today's cultural studies researchers, interested in relations between sociocultural events, media and play. Good examples from the archive are a boy's account of his interest in girlfriends in London's Coram Fields (C898/26); children's descriptions of their play in the country and park in

---

[2]   Cathy Courtney Interview with Iona Opie, 'Cathy Courtney Oral History Collection', British Library Sound and Moving Image catalogue, shelfmark C968/139/01-03.

Alton, Hampshire, and of their television viewing (C898/01); children's favourite sweets and crisp flavours in Stepney Green, London (C898/29); and problems encountered by children in Chelsea, London, when adults disapprove of their ball games (C898/67). Although the published work of *The Singing Game* can appear to privilege text over context, then, the archive reveals an intense interest in context, lived culture and the 'webs of meaning' which bind them together (Geertz, 1973).

The result of this intensely detailed research is a collection of recordings that add to the Opies' published evidence of a distinct and fiercely guarded play culture. In a period in which social commentators and scholars alike were bewailing its apparent death, Iona Opie countered that this tradition was in fact 'a truly living one' (Opie and Opie, 1985 vii).

Three questions may be posed about this extraordinarily sustained research process. One concerns the nature of the research collaboration. Since Iona Opie conducted a good deal of the research independently of her husband, it may be that conventional assumptions about their partnership need to be re-evaluated, and her own distinctive role given a greater prominence. At the same time, her collaborations with Østberg and Webb could be considered in more detail. Webb, for example, was clearly more than just the provider of photographs illustrating the Opie publications, but a skilled researcher in his own right, whose approach to what today is seen as visual ethnography both complements and contrasts with Iona Opie's greater reliance on language and audio recording.

Another question is about the theoretical basis of the research, its profound beliefs about childhood and culture. In this respect, the architects of the new sociology of childhood regard the Opies as pioneers, to be seen as predecessors of the approaches to childhood studies they advocate, with an insistence on the agency of the child and the self-sufficiency of children's play cultures (James, Jenks and Prout, 1998; Corsaro, 2009). At the same time, James, Jenks and Prout label the Opies' approach 'the tribal child', suggesting it displays an anthropological view which locates children's culture as exotic and alien, productively signalling its autonomy, but in danger of romanticizing its nature and functions. To carry forward this question, the archive might be expected to reveal something of the ethnographic method: what is included, how it is treated, what kinds of interrogation are evident, what kinds of proto-interpretation might be implied.

A third, methodological, question might be levelled at the nature of the data Iona Opie collected, and how it was captured, transcribed, notated. As we have explained, her methods relied on field notes and analogue audio recording. The photographic illustrations for *The Singing Game* were provided by Damian Webb. The tunes for the songs, meanwhile, were transcribed and notated by a friend, Michael Hurd, of whom she writes:

> Michael Hurd lived in this same village. He was a composer, and his main line was composing choral works for children, published by OUP. I knew I should print the singing game tunes. He lived just up the road, so he could take some of the tapes and write out the tunes ... It was just my luck that he was already a friend. (Letter to Julia Bishop, 1 January 2011)

The question here, then, relates to the communicative modes which make up playground games, which of these are recognized and captured, and what prominence is accorded to them. Unsurprisingly, particularly in view of the scholarly tradition of folklore studies in which the Opies are most obviously located, considerable prominence is given to the words: the mode of language. Iona Opie can often be heard in the archive recordings asking children to repeat the words of the songs. We know from interpretive work in *The Lore and Language of Schoolchildren* and *The Singing Game* that scholarly attention to historical variation and poetic form is a preoccupation of the Opies' approach, albeit balanced by scrupulous attention to the immediate cultural context in which children disown any knowledge of the history or origins of their games and songs. She is also interested in the tunes, although she does not ask the children about variants of the tunes, or about alternative tunes. In the published work, there is less explicit attention to musical variation than to linguistic variation.

The other modes at work can be seen, in terms of multimodality theory, as communicative work such as gesture, action, gaze, proxemics (e.g. Finnegan, 2002; Bishop and Burn, 2013). Some of these are not, of course, noted by Opie, though her folklorist antennae are keenly directed at the actions specific to particular games, and these are noted in careful detail in *The Singing Game*. Again, she can be heard in the recording asking children to describe these movements. An example is a sequence of movements briefly described in *The Singing Game* in relation to a song that begins 'Crackerjack, Crackerjack':

> … sung twice while the children in the circle bumped their hips into each other, and ended with the pantomime 'The boys have got the muscles' ('everyone flexes their biceps'), 'the teacher's got the pay' ('stretch out hands'), 'The girls have got the sexy legs' ('lift skirt showing off leg'), 'Hurrah, hurrah, hurrah!' ('jump up and down'). (Opie and Opie, 1985: 416)

In the recordings, this sequence is noted at the playground in London's Coram Fields in relation to a song beginning Michelle, Michelle:

> Children: Mi-chelle (boom-ba-boom-ba-boom-ba-boom)
> Mi-chelle (boom-ba-boom-ba-boom-ba-boom)
> Boys got the muscles, teachers got the brain
> Girls got the sex, what else can I say?

> Iona Opie: Now the words are – the actions that go with it are – Michelle – you clap your hands under your legs, that's twice, under each leg, as it were – um, then you've got 'the boy's got the muscles', you're sort of clenching your fists, like that, showing your biceps, you've got the muscles! (laughs). 'Teacher's got the brain' … 'teacher's got the brains', you point at your head, um, then, um, 'girl's got the sex', you sort of raise your skirt up at the side and show your legs, and then, 'what more can you say', you get down on one knee and pray! I've never heard that one before. (C898/26)

Not only is this careful attention to detail consistent with the folklorist, it shows an attention to the physical modes of expressive movement. In general, then, while in the published work linguistic form and content, variation and change are explicit preoccupations, a good deal of attention is given to physical modes of play in the recordings. Music, by contrast, is notated but rarely commented on either in the recordings or *The Singing Game*.

If we include in the picture her research collaborations, we see, as well as the musical collaboration of Michael Hurd, the ethnographic contribution of Damian Webb, not just as an illustrator, but as a complementary researcher, documenting the visual landscape of children's games which we can only imagine as we listen to the Opies' sound recordings.

In certain ways, then, Iona Opie's work foreshadows future developments in the documenting and interpretation of the lives of children. In its cultural politics and its rejection of developmental approaches to childhood, it anticipates the theories of agency, culture and play elaborated by the new sociology of childhood, though its celebration of vernacular artistry bears little resemblance to sociology. Innovations which are genuinely pioneering can be heard in the audio recordings: the deferral to children's knowledge, the delicate probing of cultural context and practice, the attention to action, movement and social function as well as the formal properties of language.

In the next section, we will look at three areas of content which the archive reveals, and which are not to be found in the publications.

The Opie Collection: What Does It Reveal?

In the light of the account given generally in *The Singing Game,* we might assume that this animated culture was one in which tradition thrived, familiar melodies persisted and scatological rhymes were shunned in favour of loud and wholesome renditions of 'A Sailor Went to Sea, Sea, Sea'. Indeed, Opie describes the children represented here as a distant reflection of the 'young people of the Middle ages' in their singing games, games that boast 150 years worth of history, and mild-mannered 'buffoonery' (Opie and Opie, 1985: 31).

An obvious question about the archive is whether it reveals broadly the same picture? Or does it demonstrate that the Opies captured something more, material that they recognized to be of significance yet due to the purposes of their own research, did not include in *The Singing Game*? In the remainder of this chapter, we will consider three areas of content that are under-represented in the published work, and which offer an expanded view of play cultures, along with the different challenges for us as we contemplate the play spaces of the early twenty-first century. The first of these areas relates to a central question of our project, how children's play cultures relate to their media cultures (see Burn, Chapter 1 of this volume; and Willett, Chapter 6). The second explores the question of variation, using specific examples from the archive. The third looks at scatological and transgressive material from the collection.

The Marriage of Oral Tradition and Media Cultures

Throughout *The Singing Game,* the Opies document instances in which references to children's experience of popular media appear. For example, we read that in Scarborough, two girls performing the song 'Sunny Side Up' include a reference to 'Larry Grayson' who presented the British television show of the 1970s *Shut That Door!* The authors also provide a short list of pop songs that girls throughout the country used as clapping songs; and in the section 'Impersonations and Dance Routines' they cite three contemporary songs: Sandie Shaw's 'Puppet on a String'; 'Save your Kisses for Me', by the Brotherhood of Man; and 'Just One More Dance', by Esther and Abi Ofarim (Opie and Opie, 1985: 414). However, the songs and performances included as full transcriptions constitute a quite specific category. Some do indeed derive from popular cultural and media sources: but ones pre-dating this generation of children by a considerable margin. In the chapter in *The Singing Game* entitled 'Impersonations and Dance Routines', for example, the songs and performances included are all adaptations and transformations of older popular songs: 'She Wears Red Feathers' from 1952 (Opie and Opie 1985: 425); 'Sunny Side Up' from 1929 (Opie and Opie 1985: 429); The 'Tennessee WigWalk' from 1953 (Opie and Opie 1985: 432). Meanwhile, performances of the hits of the 1970s are omitted. The Opies explain this selection explicitly:

> The song-dances in this section are the exception to the rule. They have taken root in oral tradition, and often words and movement have grown over the years. (Opie and Opie, 1985: 415)

Their focus, then, where it included media-derived material, was on texts which had stood the test of time, overcome the ephemerality which they saw as characteristic of media culture and had become subject to the processes of oral transmission over decades which might seem to characterize folkloric material.

By contrast, the range of material in the archive is striking. Again, the fundamental purpose of these interviews was to capture traditional singing games; not to document the children's popular media cultures. Nevertheless, the recordings demonstrate clearly that Iona Opie did take the time to capture, often in some detail, many instances in which children refer to their engagement with contemporary media. She asks them about their television viewing, finding *Scooby-Doo*, *Blue Peter*, *Secret Squirrel* and Adam Ant at Alton, Hampshire (C898.01). She explores their favourite pop songs and singers, finding a tribute to the 1970s Scottish boy-band the Bay City Rollers, sung to the tune of 'This Old Man', in Manchester (C898/69), asking children in Liss if they know the Bay City Rollers (C898/62) and recording children in Poole, Dorset singing the Bay City Rollers' 1975 hit 'Give a Little Love' (C898/80). She probes their transformations of films, finding a game based on *Chitty-Chitty-Bang-Bang* in Bedford (C898/09). An example of her interest in media culture as transgressive practice can be found in a discussion with a group of boys in Liss, Hampshire (her own village) about the popular 1970s US television series *Kung Fu* (C898/22). She asks why the programme is considered dangerous, who the central character (Caine) is and how he moves and fights, and why. Later in the recording she discovers that the boys also exchange Kung Fu trading cards, and that these have been banned by the school.

Particularly notable is the number of pop songs heard on the recordings. When asking the children what their favourite singing or clapping games are, girls often suggest a song that is topping the charts at that time. However, this distinction between songs from media cultures and those from the traditional stock of playground and street songs is not made by the children. In that moment, the song is an undifferentiated part of their culture.

A good example is contained in an interview with children in Coram Fields, a public park and playground in London's Bloomsbury, in July 1974 (C989/26). Opie asks a group of girls if they have any singing games that they enjoy playing. Having sung the often-heard singing game 'When the War Was Over and Josephine was Dead', the girls excitedly ask if their friend can sing 'Mama', and one of them reassures the interviewer: 'she does sing that in the school playground', in fact she stands on the bench and sings it to 'all the people'. The girl then begins to perform Lena Zavaroni's 'Mama, He's Making Eyes at Me', and the other girls join in on the chorus. The song, (words by Sidney Clare, music by Con Conrad) was first published in 1921, and was recorded by many artists before Zavaroni. It is a good example of the complex cultural histories of popular music, accompanied by even more complex oral hinterlands of fan performance, including playground routines. How do we know, then, that it is Zavaroni's performance which these girls are adapting? In fact, their rendition is quite an accurate presentation of Zavaroni's hit record, which opens with a single introductory 'Mama!', followed by a descending scale in the accompaniment. The girls mimic this closely, the soloist singing the song, the others singing the accompaniment in between lines, in chorus.

Having sung this the girls then move on to sing the skipping game 'Salt, Vinegar, Mustard, Cider'. The fact that 'Mama' had won Zavaroni the TV talent show *Opportunity Knocks* is not mentioned, nor the fact that the song was released as a record in 1974. Instead, it appears in and amongst their regular singing and skipping songs. Nevertheless, as indicated above, it does clearly adapt the cultural resources of Zavaroni's hit record, and these continue through the performance: the use of a characteristic vocal break, of exaggerated vibrato, of the choral representations of the accompaniment and 'shoo-wop' section. This engagement with media culture can be seen under Bishop et al's category of *mimesis* (2006). However, as Bishop et al emphasise, it is important to note that mimesis here is more than simply copying. It involves a claim to particular forms of cultural capital; it involves complex forms of musical mastery, including accurate rendition of difficult intervals in the melody, syncopation, modulation (the girls accurately produce the key change midway through the 'shoo-wop' section) and the production of a powerful vocal style. As Marsh argues (2008), these features suggest a musical sophistication considerably greater than orthodox systems of music education allow for. However, the other important factor here is context. The song has become appropriated by these girls, incorporated into their repertoire, and used to delineate, even compete over, cultural roles such as soloist and chorus. Similar performances were noted in the contemporary playground we studied in this project. In Chapter 6 of this volume, Willett considers performances of pop songs in terms of performativity, where the stylistic nature of the rendition also has the social function of performing aspects of identity, group membership and shared cultural affiliation. Opie's work here anticipates the category we have called 'cultural rehearsal', exhibiting iterative practice both for the moment and for future performance. The difference is that the iterative events we witnessed emerged from forms of repeat listening more typical of digital media (CD, DVD, iPod, YouTube) than the TV performances these children may have seen, and even the analogue records and cassettes they may have listened to.

Another example appears in an interview in the London Borough of Dulwich, in May 1976 (C898/27), in which Opie asks a group of girls what songs they use when 'Chinese Skipping' (also known as 'American skipping', 'Elastics' and 'Dutch skipping'). One of the girls asks Opie: 'can I sing a song?' and the children begin to perform Gary Glitter's 'I Love You, Love Me Love' (Glitter/ Leander, 1973). Although the children are not skipping to this song, some can be heard playing 'Chinese skipping' in the background. Having sung this, one of the schoolgirls then prompts her friend: 'Georgie, that Mamma Mia one' and the children launch into an enthusiastic rendition of Abba's 'Mamma Mia'.

Traditional singing games and the 'new' pop songs therefore appear to co-exist contentedly alongside one another. It is also clear, if we consider the recent data gathered in today's playgrounds during our project, that the pop song references are not always as ephemeral as the Opies suggested. With the benefit of hindsight, we can see that Abba's 'Mamma Mia' has returned, this time prompted by the film musical; while references to pop stars of longstanding celebrity such as Michael Jackson suggest a popular cultural tradition of some longevity (Willett, Chapter 6, this volume; Bishop and Burn, 2013).

While the archive includes this rich range of performances directly drawing on children's engagement with the pop hits of the time, the selection made for the section of *The Singing Game* entitled 'Performance' largely omits contemporary pop songs, as we have seen, and instead includes performances of songs at some historical distance from the children. These songs have worked their way into children's play cultures by circuitous routes from their origins in pre- and post-war film, musical and stage, appearing in the playground decades later, their provenance completely opaque to children of the 1970s. By contrast, the provenance of songs by Gary Glitter, Abba, The Bay City Rollers and Lena Zavaroni would have been transparent to these children, and part of their media cultures, even if the purposes and qualities of their immediate use overrode such provenance. The selection for publication, then, exemplifies the Opies' concern that immediate media culture, while important and vital, was somehow less durable than songs and games which seemed more folkloric.

Nevertheless, something about this culture obviously seemed worth recording to Iona Opie as she conducted her fieldwork. In the act of researching, her ambivalence is revealed starkly in a moment from 1970 in Ordsall, Salford. Two girls ask if they can sing a pop song, and she replies 'I'd rather not hear a pop song – it's not what I'm collecting, you see'. She immediately relents, however, and records performances of 'Big Spender' and 'Rock Around the Clock' (C898/39). In spite of the concern about ephemerality, and perhaps the kind of cultural distinction one might expect of researchers of the Opies' social class and generation, there is a sense that these performances were evidence of children's perennial appropriation and transformation of adult popular culture. The existence of these recordings offers the researcher a rich resource with which to explore the relationship between the media and the playground. Perhaps Gary Glitter's, 'I Love You, Love Me Love', enjoyed only a brief spell of popularity and the children at Coram Fields soon stopped singing Lena Zavaroni's hit, but the frequency with which these songs appear suggests that they represent something more than an ephemeral enthusiasm. As Sutton-Smith notes in his review of *The Singing Game*, the children's play culture seems almost to have 'taken on the character of modern mass media culture with its cycles of fashion and popularity' (Sutton-Smith, 1986), something that the recordings corroborate.

Something of the same sense was evident in our ethnographic studies. Certainly the hybridizing of contemporary media texts and what we have referred to as residual or sedimented texts is clear. At the same time, however, the mediascape (Appadurai, 1996) of children in the twenty-first century is different from that of the 1970s in certain ways; though there are also similarities. Both groups of children enjoyed pop songs, listened to them on TV, radio and film and learnt to perform them. Both generations enjoyed TV talent shows. However, in the interval the rise of the music video and MTV has taken place, and the variety of media platforms on which children might access this material has expanded considerably, allowing for more intensive, varied and repeated listening to vocal performances and viewing dance routines. A good example is the reference to viewing Michael Jackson videos with her cousins made by a girl in the London school, in an interview about influences on her own playground dance routines (Bishop and Burn, 2013).

Television show theme tunes and advertisement jingles also make their way onto the recordings. Of particular popularity is *The Wombles* theme tune, from the 1970s children's animated television series, based on the series of books by Elizabeth Beresford. When interviewing schoolgirls from Nottingham in June, 1977, the children discuss with Opie various singing games that they play, including 'I'm a Little Dutch Girl'. One of the girls then suggests that they sing the song that 'Michaela learnt us' and they begin to sing *The Wombles* theme tune. Significantly, the children seem unaware of the television origins of the song and explain that 'Michaela made it up, it's ever so good'. In another instance, when interviewing children in Hampshire, Opie records a small group of children performing a television jingle for fruit pastilles. They sing: 'put them pastilles round Ma, put them pastilles round, pastille-picking Mama, pass those pastilles round' (C89804-02). Again, this song appears in and amongst the other traditional playground songs and that it is borrowed from the television is not mentioned by the schoolgirls; indeed, it appears to be of little significance to them. Opie is clearly interested in what they know of the provenance of the song, asking if it comes from the TV, to which one of them replies 'Yeah', and another 'It's an advert'. Opie asks twice if they know who made the pastilles, clearly looking for Rowntrees, but they do not respond to this.

Finally, in Boughton and Salford, November 1970, when performing the widespread clapping song 'When Susie Was a Baby', a group of schoolgirls chant the line: 'when Susie was a Saint, a Saint Susie was' before beginning to sing the theme tune from the popular 1960s television show *The Saint*, aired between 1962 and 1969. Based on the novels of Leslie Charteris, the show followed the life of adventurer Simon Templar, played by Roger Moore. This kind of media reference is of the type that Bishop et al (2006) term *onomastic allusion*, here accomplished by a noun phrase ('a Saint') easily inserted into the sequence as 'a highly flexible unit which can be adapted by lexical substitution on a slot-and-filler basis' (Lennon, 2004: 166). In this case, 'Saint' does not scan, as two syllables are required for the meter; so two notes are slurred by the girls over the single syllable. However, interestingly, the word 'Saint' is insufficiently specific to function alone as the allusion, needing to be disambiguated by the melody of the theme tune. This is, then, *multimodal* onomastic allusion, pleasurable in its avoidance of the obvious citation of Simon Templar's name.

This example is indicative of the significant function that different media fulfil within play culture and raises questions which relate to themes addressed throughout this book. One of these is the way in which apparently settled traditional texts are subject to what the Opies called the processes of 'wear and repair' (Opie and Opie, 1959: 7). Here, the interweaving of TV character and theme tune into a flexible sequence (itself subject to many variations, as the Opies and others documented), along with the witty alignment of the Saint with a moment in between Susie's death and appearance as a ghost, demonstrates the process of oral composition which other researchers have noted as a feature of play culture (e.g. Marsh, 2008), while at the same time seamlessly welding together elements from oral culture and media culture.

That the children often claim to be unaware of the media origins, or uninterested in them, is a common response, confirmed in the ethnographic studies for this project (see also Bishop and Curtis, 2001). While it suggests that the dominant concern of the children is the cultural moment rather than its back story, it also brings into question the apparently secure boundary between orally transmitted lore and play derived from children's media cultures. The ethnographic studies in our project contain examples of media-derived texts taught by one child to others, so that the process of transmission is identical to that of oral tradition. How to distinguish between a folksong and a performance of media culture in these contexts becomes an impossible task, resolved here by acknowledging the merging of the two cultures and their movement through the micro-histories of children's improvisatory play.

This process also raises the question addressed elsewhere in this book of the agency of childhood. While these children are the inheritors of oral transmission and consumers of media texts, this instance and many others demonstrate their ability to transform the cultural resources they acquire, producing something new each time, determined by their interests, aspirations and tastes and preferences. This kind of agency, while it is expressive of social identities and interests, is often also referred to as a form of creativity – an idea returned to below in the context of the variations found in the Opie archive.

Variation and Its Social Context

The process of selection needed to produce a collection like *The Singing Game* inevitably narrowed the representation of variation, even producing something of an effect of standardization of songs and games. The recordings demonstrate that the variations of language, music and to some extent action are much greater than *The Singing Game* was able to show. There are instances, for example, in which a particular well-known song is sung to an entirely different tune from that often heard and from that recorded in *The Singing Game*.[3] The Opies admit in the Preface to *The Singing Game*: 'we have given more than one tune in the few cases in which there are several well-established tunes for the same game, but we have not given all variants' (Opie and Opie, 1985: vii). Though there is a brief comment in the Preface on the music, its effect is to generalize and homogenize; their interests lay more with linguistic and prosodic variation and transformation.

However, melodic variations are evident in the recordings. One striking example of this is heard when a child, recently moved to a school in Liss, in 1974, sings her version of 'Under the Bram Bush' (C898/23)[4]. Her school friends have already sung their version and this follows the familiar rhyme recorded by the Opies in *The Singing Game*. The children seem reluctant to let the 'new' girl sing her version and Iona notes that the girl has trouble trying to persuade her friends to sing it with her. Eventually, when she does sing, the tune and rhythm are entirely different from that previously heard. This episode suggests two ideas. Firstly, that variation is, as suggested above, greater than can be easily represented in collections; and greater than is sometimes suggested in academic analysis emphasizing the limited repertoire of clapping game tunes. Curtis suggests, for example:

---

[3]   The version published in *The Singing Game* was recorded in Stepney, London, in 1976 (C898/29). The words of the recording correspond exactly to the published version; though the tune does not, quite. Perhaps Michael Hurd's transcription was based on another tape (there are many instances of this song in the collection); or perhaps it is a composite derived from several.

[4]   This recording is not accessible online, as it is an off-air recording of a BBC broadcast. It can be listened to locally at the British Library.

> Girls have a great many clapping games and at a casual glance would seem to have an extensive repertoire of movements, actions and songs in their games. A closer examination, however, reveals that they build a wide variety of games from a small number of hand movements and snatches of melody. (Curtis, 2004: 421)

Secondly, that the social process of transmission is complex. Certainly, the movement of children between schools (as in this case), regions and countries is a factor in the intertextual borrowings, mergers and mash-ups – to use an expression typically applied to the combinatory bricolage of contemporary online culture (e.g. Ito, 2010) – which characterize playground rhymes and tunes. However, the temptation to celebrate such transmission as smooth, collaborative and communal is given pause by the kind of resistance found in this example, where a new and different version of the song is treated as an alien invasion, rejected in favour of familiar orthodoxy, representative of settled patterns of friendship reluctant to be disturbed.

Another variation of 'Under the Bram Bush' is sung by children from St Clement's School, Salford, November 1970 (C898/38). This tune is reminiscent of the song 'Down by the Riverside', a popular gospel song widely employed as an anthem of the Civil Rights Movement of the 1960s. Here, then, the words of the rhyme, their origins in late nineteenth-/early twentieth-century popular song (Opie and Opie, 1985: 452–3), embellished with a playground interest in adult love and procreation, are complemented by music filtering through from global protest culture – though of course there is no evidence of the children's awareness of such a meaning.

The following notation attempts to demonstrate these markedly different tunes and rhythms. The four lines represent the most commonly-found 'Under the Bram Bush' tune (Michael Hurd's transcription in *The Singing Game*), the one recorded in Salford, 1970 (C898/38), the one recorded in Liss, Hampshire, 1974, and the one recorded in London's American School (C898/02) (Figure 2.1).

The first point to note, perhaps, is that almost nothing is known of the origins of the *Singing Game* version of the tune published in *The Singing Game*. While the Opies spend a page and a half on the history of the *words* and their origins in Harry and Harriet Harndin's 1895 song 'A Cannibal King' and Cole and Johnson's 1902 song 'Under the Bamboo Tree' (parodied by T.S. Eliot in *Sweeney Agonistes*, as a matter of interest), they say nothing about the *tune*. Certainly it bears no resemblance to the tunes of either the Harndin song or the Cole and Johnson song.

The resemblance of the Salford tune to 'Down by the Riverside' has already been noted. The Liss tune is elusive, but is reminiscent of stirring film theme tunes of the time: the rhythm and melody of the four-note sequence which repeats in bars 3, 5 and 11, for example, resembles a sequence in Elmer Bernstein's 1960 theme music for *The Magnificent Seven*. It also resembles 'Under the Spreading Chestnut Tree', which, though it may derive from a traditional English dance tune (Gilchrist, 1940), has been much anthologized in campfire song manuals and more recently, websites.

Fig. 2 1   Four versions of 'Under the Bram Bush'. Transcription by Julia Bishop.

Alongside these markedly different tunes, we also hear variations that borrow from other songs. For example, in the recording of children performing 'Under the Bram Bush' in London's American School, the children concatenate the usual tune with the song 'Row, Row Your Boat' (C898/02). The girl performing sings: 'and when we're married, we'll raise a family, of forty children, all in a row, row, row your boat, gently down the stream, tip your teacher over board and see how loud she screams, ah!' This is followed by two other girls singing 'A Sailor Went to Sea, sea, sea', and then questions from Opie about where they learned the songs. A voice resembling that of the girl who performed 'Under the Bram Bush' (an English accent with a slight trace of American) tells of learning it in Boston, Massachusetts. There is no other information, but it is worth noting that 'Row Row Row Your Boat' is a traditional nursery rhyme with a likely American origin. The Roud Folk Song Index has three versions: two recorded in Nova Scotia in 1949 (S250614) and 1951 (S270014), and one text version from Canada from the 1970s (S276030). It is widely anthologized for summer camps, Scouts and Guides, and incorporated in children's TV programmes such as *Sesame Street*. It can be seen, then, as an example of the glocalisation Bennett finds in hip-hop (Bennett, 1999): a meeting of global cultural resources with local inflections and specific motivations.

The Opies had neither the time nor the space to note these variations in the published outcomes of their research. However, the recordings remind us how easy it is for these songs and rhymes to become standardised and indicate that further research into variation and the complex inventiveness of this culture is required. Bishop demonstrates how such complexity might be traced and analysed in Chapter 3 of this volume.

One response to variation can be to treat it as evidence of children's creativity, (e.g. Bishop and Curtis, 2001). However, creativity can be an unhelpful and confusing idea; and it is certainly much contested in relation to children's culture, art and education (Banaji and Burn, 2006). The Russian psychologist Lev Vygotsky proposed a specific model of creativity in childhood and adolescence (1931/1988). In his account, creativity is closely linked to play: it involves imaginative transformation of cultural resources, and traffic between external play with such transformations (through language, toys, objects and social interaction) and the internal processes of the imagination. To this extent, the kinds of transformation the Opies collected can be seen as examples of creativity. However, Vygotsky argued that true creativity also involved conscious, rational control. In this respect, it may be that the imaginative processes of game and song change are best kept within conceptions of play, rather than celebrated as creativity. Vygotsky's model certainly allows us to think of such play as a necessary foundation for creativity, just as specialists in different disciplines have seen playground games as foundations for literacy, music-making and other domains of creative activity which later become formalised as curriculum subjects and disciplines. However, while we may in this way circumscribe the forms of invention and innovation described in this chapter, we should note that other forms of play may involve much more conscious control and awareness of structure: girls constructing dance routines; children inventing rules and systems for chasing games; children controlling elaborate socio-dramatic play. We found examples of all of these in the ethnographic studies of contemporary play in our project, and they are discussed in other chapters of this volume. What all have in common, though, is an immersion in the affective flow of the moment, in the aesthetic pleasure of the game, in the dynamic social bond of collaborative play – a set of improvisatory impulses which resist distanced reflection, interest in provenance and design abstracted from performance.

Rude Rhymes in the Record

A brief glance through *The Singing Game* would suggest that the children's oral tradition of the 1970s was one largely free of scatological or offensive rhymes. There is also some evidence in the recordings that this appears to be a culture that carefully toed the line of what might be considered socially acceptable, from the girl who is too embarrassed to refer to 'Susie's bra' (lost in her boyfriend's car), to the giggling children in London who refer to Queen Mary's apparent hairiness. Elsewhere, however, the recordings suggest otherwise, as the examples discussed below demonstrate. A plausible explanation for the omission of such material from *The Singing Game* is that stringent publishing policies may have prevented the Opies from publishing such material. As Iona Opie remarks: '[…] it was editorial policy amongst publishers in the 1950s, not to include dubious material, and that prevented us including anything that was unacceptable to OUP: 'knickers' was the limit'.[5] Of course, by the 1980s we might assume that such censorship had softened, but even so, this disclosure highlights the regulatory regimes by which the Opies had to abide.

Considering these factors, it is significant that Iona Opie is vigilant in recording those instances in which the children test the boundaries of social acceptability, performing songs that range from the mischievous to the explicitly sexual. One example comes from a school playground in Poole (C898/80). While performing singing games, one young girl begins to sing: 'One plus one, we're in the bedroom, cha-nah-nah-nah-nah'. The song progresses and she sings: 'three plus three, we're jumping all around in the bedroom' before briefly noting to the interviewer, with a giggle, that this song is 'rude'. Nonetheless, she continues to sing: 'four plus four, he caught me on the floor in the bedroom, cha-nah-nah-nah-nah; five plus five, my legs are wide open in the bedroom, cha-nah-nah-nah-nah, six plus six, he's pulling down my knicks in the bedroom, cha-nah-nah-nah-nah'. The song continues and Opie can be heard laughing as the schoolgirl finishes her song (concluding with the couple 'breaking up' in the bedroom). The British Library notes accompanying the recording (produced during our project) represent further contextual information contained in the recording:

---

5   Iona Opie cited in Boyes, 1995.

The girl learnt this song when she lived in Pimlico, London. She would use this to play 'Two Balls' and explains the different actions that accompany this song. She uses terms such as 'tubble eggs' and 'nodsies'. The girl from Pimlico becomes irritated with another girl who tries to explain how this game is played and remarks: 'you don't know how we do it Jennifer with 'One Plus One' 'cos you don't even know it'. In the background a girl can be heard remarking (about the girl from Pimlico) 'she thinks she knows everything'.

The ludic function of the rhyme, then, is also to provide the necessary rhythmic accompaniment to the two-balls routine, while its more general cultural function is the entertaining appeal of its transgressive content. Its value is evident in the fierce defence of its local ownership.

Thus, although predominantly collecting traditional singing, clapping and skipping games, the fact that Opie recorded this song suggests that she was aware of its significance. Indeed, these recordings would be particularly pertinent in testing and validating theories such as those of Sutton-Smith who suggests that play can both allow children to transcend the 'normal limits' of their society and enable them to make sense of the adult world around them (Sutton-Smith, 1997). This view resembles the notion of the 'tribal child' which James, Jenks and Prout associate with the Opies: childhood perceived as a different society, operating by different rules and customs, difficult to penetrate and requiring ethnographic enquiry to do so (James, Jenks and Prout, 1998). It also echoes, however, the versions of youth culture found in British Cultural Studies in the 1970s, which conceived of young people as oppressed by adult society and urgently motivated to carve out a cultural space of resistance, albeit pursuing different strategies of resistance according to class background, and in part inheriting features of parental cultures (Hall and Jefferson, 1993).

However, there are other quite different explanations. The above interpretations construct childhood as a rebellious counter-culture, gleefully exotic, shockingly amoral, assertively ribald. By contrast, developmental approaches to childhood play see such explorations of taboo themes like adult sexuality as the child's predictable interest in future selfhoods, including the sexual identities waiting in adolescence. Our approach in this project has been to argue that these two approaches – the tribal child and the developing child – are compatible, if paradoxical. Children's play is, to echo the new sociology of childhood, about both *being* and *becoming* (e.g. Uprichard, 2008): about the self-sufficient moment of play *and* about anticipatory fantasies of adolescence and adulthood.

One interesting feature of the more extreme explorations of taboo subjects is the number of children who are willing to perform these scatological pieces beyond the regulatory regimes of the school playground. This is particularly apparent on a recording Opie collected from a housing estate in Chelsea in 1974 (C898/67). From the start of this recording, a particular boy can be heard in the background, continuously shouting rude rhymes, swear-words and insults. The fact he remains in the background suggests that he is careful to exercise some caution, unsure of his peers and most importantly the interviewer's reaction. Initially, he begins by teasing his sister who is being interviewed, mimicking her voice and answers. He then begins to shout insults, such as: 'Guess what, she [his sister] never combs her hair in the mornings' and 'Deborah I think you've got a bloody big thicky head'. As noone has reacted to these insults, he grows in confidence, shouting: 'Deborah, why don't you do a stripsys [striptease] show?' He concludes by announcing that he would like to perform a song and remarks: 'can I say another one for the old bag [presumably referring to Opie]?'. Neither the other children nor the interviewer, however, react. This defiant performance would have been unlikely on many school playgrounds, then and now: the implications of different regulatory regimes for taboo themes in play is considered further below.

Meanwhile, perhaps encouraged by this particular boy's behaviour, the other children begin to recite transgressive rhymes. One boy sings: 'ip, dip, dog, shit, who trod in it. Not because you're dirty, not because you're clean, my mum said you're the fairy queen'. Another then sings: 'Chocolate biscuits down the drain, if you want some spell your name, if you want them, fucking go away'. When Opie asks the young girl to repeat this, the schoolgirl omits the swear-word. This particular group of children also tell an assortment of jokes featuring 'bosoms' and 'willies'.

These areas of the archive raise a number of questions. Firstly, again, they reveal the well-documented preoccupation of younger children with bodily functions ranging from faeces to sex (Roud, 2010). This theme lends itself to a positive interpretation of the kind supported by some of Sutton-Smith's work, easy to characterize in terms of Bakhtin's metaphors of carnival (Bakhtin, 1965/1968). The grotesque aesthetic, humorous obsession with appetite and excretion and carnival laughter which Bakhtin identifies in Rabelais are all consonant with the ribald play of these verses and songs. At the same time, however, this kind of positive interpretation needs to be balanced against recognition of the very varied social functions of these kinds of play. Sometimes, indeed, they represent taboo bending, a pricking of adult primness and pomposity, a challenge to what Stallybrass and White see as the attempt to construct the bourgeois body through the education of the child:

> as s/he grows up/is cleaned up, the lower bodily stratum is regulated or denied, as far as possible, by the correct posture ('stand up straight', 'don't squat', 'don't kneel on all fours' – the postures of servants and savages), and by the censoring of lower 'bodily' references along with bodily wastes. (Stallybrass and White, 1986: 144–5)

At other times, like other forms of risky play, they can embody less benign functions: racism, misogyny and social exclusion. Play in its more extreme forms is a two-edged weapon, a vehicle for entering worlds otherwise inaccessible, but also an instrument of insult and inequity and the exercise of power, as Sutton-Smith and Kelly-Byrne argue in their critique of the 'idealization of play' (Sutton-Smith and Kelly-Byrne, 1984; and Richards's discussion of their essay, this volume, Chapter 4). These aspects of play were also recognized by the Opies:

The dialectal lore flows more quietly but deeper; it is the language of the children's darker doings: playing truant, giving warning, sneaking, swearing, snivelling, tormenting, and fighting. It belongs to all time, but is limited in locality. (Opie and Opie, 1959: 12–13)

Conclusion: Lessons from the Archive

To say that *The Singing Game* is an inaccurate and distorted reflection of the 85 Opie recordings would be untrue. As we have seen, the diversity of the archive gives us a better and more detailed picture of variation in language and melody than the published work is able to do, given the constraints under which it operates. The detail the archive provides of the echoes of tunes and rhymes from children's and adult worlds, along with the often-inspired compositional work of innovative details, clever juxtapositions and the mix-and-match aesthetic of singing game culture, offers robust justification for the Opies' admiration of playground culture.

At the same time, when set alongside the material found in this project's ethnographies, we can gain some sense of how continuity and change happens across the decades as well as within the micro-histories sometimes glimpsed in the Opie archive. We can see the perpetuation of the narratives and nonsense, the parody and wordplay, the rhythm and rhyme of the seventies in the songs and rhymes of the twenty-first century. We can see the disappearance of some familiar figures from folklore and the media – Cowboy Joe from Mexico, Poor Jenny, Shirley Temple and Diana Dors – and the arrival of others – Tracey Beaker, Beyoncé, Barney the dinosaur. Some figures never seem to change: perhaps Susie and her ever-varying Seven Ages of Womanhood will be with us forever. And finally, we can see the perennial preoccupations with the taboos adults impose – sexuality, fighting and bodily functions – alive and well, if a little more muted within the regulatory regimes of contemporary playgrounds.

References

Appadurai A (1996) *Modernity at Large: Cultural Dimensions of Globalization.* Minneapolis: University of Minnesota Press.

Bakhtin MM (1965/1968) *Rabelais and His World.* Translated. H. Islowsky, Cambridge, MA: Massachusetts Institute of Technology Press.

Banaji S and Burn A (2006) *Rhetorics of Creativity*, commissioned by Creative Partnerships, at www.creative-partnerships.com/literaturereviews

Bennett A (1999) Rappin' on the Tyne: White Hip Hop culture in North-east England – an ethnographic study. *The Sociological Review* 47(1): 1–24, February 1999.

Bishop JC and Burn A (2013) Reasons for rhythm: Multimodal perspectives on musical play. In Willett R, Richards C, Marsh J, Burn A and Bishop JC (2013) *Children, Media and Playground Cultures: Ethnographic Studies of School Playtimes.* Basingstoke: Palgrave Macmillan.

Bishop JC and Curtis J (2001) Introduction. In Bishop JC and Curtis J (eds) (2001) *Play Today in the Primary School Playground: Life, Learning and Creativity*. Buckingham: The Open University Press. 1–20.

Bishop JC and Curtis M with Woolley H, Armitage M and Ginsborg J (2006). Participation, popular culture and playgrounds: Children's uses of media elements in peer play at school. Paper presented at the Folklore Society Conference, *Folklore, Film and Television: Convergences in Traditional Cultures and Popular Media*, 31 March–1 April 2006, London.

Boyes G (1995) The legacy of the work of Iona and Peter Opie: The lore and language of today's children. In Beard R (ed.) *Rhyme, Reading and Writing*. London: Hodder Arnold. 131–47.

Buckingham D (2000) *After the Death of Childhood: Growing Up in the Age of Electronic Media*. Cambridge: Polity.

Corsaro WA (2009) Peer cultures. In Qvortrup J, Corsaro WA and Honig MS (eds) *The Palgrave Handbook of Childhood Studies*. Palgrave Macmillan: Basingstoke. 301–6.

Curtis M (2004) A sailor went to sea: Theme and variations. *Folk Music Journal* 8(4): 451–6.

Finnegan R (2002) Communicating: The Multiple Modes of Human Interconnection. London: Routledge.

Geertz C (1973) *The Interpretation of Cultures*. New York: Basic Books.

Gilchrist A (1940) Under the spreading chestnut tree: The adventures of a tune. *The Musical Times* 81 (Mar. 1940): 112–13.

Griffiths M and Machin D (2003) Television and playground games as part of children's symbolic culture. *Social Semiotics* 3(2): 147–60.

Grugeon, E. (1988) Underground knowledge: What the opies missed. *English in Education*, 22 (2), 9–17.

Hall S and Jefferson T (eds) (1993) *Resistance Through Rituals: Youth Subcultures in Post-war Britain*. London: Routledge.

Ito M (2010) Mobilizing the imagination in everyday play: the case of Japanese media mixes. In Sonvilla-Weiss S (ed.) *Mash-Up Cultures*. New York: SpringerWien. 79–97.

James A (2009) Agency. In Qvortrup J, Corsaro WA and Honig MS (eds) *The Palgrave Handbook of Childhood Studies*. Basingstoke: Palgrave, 34–45.

James A, Jenks C and Prout A (1998) *Theorizing Childhood*. Cambridge: Polity Press.

Jopson L (2011) Unpublished notes on an interview with Ione Opie by Cathy Courtney.

Lennon P (2004) *Allusions in the Press: An Applied Linguistic Study*. Boston, MA: Walter de Gruyter.

Marsh K (2008) *The Musical Playground: Global Tradition and Change in Children's Songs and Games*. New York: Oxford University Press.

Newall V (1980) *Folklore studies in the twentieth century: proceedings of the centenary conference of the Folklore Society*. Totowa, NJ: Rowan and Littlefield.

Opie I and Opie P (1959) *The Lore and Language of Schoolchildren*. Oxford: Oxford University Press.

Opie I and Opie P (1969) *Children's Games in Street and Playground*. Oxford: Oxford University Press.

Opie I and Opie P (1985) *The Singing Game*. Oxford: Oxford University Press.

Opie I (1988) Iona Opie. In Nakamura, J (ed) *Something about the author*. Detroit, MI: Gale. 203–17.

Opie I (1993) *The People in the Playground*. Oxford: Oxford University Press.

Opie I (1997) *Children's Games with Things*. Oxford: Oxford University Press.

Qvortrup J (2009) Childhood as structural form. In Qvortrup J, Corsaro WA and Honig MS (eds) *The Palgrave Handbook of Childhood Studies*. Basingstoke: Palgrave, 21–33.

Roud S (2010) *The Lore of the Playground: One Hundred Years of Children's Games, Rhymes and Traditions*. London: Random House.

Sutton-Smith B (1986) Review: *The Singing Game*. *The Journal of American Folklore* 99(392): 239–40.

Sutton-Smith B (1997) *The Ambiguity of Play*. Cambridge, MA: Harvard University Press.

Sutton-Smith B and Kelly-Byrne D (1984) The idealization of play. In PK Smith (ed.) *Play in Animals and Humans*. Oxford: Blackwell, 305–21.

Stallybrass P and White A (1986) *The Poetics and Politics of Transgression*. Ithaca, NY: Cornell University Press.

Uprichard E (2008) Children as 'being and becomings': Children, childhood and temporality. *Children and Society* 22: 303–13.

Vygotsky LS (1931/1998) Imagination and creativity in the adolescent. *The Collected Works of L.S. Vygotsky*, Volume 5, 151–66.

Chapter 3
'That's how the whole hand-clap thing passes on': Online/Offline Transmission and Multimodal Variation in a Children's Clapping Game

Julia C. Bishop

Hand-clapping games are a form of musical play. They are commonly undertaken by girls in groups of up to six players. The groups are often made up of friends in the same year group at school or sometimes child relatives or adults (Opie and Opie, 1985; Grugeon, 1993; Gaunt, 2006; Marsh, 2008). The skills associated with clapping are predominantly learnt through observation of other performers and peer tuition, and are honed through repeated participation in clapping games with others. Specific texts, tunes and movement patterns are transmitted during this process and exist in multiple iterations which, although recognisably similar, may exhibit difference to varying degrees. In our study, we found many instances of clapping play on the playgrounds of both schools and an overlapping but distinctive repertoire of clapping texts, tunes and movement patterns between the two.

Like all play, clapping games are multimodal (Kress and Van Leeuwen, 2001). Most obviously, they incorporate verbal text, music, movement and touch but other modes, such as proxemics and gaze, are also important. Much folklore scholarship has tended to foreground verbal aspects of clapping rhymes and has frequently adopted a comparative and historical approach to chart their potential origin, dissemination and variation over time and space (Opie and Opie, 1985; Arleo, 2001). In recent years, there has been greater attention to the music and movement elements of clapping play, including several extended studies by ethnomusicologists (e.g. Gaunt, 2006; Marsh, 2008). These have adopted an ethnographic approach to elicit participants' perspectives and examine aspects of performance, social context, transmission and creativity.

The present chapter combines aspects of both these approaches to focus on the interlinked topics of continuity and change in clapping play, and the transmission of clapping games in and between online and offline spaces. It does so by considering in some detail the clapping game 'Eeny Meeny Dessameeny' within the Sheffield school in the period 2006–2010, drawing on video recordings and the children's recollections as documented during the last 18 months of this time (see Appendix

A).[1] The role of YouTube as a source for clapping games, the ways in which the game disseminated among a network of girls, and the conscious changes they introduced into the game's words, music and movement patterns are discussed. The results of this case study illustrate the notion of 'cultural rehearsal' we propose in this book, showing that children's use of amateur clapping game videos on YouTube has much in common with their face-to-face practices of teaching and learning, but with additional affordances which offer the possibility of intense and iterative engagement. They also suggest that YouTube-referenced clapping play can carry high symbolic value in peer relations and supports the presentation of oneself or one's friendship group as both savvy and innovative. The data also exemplify the multimodal, dialogical and reciprocal nature of variation, and the subtle ways in which children draw on various cultural resources to forge their own particular meanings in clapping play.

Continuity and Change in Folklore

The study of continuity and change, 're-creation' or 'variation' has been an enduring and often a central concern in folklore studies. This is so both within older paradigms which tend to conceptualise folklore as a series of persisting cultural objects and within the performance-oriented paradigm which conceptualises folklore as 'a mode of communicative action' (Bauman and Briggs 1990: 79). Multiformity has come to be seen as a defining characteristic of folklore and is usually seen as a corollary of oral transmission (in the older paradigm) or the emergent nature of performance (cf. McDowell, 1999, in relation to the transmission of children's folklore).

The highly delimited spatial, temporal and social focus of the present study is an attempt to trace what Honko terms 'organic variation'. Honko claims that the concept of variation is under-theorised and misunderstood within folklore studies (2000). One of his criticisms is the failure of scholars to document 'real' or 'organic' variation because of the long time periods and large geographical areas from which evidence was gathered:

> There was no real 'dialogue' to be constructed between the variants, which practically never belonged to the same tradition community. The lack of contextual information made it difficult to assess the cultural representativity of data. In short, the variation was artificial, visible only to the scholar, and certainly not representative of the real, organic variation of folklore to be observed through empirical research. (2000: 8)

Honko therefore advocates the study of 'real variation' through 'thick corpus', that is, 'a "thickness" of text and context through multiple documentation of

---

[1]   References to the relevant audio and video files are given in abbreviated form in the body of this chapter. The full details can be found in Appendix A.

expressions of folklore in their varying manifestations in performance within a "biologically" definable tradition bearer, community or environment' (2000: 17).[2]

As Honko's observation suggests, a dialogic approach to the study of folkloric texts and genres, and folkloristic notions of transmission and re-creation, has begun to emerge. This approach is predicated on Bakhtin's idea that

> the word in language is always half someone else's. It becomes 'one's own' only when the speaker populates it with his own intention, his own accent, when he appropriates the word, adapting it to his own semantic and expressive intention. Prior to this moment of appropriation, the word does not exist in a neutral and impersonal language ... but rather it exists in other people's mouths, in other people's concrete contexts, serving other people's intentions: it is from there that one must take the word, and make it one's own. (Bakhtin, 1981: 293–94)

Dialogism entails a conceptualisation of communication as Janus-faced. It posits that the utterance, as part of a chain of utterances or discourse, is viewed as orientated to, and evaluative of, past utterances whilst simultaneously being shaped by the anticipated responses of those to whom it is addressed now and in the future (Bakhtin, 1986). A number of linguistic studies have made productive use of this concept in relation to children's informal talk (e.g. Maybin, 2006).

Children's play is replete with examples of such revoicings, 'the ways in which [children] take on, reproduce and represent the voices of significant people, texts and genres in their lives' (Maybin, 2008: 1). As we shall see in relation to the clapping game examined below, the players drew on local practices and texts in face-to-face interaction with peers, family discourse and performance, commercial media productions such as film, and vernacular productions globally disseminated via the participatory web (specifically, films of clapping games uploaded to YouTube). Maybin shows that children often 'reword and reframe reported utterances in line with their own intentions' in their informal talk (2006: 55). Bauman and Briggs underline this kind of transformation in folkloric speech genres, arguing, 'because the process is transformational, we must now determine what the recontextualized text brings with it from its earlier context(s) and what emergent form, function, and meaning it is given as it is recentered' (1990: 74–75).[3]

One way of thinking about this, put forward by these same scholars, is the notion of 'intertextual gap':

> The process of linking particular utterances to generic models thus necessarily produces an intertextual *gap*. Although the creation of this hiatus is unavoidable, its relative suppression or foregrounding has important effects. On the one

---

[2]   Earlier folklore scholarship is by no means without examples of this approach (see, for example, Russell, 1987). Others have shown that variation and meaning-making may arise between communities, not only within them (e.g. Green, 1970–71; cf. Bauman, 1971).

[3]   Thus, they argue that 'it helps ... if one has good data on successive points in the process, but examination even of apparently isolated texts may be productive precisely because a text may carry some of its history with it' (1990: 75).

> hand, texts framed in some genres attempt to achieve generic transparency by *minimizing* the distance between texts and genres, thus rendering the discourse maximally interpretable through the use of generic precedents. This approach sustains highly conservative, traditionalizing modes of creating textual authority. On the other hand, *maximizing* and highlighting these intertextual gaps underlies strategies for building authority through claims of individual creativity and innovation ... resistance to the hegemonic structures associated with established genres, and other motives for distancing oneself from textual precedents (Bauman and Briggs, 1992: 149)

This suggests a fresh perspective on the way in which children 're-word and re-frame' their play. Ethnographers of children's play have found that children often claim to have 'made up' games, and only sometimes articulate how they have learnt play and texts from others (e.g. Opie and Opie, 1985: 414; Opie, 1993: 3–4, 185, 191–92; Zumwalt, 1995: 23; Marsh, 2008:178; Roud, 2010: 3). Yet many games and texts have been in circulation for some time. Iona and Peter Opie contrast a child's offer of 'one you won't know because it's only just made up' with the fact that they were able to trace the text back to at least 1893 (1959: 12). They further observe that what appears to them as minor textual variation, such as the substitution of a word in a verse, is frequently claimed as authorship by children (1959: 12). Why do children commonly frame their revoicings by maximising the intertextual gap in this way?

Richards notes that:

> Though children say, repeatedly, that they 'just made it up', every act of play draws on a dense array of sources ... Their knowledge of origins may be vague and uncertain. But like any other bricoleur, their main concern is with what they can do with what is to hand rather than with where it has come from (2011: 323).

The metaphor of bricoleur is helpful here in that it stresses children's transformation, rather than the more mechanistic notion of transmission, of texts and games (cf. McDowell, 1999: 52). Bakhtin's notion of the imperative to make another's words expressive of oneself suggests that there is no contradiction between children's learning play from others and their claim to making it up. In this process, they may appear to 'repeat' texts and games, or 're-word' and 're-frame' them, or 'tinker with' them or 'rehash' them in the manner of a bricoleur, but the process is still transformative. The 'I made it up' frame looks forward to how others will respond to the game and text, playing up the intertextual gap, and allowing a child to position herself as producer, originator, authority, artist, model and/or teacher. Conversely, when a game or text is framed as having been transmitted from another, children are positioned deferentially as learners, consumers, re-producers, heirs and subordinates to the authority of sources or models.

The latter situation is illustrated by the Opies' construction of children as preservers (1959: 12), 'respecters, even venerators, of custom' in whose 'self-contained community their basic lore and language seems scarcely to alter from generation to generation' (1959: 2). Their perspective is borne of the historical and comparative lens they employed (1959: 8, 11) which leads them to minimise the intertextual gap. They acknowledge changes at various levels (e.g. 1959: 9–11, 14; 1969: 8–10), but are categorical in their view that these do not constitute creativity or inventiveness by children (1959: 8, 12; 1993: 3). Variations are viewed as occurring 'more often by accident than design' (1959: 8), '"clever wheezes", hopeful experiments, and minor games which last no more than a day, or at the most a few weeks' (Opie 1993: 12). They are attributed to such things as mishearing, misunderstanding, rationalisation and abridgement due to the intensive use of games and texts by each generation of children within a roughly six-year period (1959: 8–9). 'Thus', the Opies conclude, 'oral lore is subject to a continual process of wear and repair, for folklore, like everything else in nature, must adapt itself to new conditions if it is to survive' (1959: 9).

To illustrate this, they give an example of a playground rhyme, taken from an eighteenth-century ballad, which has been used for counting out, skipping, and the nursery, with concomitant textual changes. The Opies suggest that most of these textual changes have come about 'due to contact with newer verses' (1959: 11). There is a resonance here with Bakhtin's observation that 'when we select words in the process of constructing an utterance, we by no means always take them from the system of language in their neutral, *dictionary* form. We usually take them from *other utterances*, and mainly from utterances that are kindred to ours in genre, that is, in theme, composition, or style' (1986: 87). These may take the form of traditional formulas associated with the genre, as argued by Marsh, in the manner of oral-formulaic composition (2008: 142). The following section considers children's media cultures whose multi-modal materials increasingly permeate children's worlds and seem to offer this new and kindred or cognate quality, for they have often been drawn on in children's clapping games as well as their talk more generally (cf. Maybin, 2006; Bishop et al., 2006, Willett et al., 2013, and chapters 5 and 6 in the present volume).

Clapping Games, Media Culture and YouTube

The Opies hint that children's rhymes in general may ultimately derive from commercial popular culture and note children's ongoing adoption of media-derived elements in their games (1959: 13–14; cf. Chapter 2). Clapping games in particular have often had a productive relationship with the verbal, musical and kinetic aspects of popular music and dance, television programmes, and film (Opie and Opie, 1985; Harwood, 1994; Bishop et al, 2006; Gaunt, 2006; Marsh, 2008; Roud, 2010: 313–16; Bishop, 2010). It seems to be no coincidence that this form of play has proliferated from the 1960s on, at the same time as the development and increasing availability of electronic media (Opie and Opie, 1985: 440–43; Roud, 2010: 296).

The interaction between musical play and media is often a mutual one, resulting in what Marsh terms 'cycles of appropriation and reappropriation' (2008: 185).

These cycles are conceptualised as a recursive and reciprocal process in which kinetic, musical and verbal elements of children's play are adopted by the producers of popular culture whose products in turn influence transmission and innovation in children's play (cf. Bishop et al, 2006; Maybin, 2013). Marsh strongly contests the Opies' view that children's variation/composition is not creative: 'while some variation is inadvertent, it is clear that children also use deliberate processes of innovation to vary game material for a range of different social and aesthetic purposes, in some cases creating entirely new compositions' (2008: 199). As she shows in some detail, performance and the co-constructed nature of innovation are central to musical play and may be evidenced in a 'cycle of experimentation, regularization and control' rather than a finished product (2008: 202, 210).

Not long before the start of our project, clapping games began to be digitally transmitted, as multimodal texts, via the video-sharing website YouTube. In fact, amateur videos of clapping games have been uploaded from 2005 when the site was created.[4] These feature children or young people, predominantly girls, performing, teaching and/or demonstrating one or more clapping games. To judge from the participants' accents, the majority of videos emanate from North America but there are others from the UK, Australia, Africa and parts of Asia, They may be filmed indoors, in household spaces or classrooms, or outdoors, in school playgrounds and gardens, for example. The videos have sometimes been uploaded by parents, some clearly intended to showcase their children's talents, others perhaps to display moments in a family holiday, but more often the videos have been made by children and young people themselves, apparently using a static webcam.

The videos evidence a range in the degree of spontaneity in the performances – some are visibly stage-managed while others are more haphazard. Almost all of them comprise straight footage without subtitles, subsequent editing or special effects. Sometimes the children face the camera to introduce themselves and/or the game before playing it. Some are styled as instructional videos and may contain spoken commentary as well as segmented or slowed down demonstrations of the movements and words. Many of the uploads are less than a minute in length but others last for several minutes because the game is repeated or is one of several games shown.

As part of our project, we conducted a survey at each school relating to the children's access to and use of media.[5] At Monteney School, 73 per cent of children reported using YouTube. In a further survey relating to clapping play, we asked the children if they had ever learnt any clapping games from the following sources: radio, CD, film, television, cartoon, computer game, website or YouTube. The results are shown in Figure 3.1

---

[4]   For a history of YouTube, see Burgess and Green (2009).

[5]   The details of this survey, and further findings, are discussed in Chapters 5 and 6, and also in Willett et al. (2013).

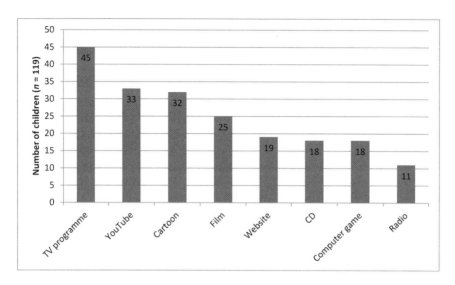

Fig. 3 1   Media sources influencing the learning of clapping games at Monteney schoolSchool

These results suggest that YouTube is among the top three media sources that may influence clapping play, along with television and cartoons, although these categories are obviously not mutually exclusive and, in particular, content from many sources is additionally accessible via YouTube. With hindsight, it would have been interesting to ascertain more information about the kinds of videos being accessed on YouTube for clapping play, especially contrasting amateur and commercial productions.

Meanwhile, it emerged during the course of our fieldwork at the school that an amateur video of clapping play uploaded to YouTube had been a source for the clapping game 'Eeny Meeny Dessameeny' (hereafter referred to as EMD), which we had already observed and filmed on a number of occasions.[6] We therefore interviewed as many as possible of those who knew or played EMD about their learning, teaching and performing of the game. Details of these children, including their ages at the time of recording and known relationships, are noted in Appendix A. This information has been pieced together to produce a 'thick corpus' relating to EMD. The following section describes how it was transmitted among a network of girls, related through family ties or friendship, in two adjacent year groups at Monteney School, during the period 2006–2010. This is followed by a discussion of the role of amateur videos on YouTube in teaching and learning

---

[6]   See also Bishop (2010) for references to YouTube videos of 'Eeny Meeny Dessameeny' and for an international study of its dissemination and cycles of appropriation and reappropriation with popular culture.

clapping play compared to other media sources and face-to-face transmission. We then turn to the conscious changes introduced by the children, considering triggers and motivations for variation, and factors affecting the nature of change and its retention and adoption.

'We got it off YouTube': Learning and Teaching 'Eeny Meeny Dessameeny' in Online and Offline Spaces

Meredith and Sally

Meredith and Sally were the first in the group to learn the game. They recall that 'it were a long time ago, when we were on the back yard in Year 2. And we got it off YouTube' (a00155). This dates the event to the 2006–2007 school year, when the girls were aged 6–7 years. They had been using YouTube to look for a pop song they were interested in and noticed that 'on the side there's little options for different videos. And it said at the top "Me and my friend doing Eeny Meeny" … People were hand-clapping on the photo so we went on it'. The girls recalled that the people on the video were not speaking in English and possibly looked 'Asian'. 'They just kept on doing it really slow, like, just to show you what to do, and with English lyrics at the bottom so you could tell what the words were' (a00155). Sally and Meredith were already familiar with the clapping pattern used on the video because it was the one they had just learnt themselves. They recalled that the people on the video also did 'little actions' on certain lines, such as the 'sleep' gesture (described below) with 'Didn't do the dishes/Lazy lazy', and rubbing their tummy on 'Stole a box of chocolates/Greedy greedy'.

Meredith and Sally learnt the game from the YouTube video by watching it about four or five times, all on the same occasion: 'It were the tune that were quite hard to pick up on because obviously the sound wasn't very good … We watched it a couple of times and then we tried it again. And, because we were getting it a little bit wrong, we watched it a couple of times again and then we got it' (a00155). Following this, they performed the game at school. This is the text as they performed it for the benefit of our research some four years later:

> Eeny meeny dessameeny
> You are the one for me
> Education collaboration
> I like you.
>
> Down town baby
> Down to the roller coaster
> Sweet sweet cherry
> No place to go.
>
> Caught you with my boyfriend
> Naughty naughty

Didn't do the dishes
Lazy lazy
Jumped out the window
Flipping crazy.

Eeny meeny dessameeny
You are the one for me
Education collaboration
I like you and you and you.
But not you. (v01636)

It is notable that the 'Stole a box of chocolates/Greedy greedy' lines which they mention as having seen on the YouTube video are not included in this performance, a point to which we will return below.

Of the time when they first learnt the game, they recalled:

> M/S   We were doing it on the playground and some of our friends came up and they said, 'Where did you learn that? Can you teach it us?' So we ended up teaching it to Naomi and Alicia and some more people.

> Julia   I see. And so do you think you're the first people who brought 'Eeny Meeny Desameeny' to the school, or had you heard of it already?

> M/S   The best bits we pick up on the tune is because we'd heard it from a few people that are in Y5.[7] So we were, like, the first people to bring it on to the back yard. But I'm not sure if we were the first people to bring it into school. (a00155)

Sally and Meredith have not been back to the video on YouTube since this time 'because we can't remember who did it, what song we were looking at' (a00155).[8] They believe that they have not modified the game since this time and perform it as they learnt it from this chance encounter.

It is noteworthy that Meredith and Sally had already come across EMD being performed by older children at school because they themselves would have spent their breaktimes in the 'back yard', on the other side of the school building, which was reserved for the younger children, whereas the Year 5s would have spent breaks in the 'front yard'. Yet, they had heard the Year 5 performers enough to marry the tune they knew with the text, movements and difficult-to-hear tune that they had found on YouTube.

---

[7]   The initial half of this sentence is hard to distinguish. Given the girls' comments concerning the Year 5 children, I take the gist of the words to be 'The bit we picked up on the best was the tune …'.

[8]   Likewise, I have been unable to locate the probable video seen by Meredith and Sally on YouTube.

Naomi, Alicia and Mary

Meredith and Sally taught EMD to their friends Naomi, Alicia and Mary at this time. Naomi was 'the first person to catch on. And, like, she were the first person that we told' (a00155). Naomi and Alicia recall that they, too, then found EMD 'on the internet' before teaching it to Mary (v01662). The girls would then clap EMD as 'a fivesome' and played it intensively:

> M   It were like our handshake thing at the time. And we just absolutely loved doing it. Like, every day when we came out. We must have done it, like, fifty times one day.

> A   And we had it bang on most of the time because we practised it that much. It were like we were synchronised. (a00138)

Mary's comment refers to what is sometimes known as a 'dap greeting', a ritualised greeting routine containing a series of gestures and body moves, developed between two friends and often particular to them (Powell, 2012a). Some of the gestures and moves are also found in clapping games. In recent years handshakes have been popularised in film and television,[9] and YouTube contains many videos in which people, especially children and young adults, either demonstrate their personal handshake or their performance of a specific handshake from a media source. Handshakes were created and practised amongst both boys and girls at Monteney during the time of our fieldwork there. Thus, Mary's reference to EMD as the friends' 'handshake' suggests they regarded, and perhaps felt others likewise regarded, EMD as an extended 'signature move' particular to, and expressive of, their friendship group. It is notable that handshakes tend to be dyadic performances whereas clapping games allow for both dyadic and group performance patterns (Marsh, 2008: 106). The frequency with which they played the game and their highly developed degree of coordination recalls the kind of multimodal calibration observed in clapping games by Bishop and Burn (2013) and 'entrainment' as described by Maybin (2013).

Emma and Lorna

Meanwhile, two years later, when they were in Year 4, Meredith, Sally, Naomi, Alicia and Mary, plus another girl, were allowed by the teacher to perform EMD in class. It was as a result of this that two more of their classmates, Emma and Lorna, learnt EMD (a00135). The six girls were 'all in a big circle and they did it', Emma remembered, 'we watched them but then they kept doing it and that. And we asked Mary to see if we could learn it and she said yes. So I, like, learned it and then Lorna. I went a bit wrong and then Lorna went a bit wrong but then we both learnt it' (a00135). Mary taught it to them:

---

⁹ For example, in *The Parent Trap* film (1998 remake), and the *Hannah Montana* television series.

E   She just said, 'Right, just copy me, girls.' And she done it with two people and she, like, just learned us. 'Right, we'll only go through one bit at a time.' So she done, like, 'Eeny Meeny Dessameeny' and then we tried it. And then tried it, like, how she done it in sections.

Julia   And do you remember what the sections were that she broke it down into now?

E   'Eeny meeny dessameeny/You are the one for me/Education, collaboration/I like you.' That's section one. Section two is 'Down town baby/Down to the roller coaster/Sweet sweet cherry/No place to go.'

L   Section two. Section three – 'Caught you with your boyfriend/Naughty naughty/Didn't do the dishes/Lazy lazy.'

E   Like, section by section by section. (a00135)

It was at the end of this school year (2008–2009) that Emma and Lorna were filmed as part of our research project (v00056).

Selina

During 2008–2009, or possibly the year prior to it, Alicia taught EMD to her sister, Selina, who is a year older than her (v01662).[10] This was prompted by the following circumstances. The family came across the film *Big* (1988) which they watched at home together on DVD. At several points in the film, the song 'Down Down Baby', often used for handclapping (cf. Marsh, 2008: 181–5), is performed by the main character, Josh, and his friend, Billy.[11] Alicia and Selina became particularly aware of 'Down Down Baby' because their mother liked the film and would sing this song from it (a00134). Although 'Down Down Baby' is a distinct text from EMD, it begins with four lines that display many similarities in their rhythm and wording to the second section of EMD:

The space [*sic*] goes
Down down baby
Down down the roller coaster
Sweet sweet baby
Sweet sweet don't let me go … (*Big*)[12]

---

[10]   Selina dated this event to the 2007–2008 school year (a00134) but Alicia remembered it as being 2008–2009 (a00138).

[11]   See the partial rendition during the opening credits (beginning at 03:09) and the full rendition, used as a recognition device in the film's narrative (beginning at 16:39).

[12]   See Powell (2012b) for a discussion of 'space'/'spades' in the introductory line of 'Down Down Baby'.

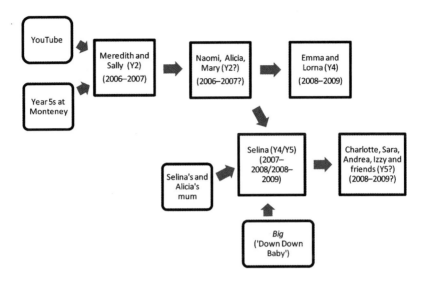

Fig. 3.2   Transmission of 'Eeny Meeny Dessameeny' at Monteney School, 2006–2010s

Charlotte, Sara, Andrea, Izzy and Friends

Back at school, Selina then taught EMD to Charlotte, a friend in her year group. When filmed as part of the project, Charlotte reported that she thought Selina's source for EMD was a television programme or that she had made it up with her sister (v00262). Selina and Charlotte's performances of EMD prompted a number of their friends to learn it from them (v00262). As shown in Appendix A, these girls clapped EMD in various combinations, including as a fivesome and in pairs, during the school year 2009–2010, at which point they were all in Year 6. In one of the films made as part of the project (v00262), Charlotte also teaches EMD to her friend's younger sister (in Year 3).

This information is summarised in Figure 3.2. Whilst it is acknowledged that this is no doubt a partial and over-simplified account, it provides detailed glimpses into the way that EMD was disseminated at the school.

Teaching, Learning and YouTube

Based on a longitudinal and international study of musical play as evidenced in school playgrounds, Marsh has provided a closely observed picture of the processes of learning and teaching. In summary, these involve:

1. Learning by 'close observation, physical contact, and modelling of new game behaviours' (2008: 138);
2. 'Recognition of known movement, textual and melodic formulae' (2008: 138), with movement patterns often being the first to be learnt (2008: 139);
3. 'Watching performing groups from outside the friendship circle and then practising them within the social safety of the observers' own friendship groups' (2008: 143);
4. Aggregative learning which takes place in relation to the whole, rather than segmentation (2008: 142, 144, 155).

Marsh's data was largely gathered prior to the advent of YouTube so we will consider here YouTube clapping game videos in relation to face-to-face transmission and other media sources. There are a number of features that distinguish YouTube videos from other media sources and, at the same time, some important parallels between YouTube videos and clapping play in offline contexts.

YouTube clapping game videos feature full-length renditions of actual clapping games being played. They thus reference and portray a vernacular practice currently undertaken in offline spaces as well.[13] The videos showcase, teach and transmit this practice. They can be seen as a subset of the numerous instructional videos of all kinds for which YouTube provides a platform and de facto library (Davies and Merchant, 2009). The vast majority of clapping game videos are amateur productions, predominantly made by children and young people themselves.[14] Children and young people feature in the videos too, usually in pairs, and these performers are evidently friends or sometimes relatives in the offline world. They are generally filmed in the kinds of offline spaces where clapping takes place. The viewer is positioned by the webcam or video camera at much the same vantage point as the interested observer in offline settings, certainly in terms of angle and often in terms of distance (commensurate with Leman's (2010) 'third-person' perspective).

In contrast, commercial media sources drawn on by children in clapping play do not feature clapping play as such but rather music, texts, songs, dances and gestures produced by adults for the purposes of self-expression, profit and entertainment. These productions are not intended to act as a source for clapping play nor to have a pedagogic function in this respect. They often show adults

---

[13] The production and style of these films would merit further attention but is beyond the scope of this chapter.

[14] See also Burgess and Green (2009) regarding the tension between the 'top-down' and 'bottom-up' aspect of YouTube, and Howard (2008) on the notion of 'the vernacular web'.

giving polished, professional performances filmed in glamorised contexts or as part of fictional constructs.[15]

In general terms, there is a high degree of fit between clapping game videos on YouTube and offline clapping teaching and learning practices, as characterised by Marsh. The videos allow close observation of peers outside one's friendship circle modelling the games. They make movement patterns, verbal text and music perceptible and sometimes come with the added affordance of a written text as well. They are perhaps even more suited to learning in the sense that they provide an unvarying performance which is available and repeatable on demand. On the other hand, they lack the possibility of physical contact and it is only via the non-synchronous tool of the comments section that one can request a slower demonstration or explanation and clarification, a request that may or may not be responded to, either by the performers/producers themselves, or by other viewers. YouTube is, then, most useful to those who have acquired a degree of competence in clapping play and are looking to improve their skill, find fresh challenges and extend their repertoire. Our concept of 'cultural rehearsal' (see Chapter 1) is intended to capture the distinctive nature of these processes, beginning with the iterative viewing and listening practices which proliferate in uses of new media, and carried into the iterative cycles of repetition, adaptation, extension and elaboration. Here, the dialogic cycle begins at the point of someone else's rehearsal-become-performance, and develops into something which may remain 'rehearsal', or may become performances of various kinds – again on YouTube; for a researcher; or for other children eager to learn the skills and specific multimodal texts.

In contrast to Marsh's findings, a number of the more explicitly instructional videos may segment the game and disaggregate the modes for teaching purposes, as well as showing the complete game. The video medium also gives the user the possibility of repeating the whole performance and certain parts, stopping and starting the performance at any point, and focusing on either the audio or the visual aspect by, for example, looking away from the screen or turning down the sound.

What did the children say about their use of YouTube? Firstly, they made it clear that they only learnt things from YouTube 'every now and then' (a00138). As suggested by our clapping play survey, it is one source among several, including television and friends, for clapping games and other forms of musical play:

> N   You watch all sorts on YouTube. We learn cheerleading chants from there as well ... We watch people do it and then you do handclap stuff, and it's just fun to watch it.

> M   Sometimes you see it on TV and you copy it from, like, on the TV. If it was on, say, Disney Channel and it was a really funny chant.

---

[15]   The clapping game performances on the American children's television programme, *Sesame Street*, which incorporates an instructional dimension within its larger social and educational message form something of a middle ground between commercial and amateur productions.

N   And *Hannah Montana*.

M   You would learn it and come to school and say, 'Look at this chant I've learnt'. (a00138)[16]

Many of the children at Monteney had access to YouTube at home and this allowed them to consult it in the same way as their peers:

Julia   So when you see a hand clap that you like, do you actually ask them to teach you?

N   Sometimes people watch. Or they go, 'Where did you learn that?' or 'How did you do that?'

A   I know it sounds strange but some people might say, 'Oh, we learn it off this person doing it on YouTube.' So we go home and type it in and watch it on YouTube … It's exactly the same. Like somebody's copied it but made it into a video. So instead of just saying, 'Can you teach it me?' to whoever started it, putting it on a video on YouTube so other people can do it. (a00138)

In practice, however, finding a specific video or even a specific game on YouTube may be a hit-and-miss affair due to the fact that clapping games do not have standard names or may have words in common with other productions. Spelling may also vary and generic titles, such as 'Awesome Clapping Games', may have been used.

Mitigating this is the large number of items available, making it likely that a search will produce at least some relevant results:

Julia   And what do you type in when you try to get it off YouTube?

A   It's loads of different things … You would just type in the name of the clap and it would just sort of come up and loads of different people, like, doing it.

N   Yeah, loads of random people. Different people change it, so it's fun to, like, watch them and see what they've put. That's why everybody knows it. Because of certain places like YouTube and stuff like that.

A   Nobody knows where they actually started. (a00138)

In addition, once a relevant video has been located, a list of related further videos appears in the right hand column of the screen. As we have seen, this led to Sally and Meredith's discovery of EMD. Thus, although a specific version learnt from YouTube and performed offline may prompt a search for the same video or game, it may not necessarily be what is found. YouTube's multiple results provide instant

---

[16]   Often the relevant programme segments can be found on YouTube as well so that a 'chant' from a television programme may be learnt via the video as uploaded to YouTube.

access to a pool of performances much larger, and potentially more culturally diverse, than those available offline. Naomi and Alicia stated that they sometimes watched them all and selected their favourite, or they watched 'the top one', or they watched them all and selected their preferred portions from each to make a composite (a00138). Thus, the children are able to 'match and mix' from the videos they find.

The girls' engagement with YouTube videos, once located, varied. Sally and Meredith viewed the film together but others watched the film on their own, as Alicia and Naomi's observations imply. Viewing together allows practice immediately following the viewing, while there is the possibility of returning to the film. The girls noted aspects of the video which aided their learning, such as the words appearing as subtitles synchronised with the performance which helps them to memorise the text (a00138) or, in the case Sally and Meredith's EMD video, they found the performers went over the game slowly. Other videos are divided into 'steps' (a00138) and it is possible that this influenced the way that Mary, unlike the children Marsh observed, segmented EMD in order to teach it to Emma and Lorna in an offline learning context. On the other hand, while Meredith and Sally repeated the EMD YouTube film that they drew on several times, they do not make reference to re-playing smaller portions, an affordance that may be more necessary when drawing on commercial productions for clapping play.

It is notable that these children did not claim to have 'made up' the clapping games that they had learnt from YouTube. Rather, they openly acknowledged YouTube as a source and reported being directed to it by friends, cousins and siblings as commonplace: 'Half of the time it's, like, your cousin would say "I've seen this on YouTube". So you watch it and then your friends watch it, and then their friends'd watch it. So that's sort of how the whole hand-clap thing passes on' (a00138). It is possible to see these references, and the access to YouTube and competency in its use that they point to, as a form of 'meaningful token' with symbolic value in the 'economy of dignity' as identified by Pugh (2009; also discussed in Chapter 5). While such tokens can be 'whatever works to gain the child entry into the ongoing conversation among his or her peers' (2009: 55), Pugh found that owning, using or knowing about (commercial) popular culture was particularly valued as a means by which to acquire or broker the esteem of others and construct a sense of belonging (2009: 56). It appears that YouTube as a platform currently has the cachet and, perhaps, the novelty value among these children to function similarly in clapping play. This leads them to acknowledge it and minimise the intertextual gap.

'Everybody just sort of change it to how they like it': Variation in 'Eeny Meeny Dessameeny'

This section examines changes made to EMD by some of these same children. The focus is on changes which have left a trace in the verbal text, music and movement patterns of EMD performances and which have emerged as a result of deliberate acts which the children could recall and explain to the researcher. On the face of it, the changes involve processes of addition, substitution (omission plus addition) and recasting as identified by Marsh (2008: 199–220; cf. Burns, 1970). They range from tiny details to more extensive re-working of aspects of the game.

Verbal Changes

Overall, there are few changes observable in the words of EMD as performed and recorded at Monteney School. The differences examined here are all associated with Naomi, Alicia and Mary.[17]

'Down to/by the roller coaster (line 6)'[18]

Alicia sometimes sings 'down *to* the roller coaster' (v00115, v01593) and sometimes as 'down *by* the roller coaster' (v01635, v01662, v01663, v01664) whereas all the other performers in her year group sing 'down *to* the roller coaster'. Her sister, Selina, who learnt EMD from Alicia, and Selina's peers, on the other hand, consistently sing 'down *by* the roller coaster'. Alicia is conscious of the difference and explained that, after watching *Big*, 'that's when we put the "down by the roller coaster" bit in' (v01662).[19] She identified the change as coming from the film:

> Me and my sister were watching *Big* and that's how I taught it to Selina. Me and Naomi had done [EMD] before and then [Selina and I] watched *Big*. And, like, that's why it's 'Down by the roller coaster' … It's not a handclap, it's just a rhythm off of *Big*. And it's really different to 'Eeny Meeny Dessameeny'. But it's got the first bit in it, 'Down by the roller coaster'. (v01662)

As shown above, however, the relevant line from 'Down Down Baby' is actually performed as 'Down down the roller coaster' in the film. Since the sisters' attention was drawn to 'Down Down Baby' because their mother used to sing it as well (a00134), it may be that she sang 'down by' rather than 'down down', a textual difference that has also been documented in versions from elsewhere (Marsh, 2008: 21; Roud, 2010: 316).

---

[17]   One further difference occurs in line 9 in which Izzy and Andrea sing 'Talked to my boyfriend' rather than 'Caught you with my boyfriend'. The change was not noticed during the fieldwork period so I was unable to ask the girls about it.

[18]   Line numbers are calculated here in relation to the text of Meredith and Sally's rendition, quoted above.

[19]   At the time of interviewing Alicia, I mistakenly assumed that she was referring to the introduction of a complete line from the film. It is only in the light of close textual comparison that the true nature of Alicia's change and her explanations have become clear to me.

For Alicia, then, the line 'down *by* the roller coaster' revoices and resonates with a song, a commercial film, her mum's singing and EMD as performed by her sister and her sister's friends.[20] Her usage vis-à-vis that of her own friendship group marks and expresses something of this 'differential' aspect of her identity (Bauman, 1971), even as she claps 'the same' game with them, and synchronises other aspects of her participation. The momentary nature of this counterpoint, and its minor nature, enables it to be accommodated within the game without threatening it and allows her to perpetuate it.

'Stole a box of candy/Greedy greedy' (between lines 12 and 13)

Naomi, Alicia and Mary made changes to their EMD text several years after it had become established within their friendship group (a00138, v01662). One of these was the incorporation of the lines 'Stole a box of candy/Greedy greedy':

A   We made the 'candy' bit at dinnertime cos-.

N   Cos we were with Mary then. And Mary in her lunch had a really big box of chocolates.

A   Malteser kind of things.

N   Yeah, they were them Malteser ones from her birthday. And we were all, like, 'Why have you brought a whole box of Maltesers in your bag?' And she were sharing them with everyone. And I remember Alicia going, 'Where did you get them from? Did you steal them?' And then we went- [*sharp intake of breath*]. And then we went, 'Stole a box of candy/Greedy, greedy'.

…

Because it was going to be 'Stole a box of chocolates, Greedy greedy'. And then I remember us doing it 'Stole a box of chocolates/Greedy greedy', and Mary just changing it to 'candy'. But we said, 'Chocolate and candy's the same thing', so we did it with 'candy'.

…

Julia   Had you heard those words before anywhere or were they new ones that you made up completely out of your heads, kind of thing?

…

N   It was just kind of out of our head a bit.

A   Yeah, just random.

---

[20] This particular line of the song may also conjure up images as well as sounds from the film for Alicia since key scenes take place at a fairground where the main character wishes he was 'big' in order to go on a ride and thus impress a girl.

N   Yeah. 'Cos it was Maltesers, chocolates. So we said, 'Stole a box of chocolates, Greedy greedy'. And then it kind of just-. After, like, two months of doing it, it just changed to 'candy' and then it's just kind of not changed back now. (v01662)

At first, then, the girls adopted the lines 'Stole a box of chocolates/Greedy greedy', and then substituted the word 'candy' for 'chocolates'. In several recorded performances, one or other of them accidentally sings 'chocolates' instead of 'candy', suggesting that the former was a prior practice and/or that the line was first known to them in that form (v01635, v01662). The lines must have been an established part of the text by the time Alicia taught it to Selina as all the performances documented from Selina and her friends contain the lines.

As described above, Naomi, Alicia and Mary initially learnt EMD from Sally and Meredith and performed it with them. In the full text from Sally and Meredith documented later as part of our study (v01636, quoted above), these two lines are absent. Lorna and Emma's text, learnt from Naomi and her friends, also lacks these lines (v00056). This suggests that all of these girls in this year group initially learnt a text without these lines. Yet, both Sally and Meredith are aware of the lines and refer to them in their recollection of the YouTube film they viewed. Moreover, in a discussion of changes others have made to EMD, Sally suggested that she and Meredith consciously omitted them: 'You're meant to say "Didn't do the dishes/Lazy lazy/Jumped out the window/Flipping crazy". But some people do, like, "Stole a box of chocolates/Greedy greedy", then they do 'lazy'. Then they do the other bit [the ending]. But it's meant to rhyme. But some people swap it all about so it doesn't rhyme' (a00155). Thus, the 'chocolate'/'candy' lines are seen as interrupting the 'didn't do the dishes' and 'jumped out the window' lines and spoiling the effect of the lazy-crazy rhyme. This time, the nature of the change means that it will disrupt the game unless both players sing the same version. When Meredith claps the game with Alicia on one of our films (v00115), she adapts to Alicia's longer text.

The formula 'Stole a box of chocolates/Greedy greedy' crops up in EMD texts as recorded elsewhere and sometimes refers to 'candy' instead of 'chocolates' (Bishop, 2010). Naomi and Alicia characterise the lines as 'out of our head a bit' and 'just random', emphasising the intertextual gap. This facilitates their framing of the change as a response to an occurrence that they shared as a friendship group, and their alignment of the speech reported to have taken place with the wording of the lines. They thus personalise and 're-brand' their version, distinguishing it textually and/or indexically from those of others circulating in the same setting and beyond.

'Flipping crazy' (line 14)

Another change to which Naomi, Alicia and Mary laid claim occurs in the final couplet of the middle section:

> A   I think it were 'crazy crazy' but we added 'flipping crazy' instead.
>
> N   Yeah, there were other bits where we were going 'Jumped out the window, Crazy crazy'. We're, like, 'That doesn't sound right. Let's change to "flipping crazy"'. Cos I remember I had a thing with saying 'flipping' all the time. And I couldn't stop. So we said 'flipping crazy'. (v01662)

This change was apparently noticed and copied by their peers in the playground:

> N   And then it was, like, contagious because everyone else saw us doing it. Then they're, like, [*sharp intake of breath*] 'You did "Jumped out the window, Flipping crazy"'. So [then] they were doing 'Jumped out the window/Flipping crazy'. And we didn't stop them. Because we knew it had just passed on. But we thought it was quite cool how other people were doing it as well.
>
> J   Yeah? You felt proud? They picked up your bit?
>
> N   Yeah. I felt like 'We did that!' (v01662)

In fact, all of the performances from the school recorded as part of our project evidence the words 'flipping crazy', as do most British versions of the game's text, although the variant text 'crazy crazy' has certainly been documented elsewhere (Bishop, 2010; Roud, 2010: 315). Again, the girls widen the intertextual gap, Naomi stressing their role in introducing the change and making the word 'flipping' a revoicing of her own speech. The intensifier 'flipping' is a slang usage with a risqué edge since it is regarded as a substitute for a stronger expletive. The response of admiration and imitation from the girls' peers suggests that this reference may have functioned within the 'economy of dignity', discussed above. In her fieldwork, Pugh observed 'children constantly lobbing new gambits by trial and error to create symbolic chits in the conversational air' (2009: 55–6). 'Flipping' may have been just such an experiment, slipped into a clapping game and deriving its symbolic value not from commercial culture but from its slang status and the taboo language it indexes (cf. Pugh, 2009: 57).

Naomi, Alicia and Mary regard the kinds of changes they have made as akin to others' practice: 'Other people, like, around school have done, like, "Eeny Meeny Dessameeny" but they've took a line out that somebody else has said and put their own line in, like, changed it' (a00138). These 'own' lines are also revoicings, as we have seen, whether or not this is recognised by the players. I have suggested that they allowed the non-threatening expression of differential identity within the friendship group, enabled personalisation and a subtle differentiation between otherwise similar texts, and were successfully transformed into currency in an economy of dignity. The texts that are fashioned may become identified with a particular group, as with Alicia, Naomi and Mary, but equally they provide, in turn, text that can potentially be further decontextualised and recontextualised (Bauman and Briggs, 1990) by their peers:

N   We were talking to some big kids and they were, like, doing hand clapping, like, teaching us. And we kind of carried it on and carried it on for, like, a couple of years and then we just decided-. We changed it through all the years and we just got 'Eeny Meeny Desameeny' of our own.

A   You see somebody else do it and you're, like, 'Oh, that looks good, teach me that'. And then everybody just sort of change it to, like, how they like it. (a00138)

This, then, seems to exemplify the 'dialogue between variants' described by Honko and to underscore the dialogical quality of children's textual practices in clapping games. We now extend this discussion to the kinetic and musical changes to EMD.

Changes in Movement Patterns

The movement patterns associated with EMD as usually performed at Monteney School comprise hand-clapping in a 3-beat pattern to the pulse of the music interspersed with mimetic gestures relating to the referential meaning of certain words in the text. Although some of the pointing gestures varied in direction, especially when the game involved more than two players and was clapped in a circular formation, the basic movements remained the same as when played in a dyadic formation. Table 3.1 presents the principal kinetic changes to EMD, with Alicia and Meredith's performance taken as the norm.

Substitution of Hand-clasping for Initial Clapping

This change was introduced by Naomi's elder sister, to whom Naomi was demonstrating her friends' modified text of EMD (v01662). The sister started to do a movement in which the performers, with elbows bent, clasp each others' hands alternately on the two occurrences of the lines 'Eeny meeny dessameeny/You are the one for me'. Naomi thought that her sister might have got the move 'from an old handshake she did with her friends' (v01662) and it is a movement formula commonly associated with this part of the text in American performances of EMD (Bishop, 2010). Naomi showed it to Alicia but it did not become an established part of their practice because they usually clapped EMD with Mary and the move is not feasible in a 3-person formation. Towards the end of our fieldwork, however, Mary left the school and Naomi attempted to re-introduce the movement. In one film (v01662), Alicia appears hesitant but goes along with the change despite finding it awkward to adjust. One reason for this is that, when the 3-way clap is resumed on the word 'education', it realigns the clapping pattern that falls with each beat, making it pick up on Down/Up, in comparison to when clapping has taken place from the start, which results in this line beginning with Clap Own. Although Naomi segments the text in order to practise this changeover from hand-clasping to clapping, she sets a rapid pace when they attempt the whole game which Alicia cannot quite match.

Table 3.1   Comparison of movement patterns in 'Eeny Meeny Dessameeny' performances

Text	Moves (Alicia and Meredith v00115)	Moves (Naomi and Alicia, v01662)	Moves (Charlotte and Sara (v000262))
Eeny meeny dessameeny You are the one for me Education collaboration I like you.	3-way Clap[a] Point[b]	Hand-clasping[c] 3-way Clap Point	The Twist[d] Twist + Point Twist + 'Cuckoo' then Writing gestures[e] Twist Point
Down town baby Down to the roller coaster Sweet sweet cherry No place to go.	3-way Clap Finger Wag[f]	3-way Clap Finger Wag	Scuba-diving[g] Undulating motion with forearm Twist Finger Wag
Caught you with my boyfriend Naughty naughty	3-way Clap Finger Wag	3-way Clap Finger Wag	Hand on hip Finger Wag
Didn't do the dishes Lazy lazy	3-way Clap Sleep gesture[h]	3-way Clap Sleep gesture	Washing gesture[i] Sleep gesture
Stole a box of candy Greedy greedy	3-way Clap Rubbing tummy	3-way Clap Rubbing tummy	Rubbing tummy Rubbing tummy

Jumped out the window
 	
Flipping crazy
	3-way Clap
	
	'Screw Loose'
	    gesture[j]
		3-way Clap
		
		'Screw Loose'
		    gesture
			Jumping to feet apart
			    position
			'Screw Loose' gesture

Eeny meeny dessameeny
 	
You are the one for me
Education collaboration
 	
I like
you.
	3-way Clap
	
	Point, both
	    hands to
	    one side of
	    each other
		Hand-clasping
		
		3-way Clap
		
		Point, both
		    hands to
		    one side of
		    each other
			Twist
			
			Twist + Point
			Twist + 'Cuckoo' then
			    Writing gestures
			Twist
			Point, both hands to one
			    side of each other

And you	Point, both
	    hands to
	    other side of
	    each other
		Point, both
		    hands to
		    other side of
		    each other
			Point, both hands to
			    other side of each
			    other

and you.	Point, both hands to first side of each other	Point, both hands to first side of each other	Point, both hands to first side of each other
But not you.	Point, both hands directly at each other	Point, both hands directly at each other	Point, both hands directly at each other

[a]   The 3-way clap comprises Down-Up clap (D/U), Clap Partner's hands (C/P) and Clap Own hands (C/O), repeated as necessary. These abbreviations are adopted from Marsh (2008: 342).
[b]   Pointing index finger of both hands at each other.
[c]   Arm-wrestling hold, alternating hands.
[d]   The same move as in the popular dance, 'The Twist'.
[e]   Index finger circling on side of head ('cuckoo' gesture), then index finger 'writing' on palm
[f]   Moving index finger from side to side in admonitory gesture.
[g]   Holding nose and bending knees to go 'underwater', first with one hand and then the other.
[h]   Hands together held alternately to each side of head, as if to indicate 'sleeping'.
[i]   Own open palms facing and moving in a circular motion
[j]   Circling index finger to either side of head, both hands simultaneously.

Naomi's gestural change parallels Alicia's verbal one ('down by') inasmuch as it re-embodies her sister's kinetic 'text'. It may also be an attempt to introduce another 'symbolic chit' in the economy of dignity. Unlike Alicia's change, however, the two must agree whether or not to incorporate the gestural one, and be able to do so successfully, or it disrupts the game. Within the gestural, and haptic, modes, then, it is harder to accommodate differential practice. This echoes Marsh's finding that 'disagreements seem to be most prominent when variation interferes with the synchronization of game elements, especially movement' (2008: 110).

EMD as a Mimetic Dance

Charlotte and Sara created a much more extensive innovation in the movements of EMD when they replaced the clapping with 'the twist' and additional mimetic movements relating to the text. This was Sara's idea and it took them only a short time to re-cast the game, Sara leading the process (a00133). They added moves that fitted with the words and that they knew from general knowledge, combining them with the moves that were already part of the game. This transformed EMD into a kind of mimetic dance, similar to those termed 'impersonations and dance routines' by the Opies (1985), 'pop songs ... either with the actions believed to have been performed by the pop groups singing them on television, or, more often, with actions fitted to them by the children ... [T]hese games usually only last as long as the pop song' (1985: 414). Although Sara and Charlotte's routine was based on a clapping game rather than a pop song, it is notable that it, too, did not last for long. In October 2009, when we filmed them, they had been doing it for a few weeks (v00262) but they were not aware of anyone else copying the routine and, when they were interviewed for the project seven months later, they could not remember the details of it any more (a00133).

The girls explained that they had made up a routine 'just sort of messing about and then we sort of got to it, knowed it better' (a00133), illustrating the 'experimentation, regularization and control' cycle identified by Marsh (2008: 210). In general, neither of them was particularly keen on dancing although they took part in the dance group organised by a friend during playtimes and both also attended the school drama club (a00133). When there was music from a CD player on the playground, they would sometimes 'mess about, just sort of, like, jumping and doing different sort of, like, "washing the windows" and "milking the cow"', with the kinds of accompanying gestures that these phrases describe (a00133). With regard to clapping games, however, they articulated an orientation to the sound and sense of the words rather than the movements:

> C   It's sort of, like, the words are really good. The movements just really go along with it.
>
> S   We just use the movements for any clap, but it's the words.
>
> C   It's the words really ...
>
> S   Like, some clicks-.
>
> C   Yeah, some of them, like, rhyme and some of them don't rhyme but they've sort of, like, got a theme to it. Like, 'Eeny Meeny Desameeny' one, that's sort of, like, got a story to it. And so has that 'My Boyfriend Gave Me an Apple', that's got a story to it. You just have to look deeper into the words and it gives you stories. (a00133)

We can perhaps view their mimetic realisation of EMD as an enactment of the story, an attempt to 'look deeper into the words'.

The girls also stressed that they were growing out of clapping now that they were in Year 6 and that 'other thoughts are going on in your head as well for, like, growing up' and 'what's happening at home and stuff' (a00133). The removal of the clapping element from EMD, and the mixing of mimetic gestures and dance, has the effect of augmenting the intertextual gap, in kinetic terms, and distancing the girls momentarily from clapping play associated with their younger years. Although the two took pride in their transformation and having it filmed for the research project, its transience precluded much 'cultural rehearsal' without which the opportunities for learning and transmission were obviously very much reduced.

Musical Changes

We did not ask specific questions about the music associated with EMD and few of the children who played the game mention it (cf. Marsh, 2008: 273). Nonetheless,

Fig. 3.3   'Eeny Meeny Dessameeny' as sung by Meredith and Sally (v01636)

a number of musical changes are evident. Firstly, Meredith and Sally were aware of finding the tune difficult to hear on the YouTube EMD video and they drew on the melody that they had heard older girls use at school. Secondly, changes in wording may require concomitant changes in the music and this is the case with the interpolation of the additional 'Stole a box of chocolates/candy' lines. As the following transcription shows, the melody of EMD as sung at Monteney consists of two parts (see Figure 3.3).[21]

---

[21]   Music transcribed by Julia C. Bishop.

The 'Eeny meeny' section takes the form of a rounded tune combined with the sudden switching to speech at the end of the first, third and final sections, while the middle section comprises a repeated sing-song pitch pattern that suggests the mock-nagging of the text and gestures at this point. The extra lines occur in the middle section and are thus easily and seamlessly accommodated by two extra repeats of the 'sing-song' bar.

Finally, the omission of the clapping element in Sara and Charlotte's mimetic dance removes the percussive element of the game including the cross-rhythm of the 3-beat clapping pattern combined with the 4-beat metre of the tune. This happens to a lesser extent with Naomi's hand-clasping gesture and, as already described, the synchronisation of the clap patterns with the words and tune has shifted when the clapping is resumed.

Otherwise, the recorded performances are quite consistent with each other both melodically and rhythmically. As Table 3.2 shows, the primary melodic differences between the performances occur in the vocal range employed, the pitching of the song (tessitura) and a tendency on the part of Izzy and Andrea to the chromatic inflection of the second and fourth beats of the bar in the central section. The difference in the vocal ranges employed is a small one and results from the final three notes in bars 2 and 16 (to the words 'one for me') being pitched in some renditions (v00056, v00262, v01593 and v01635) a semitone higher than in Meredith and Sally's performance. A number of the performers sing low in their vocal range with a tonal centre below middle C (v01636, v01033, v01664).

Tempo is probably the musical element of which the children are most aware and in which they may make conscious changes, partly because these can have a direct bearing on the success of the performance in terms of synchronisation and challenge, and the way in which the players respond to each other and potentially elicit responses from those watching too (Bishop and Burn, 2013). Here, Sally and Meredith's performance is the slowest, perhaps indicating that they had not played the game for some time, and the fastest is Naomi and Alicia during their rehearsal of the hand-clasping movement. Naomi drives the pace, perhaps to egg on Alicia's efforts to master the change and to impress and show control. Sara and Charlotte's mimetic dance, on the other hand, stays close in tempo to many of the clapping game renditions.

Conclusions

This comparative study of a clapping game within one school over a period of several years has shown that the apparently 'minor' variations, experiments and 'clever wheezes' of children can be productively viewed as subtle revoicings and re-embodyings populated, in Bakhtin's words, with their own intention and accent. Within this dialogic approach, we have seen how the notion of reducing or augmenting the 'intertextual gap' has helped shed light on the way children position themselves in relation to these revoicings and re-embodyings.

Table 3.2   Musical features of 'Eeny Meeny Dessameeny' performances compared

Performers	Range/Tessitura	Tempo (minim beat)	Duration
Meredith and Sally, v01636	Major 3rd/A–C sharp	66	35 seconds
Naomi, Alicia, Mary 1) v01593 2) v01635	1) Perfect 4th/D–G 2) Perfect 4th/C–F	90 96	1) 26 seconds 2) 26 seconds
Alicia and Meredith v00115	Major 3rd/ C–E	104	23 seconds
Emma and Lorna v00056	Perfect 4th/ E–A	84	28 seconds
Charlotte and Sara et al v00260	Major 3rd/ E flat–G	88	28 seconds
Charlotte and Sara v00262 (1st performance)	Perfect 4th/ F–A (bars 1–2), D–G (bars 3–20)	88	27 seconds
Izzy and Andrea v01033	Major 3rd/ B–D sharp	90	25 seconds
Alicia and Naomi 1) v01662 (1st performance) 2) v01663 3) v01664	1) Major 3rd/ C–E 2) Major 3rd/C–E 3) Major 3rd/ B–D sharp	112 96 100	1) 21 seconds 2) 24 seconds 3) 25 seconds

These intentions might include the ongoing negotiation of identities, on the level of individual and friendship group, particularly through bids to attract esteem and stress belonging, on the one hand, and to contribute to a sense of differentiation, on the other. They may further intersect with and amplify the aesthetic and expressive intentions identified by Marsh, 'to create something new, to increase the level of amusement and stamp their own imprimatur on the games they play' (2008: 262). This in turn is supported by children's manipulation of the intertextual gap which, with face-to-face sources, may be maximised when one is in the normally deferential role of learner ('I made it up'). Equally, the gap may be minimised with regard to YouTube clapping videos which (to paraphrase Bauman and Briggs, 1992, quoted above) render the discourse maximally interpretable through the use of new media generic precedents which are endowed with novelty value and cultural capital.

Children draw on a variety of cultural resources in their clapping play. These are characterised by a perceived kindred or cognate quality and clearly extend to the new resource of amateur clapping game films on YouTube. Cultural rehearsal here means something very close to the practices of imitation, repetition, transformation, and elaboration which the Opies observed but the potentially intense iterative encounter with the original model online is a distinctive new feature. There are also signs that the affordances of video-sharing platforms, such as YouTube, are impacting on learning practices offline (encouraging segmentation, for example). Overall, this study points to a productive relationship between children's clapping play and new media, a focus that will undoubtedly repay further investigation as technologies develop and change in the future.

References

Arleo A (2001) The saga of Susie: The dynamics of an international handclapping game. In Bishop JC and Curtis M (eds) *Play Today in the Primary School Playground*. Buckingham: Open University Press.

Bakhtin M ([1953]1981) Discourse in the novel. In Holquist M (ed.) *The Dialogic Imagination: Four Essays by M.M. Bakhtin*. Trans C Emerson and M Holquist. Austin: University of Texas Press.

Bakhtin M ([1953]1986) The problem of speech genres. In Emerson C and Holquist M (eds) *Speech Genres and Other Late Essays*. Trans VW McGee. Austin: University of Texas Press.

Bauman R (1971) Differential identity and the social base of folklore. *Journal of American Folklore* 84: 31–41.

Bauman R and Briggs CL (1990) Poetics and performance as critical perspectives on language and social life. *Annual Review of Antrhopology* 19: 59–88.

Bauman R and Briggs CL (1992) Genre, intertextuality, and social power. *Journal of Linguistic Anthropology* 2: 131–72.

Big (1979) [Film] Directed by Penny Marshall. USA: 20th Century Fox.

Bishop JC (2010) 'Eeny Meeny Dessameeny': Continuity and change in the 'backstory' of a children's playground rhyme. Paper presented at the Children's Playground Games and Songs in the New Media Age interim Conference, University of London. Available at: http://projects.beyondtext. ac.uk/playgroundgames/uploads/bishop_playground_interim.pdf.

Bishop JC and Burn A (2013) Reasons for rhythm: Multimodal perspectives on musical play. In Willett R, Richards C, Marsh J, Burn A and Bishop JC *Children, Media and Playground Cultures: Ethnographic Studies of School Playtimes*. Basingstoke: Palgrave Macmillan.

Bishop JC and Curtis M with Woolley H, Armitage M and Ginsborg J (2006) Creative engagements: Children's uses of media content in their free play. Unpublished paper, earlier versions of which were presented at the *Folklore, Film and Television: Convergences in Traditional Cultures and Popular Media* conference, April 2006, Folklore Society, London, and the *Childhood and Youth: Participation and Choice* conference, University of Sheffield, July 2006.

Burgess J and Green J (2009) *YouTube: Online Video and Participatory Culture*. Cambridge: Polity Press.

Burns T (1970) A model for textual variation in folksong. *Folklore Forum* 3: 49–56.

Davies J and Merchant G (2009) Chapter 5: YouTube as verb …iTube? weTube? theyTube? In *Web 2.0 for Schools: Learning and Social Participation*. New literacies and digital epistemologies 33. New York: Peter Lang, 53–68.

Gaunt K (2006) *The Games Black Girls Play: Learning the Ropes from Double-Dutch to Hip-Hop*. New York: New York University Press.

Green AE (1970–71) McCaffery: A study in the variation and function of a ballad. *Lore and Language* 1(3): 4–9, 1(4): 3–12, 1(5): 5–11.

Grugeon E (1993) Gender implications of children's playground culture. In Woods P and Hammersley M (eds) *Gender and Ethnicity in Schools: Ethnographic Accounts*. London: Routledge. 11–32.

Harwood EE (1994) Miss Lucy meets Dr Pepper: Mass media and children's traditional playground song and chant. In Lees H (ed.) *Musical Connections: Tradition and Change*. Tampa, Florida: International Society for Music Education, 187–94.

Honko L (2000) Thick corpus and organic variation: An introduction. In Honko L (ed.) *Thick Corpus, Organic Variation and Textuality in Oral Tradition*. Studia Fennica Folkloristica 7. Helsinki: Finnish Literature Society.

Howard RG (2008) Electronic hybridity: The persistent process of the vernacular web. *Journal of American Folklore* 121: 192–218.

Kress G and Van Leeuwen T (2001) *Multimodal Discourse: The Modes and Media of Contemporary Communication*. Arnold: London.

Leman M (2010) Music, gesture, and the formation of embodied meaning. In Godøy RI and Leman M (eds) *Musical Gestures: Sound, Movement, and Meaning*. New York: Routledge, 126–53.

Marsh K (2008) *The Musical Playground: Global Tradition and Change in Children's Songs and Games*. New York: Oxford University Press.

Maybin J (2006) *Children's Voices: Talk, Knowledge and Identity*. Basingstoke: Palgrave Macmillan.

Maybin J (2008) Revoicing across learning spaces. In Martin-Jones M, De Mejia AM and Hornberger NH (eds) *Encyclopedia of Language and Education*, 2nd edn. Vol. 3: Discourse and Education. New York: Springer, 1–12.

Maybin J (2013) Evaluation in pre-teenagers' informal language practices around texts from popular culture. In Cekaite A, Blum-Kulka S, Aukrust V and Teuba

E (eds) *Children's Peer Talk and Peer Learning in First and Second Language*. Cambridge: Cambridge University Press.

McDowell JH (1999) The transmission of children's folklore. In Sutton-Smith B, Mechling J, Johnson TW, McMahon FR (eds) *Children's Folklore: A Source Book*. Garland Reference Library of Social Science, 647. New York: Garland, 49–62.

Opie I (1993) *The People in the Playground*. Oxford: Oxford University Press.

Opie I and P (1969) *Children's Games in Street and Playground*. Oxford: Clarendon Press.

Opie I and P (1959) *The Lore and Language of Schoolchildren*. Oxford: Clarendon Press.

Opie I and P (1985) *The Singing Game*. Oxford: Oxford University Press.

Powell A (ed.) (2012a) Giving daps (intricate handshakes). Available at: http://pancocojams.blogspot.co.uk/2012/05/giving-daps-intricate-handshakes.html

Powell A (2012b) Handclap, jump rope, and elastics rhymes. Available at: http://www.cocojams.com/content/handclap-jump-rope-and-elastics-rhymes

Pugh AJ (2009) *Longing and Belonging: Parents, Children, and Consumer Culture*. Berkeley: University of California Press.

Richards C (2011) In the thick of it: Interpreting children's play. *Ethnography and Education* 6: 309–24.

Roud S (2010) *The Lore of the Playground: One Hundred Years of Children's Games, Rhymes and Traditions*. London: Random House.

Russell I (1987) Stability and change in a Sheffield singing tradition. *Folk Music Journal* 5(3): 317–58.

Strangelove M (2010) *Watching YouTube: Extraordinary Videos by Ordinary People*. Toronto: University of Toronto Press.

Willett R, Richards C, Marsh J, Burn A and Bishop JC (2013) *Children, Media and Playground Cultures: Ethnographic Studies of School Playtimes*. Basingstoke: Palgrave Macmillan.

Zumwalt RL (1995) The complexity of children's folklore. In Sutton-Smith B, Mechling J, Johnson TW, McMahon FR (eds) *Children's Folklore: A Source Book*. Garland Reference Library of Social Science, 647. New York: Garland, 23–48.

Appendix A   Data from Monteney School relating to 'Eeny Meeny Dessameeny' and profiles of children involved

Recording reference (incorporating date of recording in form YYYY-MM-DD)	Performer names	Age(s)	Known relationships
2008–2009			
MPCA2009-07-14 v00115	Alicia Meredith Louise observes	8–9 8–9 9–10	Alicia and Meredith are Y4 classmates and friends. Louise is a Y5 friend.
MPJB2009-07-16 v00056	Emma Lorna Anna observes	All aged 8–9	All three girls are in the same Y4 class as Alicia and Meredith. Meredith is Emma's 'third best friend'.
2009–2010			
MPJB2009-10-13v00260 and MPJB2009-10-13v00262 (5 performances)	Esther Sara Charlotte Louise Julie observes	All aged 10–11	All girls are in Y6 and members of a friendship group. All are in the same class except Sara.
MPJB2009-11-05v01033	Izzy Andrea	Both aged 10–11	Both in Y6. They are friends but in separate classes.
MPJB2010-05-11a00131	Izzy (interview) Andrea Esther	All aged 10–11	Esther is in the same Y6 class as Izzy and is good friends with her and Andrea.

MPJB2010-05-20a00133	Sara Charlotte		See above.
MPJB2010-05-20a00134	Selina (interview)	10–11	Selina is in the same Y6 class as Charlotte et al. She is also the older sister (by one year) of Alicia.
MPJB2010-05-21a00135	Lorna Emma	Both aged 9–10	Y5 classmates and friends. In a different class from Alicia, Mary and Naomi.
MPJB2010-07-20v01593 and MPJB2010-07-20a00138	Alicia Mary Naomi	9–10	Y5 classmates and good friends. In a different class from Lorna and Emma.
2010–2011			
MPJB2010-10-21v01635	Alicia Mary Naomi	10–11	Y6 classmates and friends.
MPJB2010-10-21v01636 and MPJB2010-07-21a00155	Meredith Sally	10–11	Y6 classmates and friends.
MPJB2010-12-09v01662 (3 performances) –MPJB2010-12-09v01164	Alicia Naomi	10–11	Y6 classmates and friends. Mary has left the school.

Chapter 4

Rough Play, Play Fighting and Surveillance: School Playgrounds as Sites of Dissonance, Controversy and Fun

Chris Richards

Introduction

I want to begin this chapter with some biographical reflections, those of Paul Gilroy (2004) but also my own. This will not be a matter of indulging 'fun' memories of childhood. On the contrary, I intend to recover some of my own memories of play because they might suggest that agonistic play, and in particular rough play and play fighting, should not be construed as, always, the creative fantasy that, almost equally, I am sure it can be (Richards, 2013a; 2013b). Violence, fighting and war have always been complex and uncomfortable issues and the historical circumstances of my own early encounters with their forms and meanings are a background to what I argue in the main body of this chapter.

In the introduction to *Between Camps* (2004), Gilroy comments:

> I have had to recognize personal motivation for turning to the relationship between "race" and fascism. I was born in 1956, the year of British folly in Suez and of the Hungarian uprising against Soviet tyranny. My first real geopolitical apprehensions came one fateful morning in 1962 when I sobbed into my cornflakes because I thought the world would end in a nuclear fireball before I could get back home after school … (Gilroy, 2004: 2)

Thus situating himself in relation to major global events, he turns next to the more immediate experience of play:

> As children, we could still see where the bombs had fallen. My own memory tells me that I was a militaristic child, but this must have been a wider generational affliction. I certainly spent much of my childhood re-enacting the glories of the Second World War. The leafy fringes of north London provided the battlegrounds across which I marched my troops and flew my imaginary Battle of Britain aircraft. We preferred these games to alternative pastimes like cowboys and Indians because we savored the fact that we always had right on our side. Our faceless, unremittingly evil enemies were Hitler's Nazis and, inspired by what we read in comics like *Eagle* and *Swift* as well as the stronger fare to be found in places like the barbershop, we harried and slaughtered them wherever they could be located: in parks, gardens and wastelands, or the disused

air-raid shelters that were unearthed all around us. This may seem to have been an eccentric pursuit for a black boy, but it was entirely unproblematic. No white playmate ever questioned the right of us not-yet-postcolonials to play that game. (Gilroy, 2004: 2)

Gilroy goes on to explore his own family history and his first perplexed discovery of the British Union of Fascists on a walk with his father in the still bomb-damaged City of London. Where to locate the threat of fascism became an enduring issue. But how to 'fight' it was also complicated by his father's stance as a conscientious objector:

> I felt a little disadvantaged when other children proudly recounted their parents' wartime exploits. My father, a twenty-year-old student when war was declared, had chosen another testing path. He said that no government could compel him to kill another human being … (Gilroy, 2004: 3)

I was born in 1952, four years earlier than Paul Gilroy, and grew up in a semi-rural area of East Yorkshire, close to Hull and to Beverley. Like Gilroy, I remember the Cuban missile crisis in 1962, talking to a friend at the bus-stop on the way to school, wondering if we would live to see the end of the day. My father was also a conscientious objector and I recall some unease in representing his position to the boys I grew up with. But perhaps because he had worked with refugees in the eastern Mediterranean, and there were plenty of photographs to confirm it, he was spared the stigma of having stayed 'at home'. As I remember it, our play, unlike Gilroy's, was not so singularly focused on the reiteration of battles with the Nazis. It was one element; I recall having a toy gun modelled on a 1940s Luger but I'm not sure why. The main fantasy in our play borrowed from the American West, 'Cowboys and Indians'. Perhaps the lack of a simple good versus bad scenario made it a more malleable narrative resource; the attractions of being an Indian were considerable and, in addition to carrying toy Colt 45s, we made bows and arrows, and 'painted' our faces. My own ephemeral favourite involved dividing my face vertically, one half green, the other brown. Reading the Opies (1959), I was reminded that I have a photograph of myself, probably aged four, standing on top of a garden shed, wearing a Davy Crockett hat, stripes of 'war-paint' on my cheeks, 'shooting' on those below with a toy rifle (Figure 4.1).

The Opies comment:

> At the beginning of 1956 Walt Disney Productions launched a publicity campaign to make Britain's youth 'Crockett conscious' in preparation for a film *Davy Crockett, King of the Wild Frontier* (released 2 April 1956). The campaign became the most ambitious adult-organized assault on the juvenile imagination since before the war. Toy manufacturers were encouraged to produce 'character' merchandise, and stimulate a Crockett cult … In April and May 1956 the campaign reached its climax, and there was a definite spasm of Crockett play. (Opie and Opie, 1959/2001: 119).

Fig. 4.1   The author, circa 1956

A great deal of our play involved staged combat with a mixture of home-made weapons and a smattering of toy replicas. As the example of Davy Crockett suggests, we engaged with the popular media and drew its imagery, and some of the merchandise, into our play scenarios (see Griffin, 1999). Though, in my experience, the American West was dominant, a mix of TV series and serials, films and comics provided a flexible resource: *The Silver Sword, Rawhide, Robin Hood, William Tell, Ben Hur, Superman, Batman* and, though too late in my own childhood to facilitate play, *James Bond* and *The Man from U.N.C.L.E.* (Opie and Opie, 1969/2008 vol. 2: 196–8).

In many ways, this was immensely exciting and imaginative play pursued mainly out of school, on lanes and in fields and woods well away from adult surveillance. The Opies mention that the '*British Medical Journal* reported a significant increase in the number of children admitted to hospital with eye injuries' in 1956 (Opie and Opie, 1959/2001: 119). There were injuries and near misses, of course. Though perhaps the worst incident that I recall, and one for which I felt responsible, happened in school. We were re-enacting the chariot race from *Ben Hur* (directed by William Wyler, 1959) and, in an excessive and reckless attempt to gain advantage at a corner of the school building, one boy was thrown into the wall and had to be taken to hospital by ambulance. But this was an accident, not a malicious act of violence.

With such a relentless preoccupation, among boys, with combat and conflict, it is obviously important to consider what enduring contribution such experience made to the formation of those involved (see Tolson, 1977; Jackson, 1990). Gilroy traces his own life-long preoccupation with 'fighting' fascism, in part, to his intense involvement in battles with the Nazis in childhood play. Translated into intellectual battle, the concern with real violence recedes somewhat, though Gilroy's ambivalence about the legitimacy of such violence lingers. With strong parental disapproval of war and violence and a great appetite for play fighting (and a year of Karate at 15, cf. Bowman, 2010: 120–21) I also have to work away at what it means to 'fight' and how agonistic play might contribute to 'combative' dispositions. The question addressed in this chapter is, most simply, what is the relationship between play fighting and real violence?

On the whole, play fighting in my own experience was exciting, collaborative fun (Newkirk, 2002). Injuries were rare and unintended. Real fights were avoided, mostly. But in the last years of primary school, at 10 and 11, I had enough encounters that were supposedly playful but were close enough to provocations to real fighting for me to recognize that play can sometimes be a mask for aggression and malice, if also, and perhaps simultaneously, a kind of homo-eroticism (Gresson, 2004: 215). Drawing on TV wrestling, a friend, defined at the time as my best friend, routinely inflicted his favoured holds and blows on me. To respond in kind would have elicited further, far more serious, violence. This was routine, prolonged and took place at school. I suppose because we were 'officially' best friends it was always construed as rough play between equals (much the same size and weight) rather than 'bullying'.[1] Some years later, while still at secondary school, he was convicted of various violent assaults in the local town. I had already fallen out with him, partly over a beating he gave a Jewish boy in our class. Eventually, he was expelled.

The School Playground

 Playgrounds in schools are very different from those spaces occupied by children outside both school and home (Richards, 2011; 2012). The playground is just as much a part of the school as the classroom. It is intricately tied into the regulation of the school day and is a space designed to privilege particular forms of play. It is also, often, designed to produce play as a complement to the learning and the discipline that are the explicit concerns of the school curriculum.[2] In the research project's London school, in June 2009, the staff notice-board had an item entitled 'Our Learning Journey 2008/9' and the last listed aim under 'Pupil development and well being' was 'To develop an outstanding outdoor learning environment/ playground'. In the stairwells, children could see (and were reminded in assembly) that the school had a set of 'Golden Rules':

> Do be gentle
> Do be kind and helpful
> Do play well with others
> Do care for your playground
> Do listen to people
> Do be honest
> Do keep to the playground safety rules
> Do not hurt anybody
> Do not hurt people's feelings
> Do not spoil others' games
> Do not damage or spoil anything
> Do not interrupt
> Do not cover up the truth
> Do not break the playground safety rules

---

[1]   Barter and Berridge (2011) comment: "Throughout our work on peer violence, the most consistent and powerful findings have been children's and young people's own testimonies on how peer relationships, and especially those involving violence, are among the main causes of anxiety and unhappiness in their lives; and that these concerns remain largely unacknowledged by, and unreported to, adults." (Barter and Berridge, 2011: 3). See also Brown, in the same volume and Brown, 2010.

[2]   School buildings are expressive indications of changing views of childhood, from the gothic piles of the first state schools of the 1880s and 1890s to the airily laid out primary schools of the 1930s and the huge, aspirational comprehensives of the 1960s. Each creates its own version of a child-shaped space, where childish impulsiveness can fight it out with school-based discipline. (Holland, 2004: 77)

On the playground itself various coloured discs condensed these rules into more situationally specific injunctions, for example:

> 'Time Out' Stop: Take time out to think about what has happened. What could you do differently next time to avoid this situation happening?

Such rules and prescriptions for proper conduct were a constant and explicit theme in assemblies and in more frequent daily reminders from class teachers. Furthermore, the playground areas were always subject to a degree of adult surveillance that aspired to be both continuous and comprehensive.

Some forms of play were regarded as safe, constructive and inclusive. Other forms – often rough play and play fighting – were not regarded as desirable and were seen as most likely to threaten the rules of conduct. Moreover, the playground was defined as a space to be kept free of the kind of conflicts that might arise among young people out of school. The playground was for learning how to cooperate with others, for learning how to play constructively, if also for 'releasing' the energy that might disrupt the more formal learning conducted inside (Stewart, 1980: 44 n.91; Sutton-Smith, 1997: 133). For teachers and other adults in schools, play that may be difficult to differentiate from real conflict was likely to be regarded as too troublesome to be left unchecked.[3]

In a key essay published in 1984, Brian Sutton-Smith and Diana Kelly-Byrne turned their attention to the prevailing view that play was a free, imaginatively creative and entirely positive component of childhood. Looking back over other contributions to Peter K. Smith's (1984) *Play in Animals and Humans*, they entitled their critique 'The Idealization of Play'. Though in some respects deliberately polemical, they highlighted the elements in play that, nearly 30 years later, are still a significant concern for some teachers and some parents. They point to the social relations of playgrounds, emphasising that play does not take place independently of the power struggles that characterize such settings:

> When we see children on the playground … that freedom is primarily freedom from the classroom. There is limited freedom of choice in the actual play of the playground itself because of the obligations to friends and to powerful other children etc (Sutton-Smith and Kelly-Byrne in Smith, 1984: 310)

> In *A History of Children's Play* (Sutton-Smith, 1982) we have detailed a host of ways in which what went on in the playground and what was commonly called children's play was often brutal and unpleasant for some of the members of the 'play group'… (Sutton-Smith and Kelly-Byrne in Smith, 1984: 311)

---

[3]   Some of our video recorded examples of pretend play involving agonistic scenarios are available on the British Library website – http://www.bl.uk Playtimes: A Century of Children's Games and Rhymes – for example Pretend Play: Action Games and Tae Kwon-do. On the whole the examples shown were regarded as acceptable by school staff on duty in the playground.

Their comments do not refer solely to play fighting – exerting power by exclusion from *any* game is clearly a possibility. The game could be football, or cops and robbers or grandma's footsteps but, however 'non-violent', to deny participation potentially inflicts damage – to the excluded children's playground identities.

However, they do also comment more specifically on the uses, in addition to tactical exclusions, of threatened aggression:

> ... if one looks at Sluckin, the Opies or the Knapps there is abundant anecdotal evidence of playground bosses, of harassment specialists, of the fact that some games are 'owned' by some children while other children are simply excluded ... children also use play to terrorize each other. That is to say, they often move between pretending and actually being aggressive. This turns out to be an extraordinarily powerful way of controlling others, for the recipients of such conflicting information have difficulty in predicting what will happen next and become uneasy ... (Sutton-Smith and Kelly-Byrne in Smith, 1984: 313)

The suggestion that victims of such behaviour are unsettled by the ambiguity of actions that may or may not be play certainly recalls the 'wrestling play' I referred to above. But the broader implication is that participants' judgements of the 'reality status' or modality[4] of play fighting are not necessarily securely consensual – and disjunctions in understanding can be deliberately heightened and exploited. From this perspective, the idea of a 'community of practice' (Wenger, 1998) in which there is a shared and stable understanding both of how to behave, and what the behaviour means, looks fragile, always contingent on the network of friendships, alliances and collaborations current in the playground. Sutton-Smith and Kelly-Byrne's argument perhaps also acknowledges wider 'popular' misgivings about what children do when they play, misgivings that are more often displaced or marginalized in the academic theorization of play. In schools, with staff informed not primarily by play theory but by such 'common sense' about children, proper conduct in the playground is not assumed. As academic outsiders, distanced from the day to day work of managing the school, we may struggle to recognize that, for teachers, the explicit and repeated statement of the rules of playground conduct is a necessary constraint, *enforcing* play on children who may not *play* with each other willingly.

The school playground might thus be understood as benignly coercive, constructing its space as strictly an arena for play, policed for infractions – children not playing or not playing properly (there was, for example, one recorded instance

---

[4] 'Modality' concerns the reality attributed to a message ... In a language such as English there are a number of words whose function is to convey modality – that is, to indicate degrees of certainty of a sentence. If we start with a simple sentence, like 'It's a monster', we have a statement that seems to claim total certainty. Thus we can say it has a strong modality. We can weaken that modality status by adding modal auxiliaries, like 'may', 'might', etc.: 'It may be a monster.' We can further weaken the claim by adding a modal adverb like 'possibly' or 'perhaps' ... (Hodge and Tripp, 1986: 104).

of a Year One boy being dragged by two other Year One boys, albeit briefly, and his escape to report it to a playground supervisor[5]). In the London school, children were recruited to the task of ensuring that everyone played where only play was allowed. A number of children, across the years, were appointed as 'Buddies' and a notice in the lower playground declared: 'If you are feeling sad or lonely you can sit at the Friendship stop. A Buddy will invite you to join in their games'. With younger children (Reception and Year One: from four to six years old) learning assistants often intervened to teach particular games. Sometimes class teachers also ventured out to join in and extend play activities with older classes. Sutton-Smith and Kelly-Byrne say that 'play is *always a "framed" event*' (emphasis in the original) but they also suggest that its status as such is precarious:

> ... *in play the metacommunicative function always retains primacy.* It is apparently essential to keep in the minds of the players that they are indeed playing, otherwise the activity will break down into anxiety or violence as indeed it often does. To this end, play requires a display of sufficient cues to keep the distinction between this realm and others in the forefront of awareness. (Sutton-Smith and Kelly-Byrne in Smith, 1984: 317)

Of course, children play willingly and, given the space, play where no adults prescribe that play should take place. They transform the available space in often unpredictable ways producing a 'realm' – or a heterotopia (a liminal space which mirrors, contests and inverts various sites in the real world, as Burn notes in Chapter 1) – that they attempt to sustain for the pleasure and satisfaction it affords. The point made by Sutton-Smith and Kelly-Byrne is that such playful transformations are somewhat insecure or, to follow Foucault's discussion of heterotopias as analogous with mirrored transpositions, are fragile and, perhaps, could be shattered at any moment (Richards, 2013). Of course, Sutton-Smith is known for his sophisticated theoretical insistence on the importance of play but he is equally known for his exploration of its ambiguities. In this respect his work is particularly salient in a period marked by heightened anxieties and uncertainties about childhood and about the nature of play, if not initially in academic enquiry (see Singer and Singer, 2005).

Childhood at Risk, Children as a Threat

To explain why such anxieties have increased, it is useful to turn to the work of Patricia Holland (2004). Her account of the shifts in popular 'common sense' understandings of childhood is grounded in a substantial collection of images from a variety of media representing childhood through many decades, mainly in the

---

5   CHCR2009-09-22v00029.

United Kingdom.[6] To some extent her argument parallels and confirms the themes outlined so far. But there are differences in emphasis that merit some discussion. For example, she identifies a tension in the formation of schools as both secure havens for children and, as concentrations of children, themselves productive of adult anxieties. She argues that the 'theme of happiness has been part of the discourse of the post-war primary school' (Holland, 2004: 78) but that:

> schools contain large numbers of the same type of person gathered in a limited and clearly defined space ....

> Such a gathering together of children carries symbolic dangers of its own. School becomes a place where order and disorder constantly confront each other ... Assembled together, children may develop autonomous activities which exclude adults. They may egg each other on or form into gangs. Their uproar and mobility are aggravated by their numbers, so that it is difficult to keep track of a single individual at every moment in time. (Holland, 2004: 79)

The play of small groups of children in and around a family, or out of adult sight, becomes in the school context a problem of control, of ensuring that play is properly contained and managed:

> ... on entering school, children find their right to undirected play limited to a designated space, the playground, and time, playtime. The playground image itself may be seen as a threat, infested by bullies and children running wild. Play itself is linked to uncontrollability and the fear that children may move beyond the reach of the school's disciplinary regime. (Holland, 2004: 79–80)

In this argument, the school playground is both a 'solution' to and the site for an intensification of the problem of play.

Like Sutton-Smith and Kelly-Byrne, Holland draws attention to the fragility of the belief that play is always constructive and harmonious. But Holland's concern is mainly with how adults represent what children do, rather than with any further investigation of what children may or may not do or what they might have to say about it. Nevertheless, her discussion of the James Bulger case (1993) and of subsequent press stories producing 'a vision of a violent world of childhood' (Holland, 2004: 120) is of continuing relevance. Though her account was published in 2004, in delineating the 'mythological construction of childhood ... interwoven with a cruel reality as newspaper narratives tell of children who are

---

[6] Commenting on the representation of play and childhood, Holland comments: The values of play are at the heart of family life and of contemporary constructions of childishness, yet they bring their own subversive influence. Playfulness and expressiveness all too easily lead to uncontrollable children, while hedonistic values may well disrupt socially cohesive family structures ... Uncontained play can all too easily topple into chaos, and ruin more than your once beautiful house. (Holland, 2004: 64–5)

both damaged and damaging' (Holland, 2004: 121) she identifies a continuing and persistent theme that undoubtedly defines the context for schools' approaches to play fighting in the present:

> Reports continue of children driven to suicide through bullying; of children who terrorise local estates, stealing cars, breaking windows, starting fires and terrifying elderly inhabitants; of gangs, whose rivalry is based on territory or race; of a growing drugs and gun culture and of suburban youth whose violence is casual and random ... now the spontaneity and irrationality of childhood, instead of being playful, has a savage and dangerous quality ... (Holland, 2004: 121)

With a regular and frequent flow of reports about violent incidents between young people (usually teenagers), the emphasis on curtailing or prohibiting play fighting in school playgrounds is likely to be justified in terms of protecting children from each other or at least of refusing to legitimate actions that may, in this view, be transposed to the real world in the children's own impending adolescence (see Cohen, 1997: 92; Holland, 2003; Robins and Cohen, 1978).

Talking about Play Fighting

I talked to a number of children about play fighting during the 2010 summer term (see Richards, 2013a). Here I want to draw on interviews, initially with Year Six boys (11 years old) in June but also with several Year Two (seven years old) children recorded just before the end of the school year in July. The Year Six boys agreed that play fighting was prohibited in the school and they identified this with the Head's disapproval, most recently voiced in an assembly in March 2010. Suavek, reporting the Head's words, and brushing aside the warnings from Rick that they were being recorded, cited her as saying 'There's something I'm very upset about, people are play fighting in our new school playground'.[7] He went on to describe her referring to the school's Golden Rules, pointing out how play fighting conflicted with many of them. Suavek also reported that the Head 'hates guns, she said if anyone's caught with guns they are missing their playtime ...'[8].

It emerged that, for the Head, play fighting was associated with 'war and crime' whereas for them play fighting was fantasy, largely informed by *Power Rangers* and *Star Wars* and most common among younger boys in Years One and Two. As Year Six boys, aged 11 and close to leaving for secondary school, they somewhat distanced themselves from such activities though they could recall them and, looking back, were always forthcoming about the sources of such play (see the discussion of origins in Chapter 2). They were enthusiastic about *Power Rangers* – especially *SPD* (*Space Patrol Delta*) – Rick saying that he 'loves it' and Suavek recalling wanting to play *Power Rangers* at his previous school (where apparently

---

[7]   CHCR2010-06-17v00239.

[8]   CHCR2010-06-17v00240.

it was dismissed as 'babyish' – presumably by the teachers). Suavek was keen to tell me about the longer history of the show and its Japanese origins though, as usual, Rick mocked and disrupted his more serious expository self-positioning[9]. Watching younger children play fighting in various video clips from March 2010, their main response was amused exasperation, animated by their sense of the inconsistency between what they understood to be a comprehensive ban on play fighting and its very visible presence as staff on playground duty looked on, apparently unconcerned. The staff's tacit acknowledgement that this kind of play fighting was not harming those involved appeared to them to be inconsistent with the school's explicit policy. They were perhaps a little envious that these younger children were left alone to play as they wished, were not interrupted and were not called 'babyish'. In practice, the school was not enforcing the kind of zero tolerance policy described and thoughtfully questioned in Penny Holland's research in early years settings (see Holland, 2003; for further discussion of Suavek and Rick, see Richards, 2013b).

A second group of boys (one each from Years Four, Five and Six) largely confirmed Rick and Suavek's account. Marwan, Mahdi and Yaman gave a shared account though Marwan (Year Six) was the most consistently articulate and it is his comments that I quote here. Referring back to the March assembly he said that the Head was 'talking about actual crimes and wars that was going on, it was quite serious'[10]. The kind of behaviour that he said she identified as unacceptable included, for example, when 'basically people pretend to stab each other like that (gestures with a downward blow to Mahdi sitting next to him)' (see Squires and Goldsmith, 2011: 208). On the whole, they seemed sceptical about the relevance of her concerns to play fighting – which they identified as 'the Year Twos play like light sabres' – and devoted much of the available time to recalling actual fights and angry confrontations, none of which actually arose out of play fighting scenarios. Marwan commented on the relationship to real violence suggested by the Head with a kind of dispassionate shrug: 'crime is happening, it's real life, it's not like it's going to change or anything'. After viewing several video clips of younger children involved in various kinds of play fighting – including shooting and throwing grenades[11] – they seemed to conclude that none of what they had seen was problematic, not least because it lacked the detail of properly simulated combat and thus had a low modality. They reiterated that the Head strongly disapproved of shooting but indicated that for such actions in the playground to be checked they would have to be seen by her (and not just by other staff) and would also need to be much more explicitly modelled on, for example, firing a sub-machine gun, which Marwan demonstrated with appropriate sound effects.[12]

---

[9]   CHCR2010-06-17v00242.
[10]   CHCR2010-06-17v00243.
[11]   CHCR2010-03-03v00186.
[12]   CHCR2010-06-17v00245.

I asked Lena, at the end of Year Two, about playing *Star Wars*.[13] She shook her head and said: 'I don't play that anymore'. I suggested that she'd been playing it some two or three weeks ago and she again shook her head and said firmly 'one month ago'. Despite this unpromising beginning she went on to explain that each time she played *Star Wars* she was a different character (see Edmiston, 2008): 'when people want to join in the game they have to wait until the next, until I change character, and when I change character ... and everyone moves along, if you're the last character, then you're out of the game'. This rule governed game structure was possibly exaggerated in her account – as it enabled her to amplify the degree of control she exercised – but it was also characteristic of 'pretend play' that a negotiated and consciously 'managed' order was maintained between the participants (see Chapter 1, this volume; and Burn, chapter 6, and Willett, chapter 7, in Willett et al, 2013). Sutton-Smith comments:

> To understand a group of well-acquainted children at play, it is often useful to think of them like a traveling troupe of medieval players who arrive, set up their theater, and then begin performing. It is a world that is run more like a theater is run than like an everyday world. Children play the parts of stage managers, directors, and actors all at the same time, moving freely about the parts as they get ready to put together their own shows for themselves ... (Sutton-Smith, 1997: 159)

Such a movement between participation and management highlights the crafted pretence of their play fights. Getting lost in the action would risk moving too close to the reality of physical conflict but with attention divided between the maintenance of the game structure and the enactment of combat, the risk of such a slide from play to fight is much reduced. Moreover, the movement from one character to another implies an exploration of different perspectives within the combat narrative rather than a fixed identification with one 'actor'. As Edmiston notes in his detailed account of his own son's play, 'Michael effortlessly moved among multiple points of view as he took up the perspectives of different people along with their relative power and authority' (Edmiston, 2008: 150; see also Spina, 2004). Lena attributed the 'idea to play *Star Wars*' to Eyal. Nevertheless, though she claimed that she was not allowed to watch television during the week (only at week-ends and during the summer) she was unequivocal in naming her preferred viewing as *Ben 10: Alien Force* and *Star Wars*. She was thus a knowledgeable participant in these combat scenarios, well able to negotiate her characters and their inflections with the boys who appeared to initiate these games. If she had significant misgivings about the game, they seemed to lie in being the victim in some permutations of the narrative: 'I like all of it, the only bit I don't like is when I get killed ... I die because when I'm not looking Darth Vader just creeps behind me a puts a light sabre in my body somewhere ... if it touches you anywhere it burns you and you die'.

---

[13]   CHCR2010-07-22v00267.

Lena's account of her interests *in play* favoured fantasy and not the more realistic domestic simulations often associated with girls: she identified 'the worst game I've played in my whole life – Mummies and Daddies – because I don't like the game, I've already got a Mummy and Daddy'. By contrast she spoke enthusiastically about, and briefly enacted, her participation as a big cat – a feature of play among children in the Year Two class in the preceding weeks – 'my favourite is a cheetah, my favourite animal, because it's the fastest in the world or the universe I don't know … every night I get food … chicken … this is not what I eat but what I bring to eat … meat of a cow, milk of a cow [demonstrates being a cheetah] I only have fights with leopards and jaguars … two of them are cheetahs and two of them are leopards'. But her activities as a cheetah, or her death by light sabre, were only 'pretend', in games from which she had perhaps moved on. Indeed my one to one interview with her was marked by her quite insistent shift into talking about her autistic younger brother and his very different prospects in school. I wanted to talk to her about pretend play and she told me enough about her enjoyment of it to satisfy the questions that I asked. But it seemed to me that she had other more real world preoccupations that she wanted to explain (see James, Jenks and Prout 1998: 87). Given the opportunity to talk to an adult, familiar to her through quite a lengthy period, to talk about play may have seemed inconsequential and inappropriate. Play was what she did with other children, whereas the real circumstances of her immediate family life were more properly the stuff of conversations with a teacherly adult in school.

I also interviewed another Year Two girl, Anabel[14]. I was curious about an event that I had encountered and video recorded in the later stages of its development and initially understood to be a violent scene in which girls seated at desks were being machine gunned by their teachers[15]. This event is discussed further and in more detail by Willett (Chapter 6, this volume). Quite a large group of girls, mainly from Years Two and Three, had used wooden blocks and planks to assemble a row of desks or tables in a covered area of the playground – the Brick Area. My misunderstanding was illustrative of the difficulty faced by adult observers in judging the modality of the play events taking place. I had assumed that the girls participating in this event were all playing in the same reality domain. Anabel, though very shy and reluctant to give extended answers to my questions, explained clearly, and very straightforwardly, that I had not understood the structure of the game: 'We were playing a game where they make a table and we were the TV and we're 3D so we come out of the TV and we're trying to be pirates'. The game began with a domestic and mundane setting: 'we started off with a table and wanted to eat dinner and we just decided we wanted TV'. Though negotiated between the participants, it seems that the game did not have a fully predetermined form and, as it developed, it became a play with the status and boundaries of differing modalities. Sutton-Smith observes that:

---

[14] CHCR2010-07-22v00268.
[15] CHCR2010-07-14v00260.

> Play proceeds, as it were, within itself, every subsequent action playing off the preceding ones, sometimes with increasing transformation, even with increasing nonsense, from play to playful. (Sutton-Smith, 1997: 195)

So those having dinner find themselves, though just watching TV, apparently assaulted by pirates, screaming and laughing as the 3D TV characters intrude into their domestic space: 'those two have got guns and that's a knife'. They had elaborated a complex heterotopian fantasy, opaque to uninformed outsiders. Of course I asked about the pirates but she was quite vague about their origins. She had not seen any of the *Pirates of the Caribbean* films but mentioned *Blackbeard* and CBBC's *Horrible Histories*. Pirates may have been a class topic too (see Willett, Chapter 6, this volume). But she had no particular interest in or attachment to being a pirate beyond, it seemed, the occasion of the 3D TV game and the ephemeral heterotopia it allowed them to construct. I asked her if she did have a favourite pretend play character that she liked to be; she answered: 'A fish ... you know *Nemo*? I was pretending that every time I say something I forget'.

A similar emphasis on the ephemeral and rapidly receding interest of past games emerged in a further interview with a member of the Year Two class, a boy, Tom.[16] I showed him a video clip[17] in which he appeared among many others but adopting quite striking East Asian martial arts poses (for the wider history, see Bowman, 2010; Willis, 1985). I asked him who he was fighting against: 'Ninjas ... I wouldn't do that anymore [Why not?] because it's a bit boring [It looks like you were having really good fun to me] I know *then* we would be but we wouldn't be *now*'. This interview took place during the 2010 Football World Cup and he was far more interested in telling me about their pretend play final in which Australia beat Spain 4:3. The play presented to him (from April) was firmly in the past: 'I used to go to karate class, club ... but anyway they're made up moves [so where's the karate club you go to?] I don't go to it anymore'. Somewhat disowning his own apparently past interest, he was more interested in commenting on others in the same video clip: 'Li gets told off for it ... there's Eyal he's probably being the bad guy – he's got the best karate skills because he goes Tae Kwon Do ... I was a good guy, I was on Li's team and he's fighting Li which means he's [a bad guy]'. To some extent he engaged with the events in the clip by re-enacting them, rolling on the floor and sometimes demonstrated other things that had happened like a boy being pushed backwards. But at one point he asked me a question: 'Have you ever been in a fire?' I said that I hadn't and he told me, albeit briefly, about a fire at his home. Like Lena, he appeared to want to move away from talking about play and to engage me in talk about something more dangerously real.

Though Tom refers to Li being 'told off', there is little evidence in any of these interviews, with either Year Six or Year Two, that, in practice, teachers intervened in fantasy play fighting. However, the children did judge what they could do without

---

[16]   CHCR2010-07-22v00269.

[17]   CHCR2010-04-20v00201 see Playtimes: Pretend Play: Tae Kwon-do at http://www.bl.uk.

getting into trouble with teachers and there were references in other interviews to making choices informed by the presence or assumed absence of teachers and other adults. For example, Nur (Year Three)[18] suggested that there were some real world precedents for imagining that the apparently friendly and familiar midday meal and play supervisors could be a threat: 'if you're in trouble ... well you have to sit on the bench and miss some of your playtime, if you're naughty'. The bench, it seemed, was where they might be confined if, in his account of their play scenario, one of them was caught in running from one hiding place to another. At one point, late in one play event, where he was crouching down behind a wall, he explained to me (in the subsequent interview): 'See what I mean, Lyn almost caught me, so I run back up the steps'. In this example, discussed elsewhere (Richards, 2013a), he heightened the surveillance activities of the playground supervisors to construct a greater sense of risk, and of pleasure, in the game. The game involved running, hiding and some occasional simulation of firing arrows. It was formed and judged with, and within, the contextual fact of adult supervision. In effect, he inhabited a heterotopian pretence that the open areas of the playground were exposed and dangerous zones to be crossed swiftly and with careful timing.

Play that might be construed as play fighting by the playground supervisors *was* avoided: 'I only play fighting when the teachers ain't looking ... if they're looking, I just stop'. Another boy, Agon in Year One (March 2010), also talked to me about the issue of play fighting, commenting that: 'when teachers are there we pretend, when teachers are not there, we do real'. He had interests in well known and enduring combat fantasy narratives such as *Teenage Mutant Ninja Turtles* (TV, film and computer game) and *Power Rangers.* Of course, it was difficult to know exactly what he meant by his comment, 'we do real'. But, at the very least, it suggested an ability to judge the modality level of play fighting to accommodate the presence, or otherwise, of adult surveillance. For him, it seemed that the *boundary* between the real and the pretend was familiar and routinely deployed in deciding *how* to play (see Robins and Cohen, 1978: 102; also Cohen, 1997: 99).

Gender War

When we first visited the school, there was some concern among staff at the supposedly disproportionate number of boys, especially in the upper years. Such concerns seemed to decline somewhat after the departure of the then current Year Six and also after the opening of a new playground area. But the view that, in the playground, boys were most likely to be troublesome did persist (an observation recorded in field notes 9 June 2009).

One example of boys playing in a way that drew supervisors to intervene, from October 2009, is worth describing in some detail.[19] I want to focus on one

---

[18] CHCR2010-06-15v00232 See Playtimes: Pretend Play: Action Games at http://www.bl.uk.

[19] CHCR2009-10-05v00061.

boy in particular, Isamu, then in Year Four. The events took place on the rooftop playground before the opening of the new playground area at ground level. The space was always congested and multiple activities took place in close proximity. In this case, in the Quiet Area (an ironic designation on most days that I was there), some boys were playing with pogo sticks, laughing and falling over and into each other. From time to time two supervisors wandered over to check that their play was not getting too dangerously wild. When Isamu arrived he seized a pogo stick and immediately pretended that it was a machine gun, shaking with the rapidity of the fire. He threw down the 'machine gun', and chased after a girl, arms wide apart, screaming. When she returned, he directed some mock blows at the girl, threw himself on the floor, then jumped up and chased her out of the area. When he returned, he grabbed a cushion and began shouting and hitting himself in the face with it before throwing it, repeatedly, at other boys (David in particular). Two girls, Alice and Nadine (discussed further below) and others arrived and Isamu redirected his wild assault towards them – all of this was met with good humour, laughing and reciprocal counter assaults. But one of the supervisors came over and intervened saying 'You know the rules'. When she had gone, Isamu screamed and chased the girls, throwing himself about with a kind of gleeful hyperbole. None of this was in any way obviously problematic for any of the children involved and their conflict was staged with extremely noisy hilarity. Throwing cushions and, perhaps, making quite so much noise in the Quiet Area – where one girl sat reading throughout all of this – were the most obvious breaches of the rules. But there seemed little real risk of injury or of offence to each other in what they were doing.

Isamu's own comments on his style of play were elicited some months later[20] and were mainly framed by a discussion of his energetic war play in the new playground (video recorded[21] and also viewed with several older boys, discussed above). Isamu's battlefield fantasies were allowed to unfold without much adult intervention – though the events I recorded preceded the assembly forbidding play fighting later that March. Lying on his belly, half hidden by a mound and a tree stump, he repeatedly threw grenades and jumped to his feet to fire what appeared to be a machine gun. From time to time, he ran towards a decked area and engaged in 'violent' close combat with two or three of the boys half-hiding there. As in the previous event in the Quiet Area, some of his actions, for example an apparent attempt to strangle himself, served as dramatic enactments of assaults of which he was the *victim*, and not only the aggressor. In this respect, he was shifting between positions in a fantasy scenario rather than 'identifying' with and enacting only one (Edmiston, 2008). In the account given by Isamu in the subsequent interview, my emphasis on his relatively solitary activity in the battle fantasy he enacted was strongly countered by his explanation that he was playing with other boys from his class and that six of them were divided into two teams of three. Attempting to trace some of the sources for his play fantasies, I asked if he watched war films but he dismissed this: 'Nah can't be bothered, rather play them, can't be bothered to watch

---

[20]   CHCR2010-06-15v00238.
[21]   CHCR2010-03-03v00186.

them, watching them is a bit boring. I like watching football'. He went on to talk about five-a-side football on the rooftop playground and his enthusiasm for 'boys against girls football matches'. There seemed to be a significant continuity with the team against team structure of his war game and he represented these various adversarial scenarios as gender polarized: 'boys versus girls all the time, boys had to catch the girls, attack them, put them in jail; either that or gangster stuff'.

Such ordered conflict may fulfil a variety of purposes. For Thomas Newkirk (2002), who has written extensively about boys' preferred modes of writing, combat narratives facilitate engagement *between* boys. Newkirk remarks:

> There is often a deeply *social* subtext to stories that might appear individualistic and combative. For many or even most boys it makes no sense to claim that competition (or conflict) and collaboration are *opposed* ideals; rather, boys regularly collaborate *through* combative play. (Newkirk, 2002: 121)

In combative play, boys were able to be together, to touch each other and to share in intensely exciting fantasies of power and vulnerability. Though it was not at all easy to elicit any kind of fully articulated account of the pleasures and satisfactions of such play for boys from the participants themselves, the concluding arguments offered by Sutton-Smith and Kelly-Byrne (1984) in their essay on the idealization of play (discussed in the introduction to this chapter) suggest a plausible interpretation:

> ... the very point of play's paradoxes are that they permit us to communicate such subjectivity to others in a disguised fashion. They permit us to say the opposite of what we mean in order to mean the opposite of what we say ... Being weak we (child or adult) play at being powerful in order both to disguise that we feel weak and yet to reveal to any other that weakness is our problem. (Sutton-Smith and Kelly-Byrne in Smith, 1984: 319)

> ... play is a very special kind of 'language of expression' within which we share our secrets with others. It proceeds by paradox and dialectic in order that our subjective worlds, our wish-fulfilments, can see the light of day and enter into the human community without directly overthrowing or directly tampering with the everyday order of normative expectations. Through sharing these secrets of infirmity and desire we are bonded to those with whom we play and feel the validity of our membership in their community. (Sutton-Smith and Kelly-Byrne in Smith, 1984: 319)

It is possible to speculate that, to some extent, play fighting for these boys involved an exploration and recognition of a shared vulnerability, that being weak was an issue that none of them could escape. On warm dry days in the new playground, boys rolled around together, wrestling each other to the ground in a prolonged and diffuse series of encounters below the threshold of more fully elaborated fantasy play. To an adult onlooker this may look like an irritating and occasionally uncomfortable way to spend time on the playground but through its possible exploration of 'secrets of infirmity and desire' it may well sustain a sense of conviviality and belonging. In addition to such loose wrestling, boys played football together, hung out together trading cards (Match Attax, Pokémon, Bakugan) and clustered together to chat, rest and pass the time. Of course, in any of these mainly, if not always exclusively, homosocial situations other tensions and conflicts between the boys may well have been present but, to the extent that they were together, such troubles appeared to be contained, perhaps displaced by shared recognition of their common circumstances. After all, whatever the constraints of the school site, they could, if they had wished, have gone elsewhere, avoided each other and sought out more solitary or less exclusively male dominated spaces – the hall, the library, or areas of the playground used by younger children (Reception and Years One and Two).

In mixed gender playgrounds of the kind discussed here, play was not always – with the notable exception of football – sustained as exclusive of girls for very long. Through to the end of Year Two, and to varying degrees thereafter, there was considerable mixing among girls and boys in their play. With respect to specifically combative modes of play, I asked Li if any of the girls also did Tae Kwon Do.[22] He replied, commenting on Lena (interviewed above): 'she always plays fighting games with us, nearly every day she plays with us fighting …'. He added that Lena had not taken classes and did not do 'the hard moves because we told her not to'. In these comments, though acknowledging a girl's participation, he firmly constructed a shared male position, implying authority and control. His own male combat persona was also asserted through typifications of girl behaviour as responsive to his agency: 'nearly all the girls in the class are scared of me because I [like] fighting and they're like "aaaargh" they keep running away and go in the girls' toilets. Sometimes Lena helps me so, she can go in, she gets them out and then I get them and bring them to jail'. In this account the divide between girls and boys was reasserted through the reiteration of a pattern of gendered adversarial play. Lena became something of an exception, a transgressive figure helping the 'wrong' side. The wider game pattern he alluded to was one of collaboration in staging threat, pursuit and capture, often drawing on the toilets as gender segregated forbidden zones. The girls ran away screaming not because they were really afraid or felt threatened but because that was what they were supposed to do within the terms of their play – and because they enjoyed screaming and being chased.[23]

Isamu's sporadic pursuit of a girl in – and out of – the Quiet Area and Li's chasing of the girls into the toilets were consensual forms of play. Some episodes witnessed in the Brick Area – a space under an arch where wooden blocks and

---

[22]   CHCR2010-06-17v00248 See Playtimes: Pretend Play: Tae Kwon-do at http://www.bl.uk.

[23]   Caroline Pelletier's observations on gender in computer game participation are helpful here: 'The students do not portray games in stereotypically gendered ways because they *are* boys and girls, but because they wish to produce and *identify* themselves as such' and 'It is by constructing games as gendered that the students are able to construct themselves as gendered. It is precisely by drawing on popular stereotypes about games for boys and games for girls that young people come to recognize and assert their gender' (Pelletier, 2007: 140).

planks were available – may have been less fully participatory. Several Year One boys[24] using planks as machine guns to attack groups of girls otherwise uninvolved in their combat fantasies involved positioning girls, who may or may not have been willing participants, as adversaries to be eliminated. The boys played together, with each other, but in what sense the girls were collaborating was unclear. Going beyond a description of the boys' collective action, it is essential to ask what the girls' perspectives on such events might be. In a comparable event, though marked, unusually, by shooting outside the designated Brick Area, one boy (Benjamin, Year Three) turned to speak directly to me (and the Flip camcorder) saying 'I'm telling you this, a man's got to do what a man's got to do!'. This almost self-consciously 'cliched' self-positioning suggested that even in the midst of the excited 'shooting' that persisted through quite a long episode it was possible to step to one side of the action and offer a possibly parodic aside. However, such slightly 'out-of-role' comments, from boys in Year One, were more improbable.

To some extent, the girls observed in this school did contribute to play that was polarized in gender terms. In particular, some seemed to enjoy teasing and provocation. For example, Alice and Nadine (Year Four), who always played together, often spent their time hanging around groups of boys and 'intruding' into their play to provoke a chase or an occasion for loud screaming.[25] Perhaps the most striking examples of this arose when Alice positioned herself outside the boys' toilets, half concealed by the door frame and a recess in the wall, and repeatedly kicked the door provoking the group of boys inside to peer out and eventually to chase and retaliate, pleading or demanding that they 'Stop it!'.[26] Both girls enjoyed this enormously and persisted despite the indignant protests made by the boys. Writing of their own undergraduates, Sutton-Smith and Kelly-Byrne (1984) remark on the common tendency to seek out 'deep play' experiences reported by many of them. Citing Geertz (1973) they suggest that in 'deep play' 'the stakes are so high that it is irrational to participate' (Sutton-Smith and Kelly-Byrne, 1984: 314). Their examples include, from young men, 'physical danger … often with drinking added to deepen the risks' and from young women 'various forms of blind dating, flirting with strangers, provoking jealous boyfriends and rough sexual activity … the most widely reported instance of deep play (puns apart) was sex without contraception' (Sutton-Smith and Kelly-Byrne, 1984: 316). For eight or nine year old girls, and in the school playground, the comparison will seem inappropriate. But the broad point here is that play is not emotionally bland; it does involve provoking quite strong and sometimes disturbing emotions. Mostly, in a school context, the risks entailed in participation are minimal (running at high speed, jumping, hanging upside down or provoking a race or a chase) but without some element of risk, the heightened emotionality of many forms of play, including play fighting, cannot be achieved. For *both* girls and boys some of their favoured forms of play depended on the sense of risk, of threat or of uncertainty.

---

[24] CHCR2009-10-05v00059.

[25] CHCR2009-10-12v00068; CHCR2009-10-12v00069.

[26] CHCR2009-10-12v00070.

Conclusions

Play fighting is a fluid and variable phenomenon. Often, and this is supported by the examples from the playground discussed in this chapter, it is a consensual heterotopian fantasy in which participants take positions and enact scenarios that both draw on and extend aspects of the media texts most familiar to them – and sometimes more marginal sources introduced to them in the classroom or by a particular participant. But to argue that it is always and only a consensual fantasy would imply a rigid, abstracted and overly essentialising view of play fighting, as if its form is sustained in those terms whatever the particular social circumstances of those taking part. Stephanie Spina's (2004) defence of video game play, which I mostly accept, examines a kind of play that, though it might depend on and further facilitate social exchange, is largely a matter of fantasy removed from the actual lived social relations of friends, cliques and playgrounds. To discuss play fighting in the same way is difficult. The resources for play fighting may include TV and film viewing, video game play and collaborative computer game play, where the *fantasy engagement* with the text may prevail. But the *playground* enactment of play fighting is embedded in the particular social relations of children in specific social sites. This makes play fighting – and other forms of play too – a shifting form, strongly inflected by the dynamics of gender, age, friendship, class, ethnicity and power. It would be misleading to imagine that play fighting is a secure, stable and autonomous fantasy that somehow suppresses or displaces all these other elements in the relations between children. Play fighting is an important and constructive strand in children's play and its routine proscription is neither productive nor, ultimately, enforceable. But it is equally important to acknowledge that play fighting may not always be benign and that it should not be simply and routinely construed as always 'only playing' (Boulton, 1994). As I suggested in my introductory and partly autobiographical reflections, playing and pretending may appear to be what play fighting is about but other, additional, and less mutually satisfactory conflicts may also be present. The conclusion here is thus that play fighting is likely to be an enjoyable, intensely exciting and consensual fantasy but that exactly what it may be in any particular social circumstances can only be determined by giving it considered attention, by engaging with those who participate in it and by reflecting carefully on how they represent its forms and pleasures (Robins and Cohen, 1978; Walkerdine, 1986; Willis et al, 1990; Seiter, 2005: 63–82; Edmiston, 2008; Edmiston and Taylor, 2010).

There is little doubt that adult anxieties about the longer term consequences of play fighting will persist. The belief that it will contribute to a habit of violence in interpersonal relations or to a wider acceptance of force in human conflict is well established among teachers and others who work with young children (Holland, 2003). To argue otherwise goes against the grain of both popular common sense and much, perhaps mainly psychological, research (reviewed by Spina, 2004). But Gilroy's (2004) recollections of 'harrying' and 'slaughtering' suggest, through their contextualization in a nuanced and complex auto/biographical sketch, that such early experiences of violent fantasy are articulated with an array of other, and contradictory, elements in family history, schooling and wider historical circumstances (Walkerdine, 1986; Holland, 2004). The simplistic causality of the equation between play fighting (then) and real world violence (now) in individual life-histories cannot be sustained. I would not, for example, want to use my childhood friend's relish for (very) rough play and his subsequent criminal conviction for street violence as evidence to support such reductive causal explanations. Such instances highlight the anxieties that, rather than being dismissed as 'moral panic', should be engaged and debated but they are *starting points* for enquiry not, ever, singular and unequivocal proof of the consequences of allowing play fighting to continue.

References

Barter C and Berridge D (2011) *Children Behaving Badly: Peer Violence between Children and Young People.* London: Wiley-Blackwell.

Boulton MJ (1994) Playful and aggressive fighting in the middle-school playground. In Blatchford P and Sharp S (eds) *Breaktime and the School: Understanding and Changing Playground Behaviour.* London: Routledge, 49–62.

Bowman P (2010) *Theorizing Bruce Lee: Film-Fantasy-Fighting-Philosophy.* Amsterdam and New York: Rodopi.

Brown J (2011) Understanding dimensions of 'peer violence' in preschool settings: An exploration of key issues and questions. In Barter C and Berridge D (eds) *Children Behaving Badly: Peer Violence Between Children and Young People.* London: Wiley-Blackwell, 21–32.

Brown J (2010) 'They are just like caged animals': surveillance, security and school spaces. http://www.surveillance-and-society.org/ojs/index.php/journal

Burn A (2013) Computer games on the playground: Ludic systems, dramatized narrative and virtual embodiment. In Willett, R, Richards C, Marsh J, Burn A and Bishop JC *Children, Media and Playground Cultures: Ethnographic Studies of School Playtimes.* Basingstoke: Palgrave Macmillan, 120-144.

Cohen P (1997) *Rethinking the Youth Question: Education, Labour and Cultural Studies.* Basingstoke and London: Macmillan.

Edmiston B (2008) *Forming Ethical Identities in Early Childhood Play.* London: Routledge.

Edmiston B and Taylor T (2010) Using power on the playground. In Brooker L and Edwards S (eds) *Engaging Play.* Maidenhead: Open University Press/ McGraw-Hill, 166–81.

Geertz C (1973) *The Interpretation of Cultures.* New York: Basic Books – HarperCollins.

Gilroy P (2004) *Between Camps: Nations, Cultures and the Allure of Race.* London: Routledge.

Gresson AD (2004) Professional wrestling and youth culture: Teasing, taunting, and the containment of civility. In Steinberg SR and Kincheloe JL (eds)

Kinderculture: The Corporate Construction of Childhood (2nd edition). Boulder, CO: Westview Press, 207–27.

Griffin S (1999) Kings of the wild backyard: Davy Crockett and children's space. In Kinder M (ed) *Kids' Media Culture*. Durham, NC: Duke University Press, 102–21.

Hodge R and Tripp D (1986) *Children and Television: A Semiotic Approach*. Cambridge: Polity.

Holland Patricia (2004) *Picturing Childhood: The Myth of the Child in Popular Imagery*. London: I.B. Tauris.

Holland Penny (2003) *We Don't Play with Guns Here: War, Weapon and Superhero Play in the Early Years*. Maidenhead: Open University Press.

Jackson D (1990) *Unmasking Masculinity: A Critical Autobiography*. London: Unwin Hyman.

James A, Jenks C and Prout A (1998) *Theorizing Childhood*. Cambridge: Polity Press.

Levin D and Carlsson-Paige N (2006) *The War Play Dilemma: What Every Parent and Teacher Needs to Know*. New York: Teachers College, Columbia University.

Newkirk T (2002) *Misreading Masculinity: Boys, Literacy, and Popular Culture*. Portsmouth, NH: Heinemann.

Opie I (1993) *The People in the Playground*. Oxford: Oxford University Press.

Opie I and Opie P (1959/2001) *The Lore and Language of Schoolchildren*. New York: New York Review of Books.

Opie P and Opie I (1969/2008) *Children's Games in Street and Playground*, Volume 1. Edinburgh: Floris Books.

Opie P and Opie I (1969/2008) *Children's Games in Street and Playground*, Volume 2. Edinburgh: Floris Books.

Pelletier C (2007) Producing gender in digital interactions: What young people set out to achieve through computer game design. In Weber S and Dixon S (eds*) Growing Up Online: Young People and Digital Technologies*. Basingstoke: Palgrave Macmillan, 129–48.

Richards C (2011) In the thick of it: interpreting children's play. *Ethnography and Education* 6: 309–24.

Richards C (2012) Playing under surveillance: gender, performance and the conduct of the self in a primary school playground. *British Journal of the Sociology of Education* 33: 373–90.

Richards C (2013a) Agonistic scenarios. In Willett R, Richards C, Marsh J, Burn A and Bishop JC *Children, Media and Playground Cultures: Ethnographic Studies of School Playtimes*. Basingstoke: Palgrave Macmillan, 170–95.

Richards C (2013b) 'If you ever see this video, we're probably dead' – a boy's own heterotopia (Notes from an inner London playground), in *Journal of Children and Media* 7(3), 383–98.

Robins D and Cohen P (1978) *Knuckle Sandwich: Growing Up in the Working Class City*. Harmondsworth: Penguin.

Seiter E (2005) *The Internet Playground: Children's Access, Entertainment, and Mis-Education*. New York: Peter Lang.

Singer D and Singer J (2005) *Imagination and Play in the Electronic Age*. Cambridge, MA: Harvard University Press.

Sluckin A (1981) *Growing Up in the Playground: The Social Development of Children*. London: RKP.

Spina SU (2004) Power plays: Video games' bad rap. In Steinberg SR and Kincheloe JL (eds) *Kinderculture: The Corporate Construction of Childhood* (2nd edition). Boulder, CO: Westview Press, 254–83.

Squires P and Goldsmith C (2011) Bullets, blades and mean streets: Youth violence and criminal justice failure. In Barter C and Berridge D (eds) *Children Behaving Badly: Peer Violence Between Children and Young People*. London: Wiley-Blackwell, 199–215.

Stewart S (1980) *Nonsense: Aspects of Intertextuality in Folklore and Literature*. Baltimore, MD: The Johns Hopkins University Press.

Sutton-Smith B (1997) *The Ambiguity of Play*. Cambridge, MA: Harvard University Press.

Sutton-Smith B and Kelly-Byrne D (1984) The masks of play. In Sutton-Smith B and Kelly-Byrne D (eds) *The Masks of Play*. New York: Leisure Press, 184–99.

Sutton-Smith B and Kelly-Byrne D (1984) The idealization of play. In Smith PK (ed.) *Play in Animals and Humans*. Oxford: Blackwell, 305–21.

Tolson A (1977) *The Limits of Masculinity*. London: Tavistock.

Walkerdine V (1986) Video replay: Families, films and fantasy. In Burgin V, Donald J and Kaplan C (eds) *Formations of Fantasy*. London: Routledge and Kegan Paul, 167–99.

Wenger E (1998) *Communities of Practice: Learning, Meaning, and Identity*. Cambridge: Cambridge University Press.

Willett R (2013) Superheroes, naughty mums and witches: Pretend family play amongst seven to ten-year-olds. In Willett, R, Richards C, Marsh J, Burn A and Bishop JC *Children, Media and Playground Cultures: Ethnographic Studies of School Playtimes*. Basingstoke: Palgrave Macmillan, 145–69.

Willis B (1985) Kung Fu films. In Points C (ed) *Working Papers for 16+ Media Studies*. Clwyd Media studies Unit in association with the Centre for Contemporary Cultural Studies, 147–62.

Willis P with Jones S, Canaan J and Hurd G (1990) *Common Culture: Symbolic Work at Play in the Everyday Cultures of the Young*. Buckingham: Open University Press.

Chapter 5
The Relationship between Online and Offline Play: Friendship and Exclusion

Jackie Marsh

In this chapter, the relationship between children's play in online and offline environments is explored. For children in contemporary societies, the boundaries between these two domains are becoming increasingly blurred as children's play spaces expand to include online sites. In the project outlined in this book, we were interested in the way in which children's play has changed in recent decades, especially with the influence of media and new technologies. Given that children are spending increasing amounts of time online, it is inevitable that their play activities now move across virtual and non-virtual domains. The chapter identifies both the continuities and discontinuities in this play, focusing on children in Monteney Primary School in Sheffield. The extent and nature of children's engagement in online activities is outlined and the way in which friendships are constructed across online and offline spaces is analysed. The chapter concludes with a consideration of the implications of this analysis for the study of play.

Children's Online Activities

Online activities are now prevalent in many children's lives (Livingstone, 2009). Ofcom[1] (2011) report that 91 per cent of children aged 5 to 15 in the UK have access to the Internet at home. Children are engaged in online activities in their earliest years of life, often supported by their families as they access Internet games and communicate with family members (Blanchard and Moore, 2010; Marsh et al, 2005). These practices create alarm for some who suggest, despite an absence of convincing empirical data in this area, that young children should not be encouraged to engage with such technologies as they can be detrimental to development (Levin and Rosenquest, 2001; Palmer, 2006). But many families encourage and celebrate their young children's emergence into the digital age. For example, babies engage in Skype conversations conducted by their families, toddlers navigate complex online screens and take immense pleasure in their interactions with iPads and iPhones and some of this activity is video recorded by proud parents and placed

---

[1]   OFCOM (Office for Communications) is the UK media regulator.

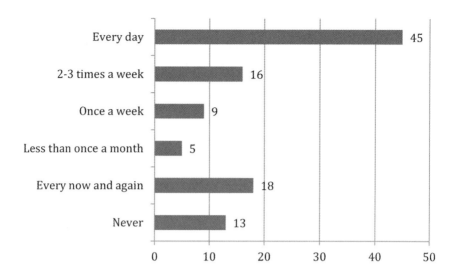

Fig. 5.1   Per cent frequency of Internet use (n=173)

on YouTube[2] as a testament to their 'toddler netizens' (Luke, 2000). Given the extensive engagement that many children have in family digital literacy practices in their earliest years it is inevitable that by the time children attend primary school, many of them are already competent users of the Internet.

This was the case with the children in the present study. At Monteney Primary School, 180 children aged 5–11 completed a survey of their media-related activities. One hundred and seventy three children completed a question which asked them to report on the frequency with which they accessed the Internet. Figure 5.1 outlines the responses.

Given that 70 per cent of children reported using the Internet at least once a week or more frequently, it is of no surprise that the range of Internet activities in which they engaged was wide and included the use of websites related to media brands (e.g. Disney) and favourite television channels and programmes, virtual worlds, Massively Multiplayer Online Games (MMOGs), games and social networking sites. Children were asked to list their favourite websites and the sites listed are outlined in Table 5.1.

------

[2]   See, for example: Skype: http://www.youtube.com/watch?v=HIr0O-IAoxQ; Internet site: http://www.youtube.com/watch?v=aYUYpzN-P8g; iPad: http://www.youtube.com/watch?v=MGMsT4qNA-c; iPhone: http://www.youtube.com/watch?v=oZwKPDvYA 2M&feature=fvsr.

Table 5.1   Children's favourite Internet sites

Type of site	Sites named
Browsers	Google; Firefox; Internet Explorer
Social networking sites	Facebook; Bebo; MySpace
Virtual worlds	Club Penguin; Moshi Monsters; Farmville
Massive Multiplayer Online Games (MMOGs)	Age of War 2; Runescape; Sacred Seasons; Evony
Sites related to favourite brands/toys/films/TV programmes/videogames	Barbie; Mario Bros; Gogo's Crazy Bones; Hannah Montana; Doctor Who; Simpsons; Mister Maker
Sites related to television channels	'Watching TV on the Internet'; CBBC; CBeebies; Cartoon Network; Disney
Video sites	YouTube
Shopping sites	eBay
Music sites	Limewire; Grooveshark; Monstrosity
Email/chat sites	MsN; Hotmail; Google Mail
Creative/arts sites	Pizco; Capzles; Tux Paint
Education sites	Smart Kiddy; Studywiz; Education City
Various games sites	'Free online games'; mostfungames.com; bored.com; stickpage.com; Miniclip; crush the castle, motorbike games, car/parking games, racing games, drifting games, animal games, girls go games; Roblox; Playfg; Orsinal; Friv; Poker games; Games for girls; Dressing up games (e.g. Stardolls); Game station; Cartoon games; E zone; Flonga

It can be seen from Table 5.1 that many of these sites were not aimed primarily at children aged 11 and under (such as Facebook, which has a registration age of 13), but younger children have always accessed media texts that are considered more appropriate for teenagers and adults (Buckingham, 1993). For the children at Monteney, online activities were embedded in their everyday lives and it is, therefore, inevitable that traces of these activities can be discerned in the children's playground culture. As Rebekah Willett's chapter reporting the parallel study at Christopher Hatton indicates, numerous episodes of play related to some of the texts above were observed or reported in this study, such as Disney texts, *Super Mario* and *Doctor Who*. These have been embedded in children's cultural worlds for many years and, indeed, the studies conducted by Iona and Peter Opie documented the way in which children drew on pop music, television and films in their play (Opie and Opie, 1988). A relatively new phenomenon, however, is children's developing interest in online virtual worlds, a number of which appeared as children's favourite Internet sites in Table 5.1. In the next sections, I move on to consider the prevalence of these sites in children's cultural practices and outline their use by children in this primary school in order to explore the offline-online continuum.

Virtual Worlds for Children

Children's toys and cultures reflect the zeitgeist of a given era (Warner, 2009). It is no surprise, therefore, that there has been an increase in the development of virtual worlds for children, given the general interest in these sites. Online virtual worlds are immersive 2D or 3D simulations of persistent space in which users adopt an avatar in order to represent themselves and interact with others. They may or may not include game elements. The burgeoning of the children's virtual world market began around the mid-point of the first decade of the twenty-first century, with some of the current major players, such as Ganz's *Webkinz* and Viacom's *Neopet* beginning to attract large numbers of users around that time. Since then, this has been an area of rapid development, with some reports that the fastest growing demographic of virtual world users is children between the ages of five and nine. It has been reported that there are now over 150 virtual worlds either operating or in development that are aimed at children and young people under 18 years of age, with approximately 355 million users aged five to 10 of virtual worlds.[3]

The majority of children's virtual worlds involve playing games as a major activity. This is not to suggest, however, that the worlds should be categorized primarily as games. As Meyers (2009) argues, the activities undertaken in what he terms 'shared virtual environments' (SVEs) have more in common with virtual worlds for adults, such as *Second Life*, than other online game sites. Many of the sites enable users to manage an avatar (clothe and manipulate an online representation of themselves) create home environments, chat to others through the use of instant messaging and engage in shopping for virtual artefacts. These virtual worlds promote a range of types of play from the more restricted rule-bound play involved in games constructed by the site producers to imaginative play, which can involve fantasy and socio-dramatic play (Marsh, 2010).

In order to avoid the difficulties faced in any simplistic dichotomization of the 'real' and 'virtual' (see Marsh, 2010, for further discussion of this binary), in this chapter I use the terms 'offline' and 'online' to distinguish between those periods when children use online virtual worlds and those periods when they are not engaged in the use of the Internet or computer in their play.

Children's Use of Virtual Worlds

In the survey of media use completed by children in Monteney Primary School, 168 children responded to the question asking whether or not they used virtual worlds. Ninety per cent stated that they did so and the virtual worlds they reported using included *Club Penguin, Moshi Monsters, Bin Weevils, BarbieGirls, Webkinz, Habbo Hotel* and the MMOGs *Runescape and World of Warcraft*. This was in contrast to a survey conducted at the same school two years previously, in which 52 per cent of 175 children surveyed stated that they used virtual worlds (Marsh,

---

[3]   KZero, http://www.kzero.co.uk/universe.php.

2010; 2011), supporting the arguments made by Gilbert (2009) about the growth in the use of these worlds over time. Children at Monteney were thus familiar with the concepts of virtual worlds and avatars at an early stage of their commercial development, and this may be in part because the ICT teacher, Peter Winter, had undertaken activities in his classes in which children developed avatars in the form of 'Weemees'.

Children were asked which websites they discussed with their friends. Responses included: *Runescape, Moshi Monsters, Bin Weevils, Club Penguin* and *World of Warcraft*. One child described *Moshi Monsters*:

> moshi monster it is a pet you look afther and you can chat to your frinds at home and you have to feed you moshi monster and play daily games on it so yoju can get monmey to feed it with and by it stof.

For younger children, playing games offers a strong attraction for engaging with virtual worlds. The UK Children Go Online Survey identified that 70 per cent of nine to 19 year-olds in the UK played games on the Internet at least weekly (Livingstone, 2009: 45) which indicates the attraction of online games for tweens and teenagers and their younger counterparts are no exception. As the survey quote above indicates, these sites frequently enable users to adopt and look after pets which need constant attention, otherwise users receive reminders about the need to look after them or even, as in the case of *Club Penguin*, are informed that their neglected pets have run away. These requirements are very much related to the producers' desire to promote 'stickiness', that is, to ensure children keep returning to the sites over time.

This child's comment about getting money to feed a pet on *Moshi Monsters* also indicates the way in which commercialised practices are embedded in these sites. Users earn in-world currency through the completion of games, currency which they then use to buy virtual items for their avatars, pets and virtual homes. Embedded within the moral panic discourses surrounding children's use of technology, the child is frequently constructed as the '"subject of consumption" the individual who is imagined and acted upon by the imperative to consume' (Miller and Rose, 1997:1). Children are, most certainly, embedded in commercial play worlds that drive consumption of economic goods from an early age.

Cook (2010), however, argues that we need to move beyond the traditional discussions of children's socialisation into commercial activity, as these discussions frequently do not acknowledge the complexity of children's engagement in consumer culture. Instead, he posits the concept of 'commercial enculturation' as a means of signifying that participation in commercial activities does not follow a linear trajectory in relation to age, but rather children's consumption is culturally defined and shaped through social relationships. Further, Pugh (2009) suggests that the kind of social practices in which children develop peer networks through shared economic interests, such as collecting and swapping consumer items linked to popular cultural interests (at Monteney, for example, children collected *Club Penguin* cards), should be seen as 'an economy of dignity'. She argues that children 'collect or confer dignity among themselves according to their (shifting) consensus about what sort of objects or experiences are supposed to count for it' (Pugh, 2009: 6–7). The key motivation for engaging in these collective expressions of consumerism is to seek a sense of belonging. This is not to suggest, however, that we need to be unconcerned about the way in which children are positioned as consumers. As Buckingham (2011) contends, there is a need to explore the complexities embedded within the relationship between childhood and the commercial world in order to identify the ways in which children are positioned within markets and to develop strategies for facilitating their critical engagement with this positioning. In this way, a reductive and narrow rejectionist agenda is avoided and children's own agency in navigating these waters will be enhanced.

A further question on the survey asked children to say something about media-related games they played in the playground. Two children mentioned games which included an avatar:

> its called mythical people and I am a made up greture called an avater who can do anything and my best friend aiden is a wizard

> it is called mythical people i am a wizard and angela is an avatar how can do eneything

In these two examples, the children grafted aspects of virtual worlds (i.e. avatars) onto sedimented play practices related to wizards and mythical creatures, staple characters in children's play over time. As Burn suggests in Chapter 1, this can be characterised as cultural rehearsal, a process in which the old and new are remixed in a single practice. We can also see it as an example of heterotopian games, in which cultural resources for game-making are imported into the playground from the online world.

There is a growing relationship between children's online and offline play. Lauwaert (2009) suggests that the 'geography of play' now consists of physical and digital artefacts and practices, both core and peripheral, many of which are connected to each other. This is very much the case in relation to recent developments of virtual worlds, in which 'clickable' technologies are used to create artefacts that can store information from the virtual play and be transferred to other players. For example, Disney has in recent years launched a virtual world titled *Pixie Hollow.* Children are able to purchase bracelets that can be used to exchange game credits with other players. Many virtual worlds for children are linked to key brands (e.g. *Barbie*, *Lego*) and therefore the spatial boundaries of play are becoming blurred as children move across online and offline worlds. At Monteney School, children reported owning a range of toys and artefacts related to their use of virtual worlds, such as *Club Penguin* collecting cards and puffles. *Club Penguin* is also available on different platforms, such as Nintendo DS, and children reported playing across these platforms. Games related to *Club Penguin* were played on the playground and thus the circulation of the *Club Penguin* narrative and associated discourses occurred across a range of online and offline spaces. Whilst it is becoming increasingly clear that there is a continuum between online and offline play, this does not mean that there are no palpable distinctions between them. As Boellstorff (2008) suggests, engaging in online activity is qualitatively different from offline activity. There are obvious modality differences. Manipulating an avatar is not the same as navigating one's physical body through space. Nevertheless, there are overlaps between online and offline identities. Malpas notes that:

> A basic starting point for any serious discussion of the virtual must be recognition of the *non-autonomy* of the virtual – a recognition of the fact that the virtual does not constitute an autonomous, independent, or 'closed' system, but is instead always dependent, in a variety of ways, on the everyday world within which it is embedded. (Malpas 2009:135).

Online and offline identities inter-relate (Robinson, 2007), although there is evidence that suggests that Internet users do play and experiment with their online identities, developing aspects of their identity which they would not perform in an offline context (Boellstorf, 2008; Nardi, 2010; Kafai, Fields and Cook, 2010).

Given the extent to which children played online in virtual worlds, I was interested in the impact this had on their friendships. How far did children play with other children online that they played with in the playground at school? Did children who were not engaged in extensive online play feel more excluded from playground activities? In order to explore these questions, I asked children to create sociograms and then interviewed a group of children about peers they played with online and offline, drawing on the diagrams they had created. Sociograms are, according to Rapoport and Horvath (1961: 279), 'a description of the population in terms of relationships between pairs of people in that population'. In this method, research participants indicate their connections to other people in a specific group, relationships that are then mapped through network diagrams. In the following section, I outline the process of collecting these data before moving on to examine the themes that emerged from the analysis.

Online and Offline Friendships

Children in 11 of the 12 Year One to Six classes across the school were given a list that contained the names of all the children in their class inside individual circles. They were then asked to draw a black line to a circle that contained the name of a friend they played with in the playground and a red line to a circle that contained the name of a friend that they played with online, in the range of sites outlined in Table 5.1. One hundred and forty-five children completed the diagrams. The data were then analysed at a whole class level for six classes, as not all children in the other five classes completed the diagrams. An example of a sociograph of online and offline friendships developed from the data from children in one class can be found in Figures 5.2 and 5.3.

Class 4 Offline

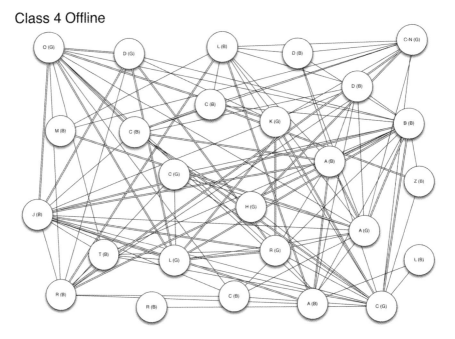

Fig. 5.2   Offline friendships in Class 4

These diagrams indicate the variation across the class in terms of the numbers of friends in online and offline friendship groups, with some children having no or few online friends and others having many. From an analysis of the data collected from all 145 children, the following patterns emerged:

- 68 per cent of children had online friends in their class.
- Children who had only offline friends and children who had both online and offline friends had an average of nine offline friends each.
- Older children were more likely than younger children to play online with children they did not play with offline.
- Boys who played online had twice as many girls as friends (average 4.6) as boys who only played offline (average 2.3).
- Girls who played online had almost twice as many boys as friends (average 7.1) as girls who only played offline (3.6).

The greater propensity to play online with children of the opposite gender is of interest, given the way in which gendered patterns are often entrenched in children's offline social relationships (Renold, 2005; Thorne, 1993). It is also of note that children played online with their classmates, which resonates with data from older groups that suggests that online and offline friendships overlap (Subrahmanyam, Smahel and Greenfield, 2006) and that online use thickens existing social ties (Davies, 2008; Ito et al, 2009).

Class 4 Online

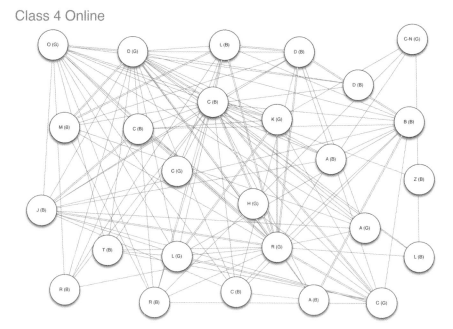

Fig. 5.3   Online friendships in Class 4

Following the completion and analysis of the sociographs, I interviewed 12 children across the three year groups in Key Stage 2 (Year Three, seven- and eight-year-olds; Year Four, eight- and nine-year-olds and Year Six, 10- and 11-year-olds) in order to explore potential issues of social exclusion due to lack of online activity. I wanted to identify how far children who did not participate in online activities felt excluded from offline activities. I did not interview children in Key Stage 1 due to the sensitivity of questions about social exclusion. I stressed to children in Key Stage 2 that they could refuse to answer questions and could stop the interview whenever they wished to do so. I identified a girl and a boy in each of the year groups Three to Six who, according to the sociographs had few (three or fewer) or no online friends, and girl and a boy in each of these year groups who had reported having lots of online friends (10 or more). I asked them about their online and offline friendships, who they played with, how they made their friendship choices and whether or not they felt the children who did not play online felt excluded from offline play in the playground. The interviews took place in the academic year following the completion of the sociographs, due to the summer holiday. Children were therefore asked to reflect on their friendships of the previous academic year, which may mean that their recollections were hazier than if they had been interviewed prior to the summer vacation.

In examining children's online friendships, it is worth noting that online behaviour in terms of befriending and de-friending is fraught with tensions, tensions which were not particularly evident in the interviews with this group of children. It would be useful to trace children's developing sense of the issues prevalent in managing online relationships over time in order to identify how and when particular patterns emerge. For the children at Monteney, means of managing their online relationships appeared to be implicit in nature, based on intuition, and drew from their offline experiences. Holmes (2011) suggests that the complexity of navigating online friendships requires an 'emotionalisation of reflexivity' and it could be argued that the children in this study were in the early stages of developing the capacity to engage in this process.

The six children who had few or no online friends did not, in the main, appear to be affected. Tom (Year Four) and Casey (Year Six), for example, reported that they were not aware that their peers were playing online with each other and therefore were, seemingly, unaffected by this. Similarly, John in Year Three was not aware that his friends were playing together online when he was in Year Two. John's father would not let him play on the Internet because of his fear that John would be the object of predatory behaviour by adults. However, this had now changed as John progressed to Year Three and he had been allowed online. I asked John if his dad let him play online with his friends:

John   *No.*

Jackie   *Did you ever ask him?*

John   *Yeah, but he said still no. When I asked him over and over he said, "No, no, no".*

Jackie   *And did you feel upset or sad about that?*

John   *No, I didn't thought I was missing 'owt [anything].*

John then went on to mention a game he felt he was missing out on playing, however, a game which was undertaken in the playground:

John   *Well one game I missed out is playing dogs when I was in Y2 and in Y1.*

Jackie   *You missed out playing ...?*

John   *Dogs.*

Jackie   *Dogs? Why did you miss out on that?*

John   *'Cos people say it's ... people don't play with me any more if I play dogs.*

Jackie   *Oh right. They didn't want you to play? Why do you think that was?*

John   *Because I played dogs.*

It would seem that in this case, a feeling of exclusion came about not because of lack of opportunities to engage in online play, but because John wanted to play a game that others did not wish to play in the playground. Such face-to-face interactions, significant in matters of social exclusion, might suggest that recent concerns about the negative consequences of online activity for intimacy and trust in offline relationships (Turkle, 2011) can be given undue emphasis.

Lara, in Year Six, was aware that her friends were playing online, but she made a conscious decision that she did not want to play online very often and this did not impact upon her sense of being included in offline contexts:

Lara   I knew that other children were on it, it's just like I didn't like want to get all fussy and everything because I don't go on it that much.

Jackie   Yeah, what do you mean, "You didn't want to get fussy", what does that mean?

Lara   Like I didn't want to go through all the trouble to not go on it so much, like.

Jackie   Now explain to me. So if you made friends you'd have to go on it not as much?

Lara   Well if I made like a lot of friends, a lot a lot of friends then I'd go on it a bit more, but I didn't really go on it so I only had that one friend.

Jackie   And did you ever feel left out of any games because you didn't go online or make online friends?

Lara   No.

Lara expresses a reluctance to become engaged in spending extensive time developing online friendships, a phenomenon also identified with older users of the Internet, who have complained about 'communication overload' (Agosto and Abbas, 2010:7). There appeared to be both time and technological constraints in terms of developing online networks. Jay in Year Four had only three online friends and he suggested that this was down to the management of the process:

Jay   I played with lots of people on the playground but I played with a couple on the Internet.

Jackie   Yeah, why didn't you play with everybody on the Internet?

Jay   Because I would have to get up like 28 tabs and I could fit three on my screen.

Only one child in this group of six stated that she felt negatively about not playing with online friends. Gilly, in Year Three, was not allowed to use her parents' computer, 'Because someone might send me a nasty horrible e-mail'. She said that this lack of opportunity to engage in online play with her friends made her feel 'lonely'. In this instance, Gilly was being presented with different adult agendas: the parental one emphasising risk and the researcher's agenda relating to the exploration of patterns in friendship and social exclusion.

In the interviews with the six children who had many online friends, there were similar comments made about the perceived lack of impact for children who did not have many online friends, and the way in which online activities did not really influence playground friendships. I looked at the sociograph developed by Kate, in Year Three, with her.

> Jackie   So if we look at James, you played with James in the playground and online didn't you?
>
> Kate   Yeah.
>
> Jackie   But with Tony, you only played with him in the playground and you didn't play with him online. So I'm interested in why some children you play with both in the playground and online, and other children only in the playground?
>
> Kate   Well it's simple for some reasoning, because some people haven't got a computer.
>
> Jackie   Do you know they've not got a computer?
>
> Kate   Yeah.
>
> Jackie   How do you know?
>
> Kate   Because I ask if they've like got a Club Penguin or something and they say, "I haven't got a computer".
>
> Jackie   Oh right, OK. So how do you find out which friends you're going to play online with?
>
> Kate   We just arrange it at school and say, say go on it when we get back from school like, Moshi Monsters and stuff ...
>
> Jackie   And do you think you were more friendly with children that you played with on the Internet, or it was just the same?
>
> Kate   It was just the same.
>
> Jackie   You didn't notice?
>
> Kate   No, I didn't notice.

Kate dismissed my seemingly naïve question about why she played with some children online and not others by pointing out the 'simple' fact that some children did not have access to the Internet. This did not impact on her friendship choices in the playground. Similarly, Carl (Year Three) did not feel that there was a negative impact of children not being able to play online and reported playing in the playground with children who had no online presence.

Children reported playing online with other children that they played with in the playground, but also other children in the school who were not regular playmates. They would then not seek to play with these children in the playground, as this interview with Mandy, in Year Six, indicates:

> Mandy Well usually the people online I usually … the people that are online I usually just play with them, and then if I go out and play in the yard I kind of just play with all my friends and people like if they're not playing with anyone else and then go and talk to them and see what's the matter.
>
> Jackie So you don't seek out people that you play with online?
>
> Mandy Erm … no.
>
> Jackie Does it make any difference do you think in the playground or play with Moshi Monsters "I'll play with her today" or do you not think about it or …?
>
> Mandy No I don't usually think about it, I just like go to school and see who's there and play with them.
>
> Jackie And are there some people that you wouldn't play with online?
>
> Mandy Erm … probably just people who I haven't got as a friend on Moshi Monsters, or people who aren't on with … online or stuff like that. But I usually talk to everyone that's on.

For some children, therefore, online and offline networks appear to be distinct in nature, and children are content to play online with peers and then not pursue those friendships in the playground. This pattern was more likely to occur in the older year groups, as the younger children played primarily online with people they knew offline. Carl (Year Three) reported how he made decisions about who to play with online based on their offline behaviour:

> Jackie … So when you choose children to play with online, what makes you choose them?
>
> Carl Because they're nice friends and I think they would love to play with me lots of time.
>
> Jackie And when you play with children in the playground what makes you choose them?

Carl   I like them people but if they're online I think they would say bad words and that means they would get banned from it.

Jackie   Who is that, who would do that?

Carl   Someone like James because he's naughty.

Jackie   How can you tell he's going to be naughty online?

Carl   Because if they're naughty online you have to do something like a tick to show you're going to be good on it, and if you break that your account's going to get banned from Moshi Monsters.

Jackie   Oh right OK, so it actually could hurt you if you played with children who did break the rules?

Carl   Yeah, 'cos it would talk me into the [indistinguishable] and they would ban … if I did it, it would ban my account as well.

Jackie   So how do you think you can tell the children who might break the rules then?

Carl   Because erm … if like they shout out and they thump people in faces sometimes …

Jackie   In the playground?

Carl   Yeah. And if they're going to say something like "I don't like you", and like Casey when I've gone to his house, my nan – nan lives next door to him and I go to her house every night, Casey swears when we go round to play football, and that's why I didn't ask him to my accounts.

Jackie   Oh right OK, because he might get you into trouble.

Carl   Yeah.

Jackie   And get you banned.

Carl   Yeah. Because if they're banned we can never add that account on to Moshi Monsters ever again.

Jackie   Oh gosh. And did Casey ever ask to be your friend on the Internet?

Carl   Mmm, about 5 times.

Jackie   And what did you say to him?

Carl   I said "sorry, I don't want to get banned from it".

Jackie   And what did he say?

Carl   "Please!" like that. And I said, "No because I don't want to get banned, I want to play nice with my friends".

Jackie   And did that make him change his play with you in the playground or not?

Carl   No he's still hurting people, and he's still swearing when we go round to play football.

Carl's concern not to get banned from a virtual world appeared to have shaped his decisions about who to accept as an online friend. Jay (Year Four), had few online friends, as indicated previously, and he also made judgments about who to play with based on his offline experiences:

Jackie   Was there anybody else that you would say, "Oh no I wouldn't play with them online"? You don't need to say names but is there anybody that …

Jay   Yeah, because he gets too competitive.

Jackie   Oh, really, one of your friends?

Jay   Like, "Oh, I really want to win it".

Managing online friendships was, for these children, a matter of making judgments based on observable behaviour of their peers in the offline world. Reputation is an important concept in terms of managing online relationships (Taylor, 2006). Trust with others is developed through perceptions of their online reputations, and aligning oneself with Internet users who may create problems is avoided by some through the practice of engaging only with Internet users they have some long-standing knowledge of (Xu, Cao, Sellen, Hebrich and Graepel, 2011).

Children in the study arranged to meet each other online at specific times and shared online usernames so they could track each other down. There was no suggestion in the interviews that children were sharing online usernames in a quest to gain as many online friends as possible, a practice which has been noted with teenagers and adults. Holmes (2011) in a study of adults' use of Facebook, cites the case of an individual called Margaret, who stressed how she accepts all friend requests on Facebook. Holmes notes that:

> Those overly free in friending may be accused of 'friend farming' (collecting friends to look good) (Hardey 2008: 132) and Margaret's strategy of accepting all friend requests may lead to being labelled as a *Facebook* 'whore' who has too many friends and is interested in self display (Holland and Harpin 2008:1 to 6 to 8).

Whilst this description might dismay those of us who object to the use of vocabulary which deprecates women ('whore'), it points to the way in which online behaviour in terms of befriending and de-friending is fraught with tensions.

Through the sharing of usernames and developing of peer networks online that were based on school networks, the children were constructing online friendships that, in the main, demonstrated homophily, exacerbated by the fact that the school served a primarily white, working class community. Emergent research in this area suggests that adolescents demonstrate greater homophily in their online social networks than adults (Mazur and Richards, 2011) and this phenomenon deserves further attention in relation to the online practices of children under the age of 11. The findings from this study would suggest that for children at Monteney, online and offline social networks and practices overlapped in complex ways and shaped both their online play and their playground activities. In the next section, I explore the relationship between online and offline play.

Online and Offline Play

In a previous study of the use of virtual worlds by children in Monteney Primary School, I explored the relationship between online and offline play and identified that forms of offline play could be found online, such as fantasy play, socio-dramatic play and games with rules (Marsh, 2010). For example, in the third category here, games with rules, children reported importing games such as hide-and-seek and musical chairs into their play in the virtual worlds *Club Penguin* and *Habbo Hotel*. In the study reported in this book, there were numerous opportunities to identify how online practices informed offline play. Across both school playgrounds, there appeared to be three ways in which online play permeated offline activities, which I have categorized as: naming the game, playing the game and gaming the game. In this context, 'game' is a term used to refer to online play in specific sites which contain game elements, such as virtual worlds and MMOGs.

Naming the Game

In this category, instances of play occurred in the playgrounds in which children were playing a game that did not utilise the specific characters or narrative structures of an online game, but, nevertheless, the offline play was given the title of the online game:

> Sarah-Louise   Sometimes I play with my friend and we take turns being 'Club Penguin'.
>
> Jackie   What do you have to do when you're 'Club Penguin'?
>
> Sarah-Louise   When you're 'Club Penguin' someone … when you're standing like a star, you have to try and pass 'em and they're going sideways they try and stop you passing 'em but you have to try and unpass 'em … when you dodge 'em you jump over a log and if you touch a bench you win and someone else is 'Club Penguin'.

What Stacey describes is a tag game which has been badged with the *Club Penguin* label. Similarly, as reported in Burn (2013), a five-year-old boy from Monteney suggested that he and his friends sometimes refer to their game as *Call of Duty*, even though what they actually played was a generic shooting game. These can be seen as examples of what Bishop et al (2006) term *onomastic allusion*, when children refer to the names of favourite characters, television programmes, films and other elements of popular culture, but the source text/artefact is not drawn upon in an extended manner. Such practices may serve to signal children's ownership of the right sort of cultural capital in order to extend friendships.

Playing the Game

In this category, children reported, or were observed, playing games in the playground that they had played online. Burn (2013) discusses this in relation to computer games and outlines how children adopt both the ludic system of the game (the game-like elements, such as its rules for winning, its economic system) and the representational system:

> This provides landscapes, imaginary worlds, characters, narrative possibilities, and the resources for a dramatised experience analogous to, though in certain ways structurally distinct from, the narratives and representational systems of novels, films and plays (which also, of course, both resemble and differ from each other). (Burn, 2013)

It may be the case that play under this category may not relate just to the online form, but also representations of that text in other media. For example, I observed a group of boys in Key Stage 1 in the Monteney playground involved in an extended play episode based on the 'Avatar' theme. I had assumed that this play was informed by the film of the same name, but it could also be the case that such play may have been influenced by the children's engagement with the narrative in other forms, such as books or computer games, given the transmedia intertexuality prevalent in children's cultural practices (Kinder, 1991). Such play provides an example of 'heterotopian games', as described by Burn in Chapter 1, in which themes and characters from the virtual online world can be transposed into offline imaginative play, which evokes the virtual realm of fantasy.

Gaming the Game

This category refers to the way in which children might take the ludic elements of online games and use them to inform the structure of an offline game. In Chapter 1, Burn suggested that this structural borrowing, which can be viewed as 'ludic bricolage', can be seen in the example of a group of girls in the Christopher Hatton playground who introduced the ludic structures of computer games, with the various levels players have to go through, into a game played with hoops set onto the playground surface.

Similarly, in the Monteney playground, I observed a group of children playing a game in which a boy (the protagonist) was situated across a table from three other children. He pushed the children's heads so that they sank down onto the table. One of the girls stated that they had been poisoned and then the group all ran to a different part of the playground as the protagonist chased them. On questioning the group, they informed me that they had been playing the game 'Hotel', which I later identified as the free online game *Hotel Management*. This is not a particularly complex game; it involves a hotel receptionist who hands out keys to residents who then collect goods, which earn them money. In the Monteney example, just as in the Christopher Hatton 'Hoops' game, the children demonstrated the way in which they merged elements of online games with the more standard fare of playground pretend play, for example being poisoned by a wicked protagonist. In these activities, children are demonstrating well-established patterns, of course. Bishop and Curtis (2006) and Willett (2013) all discuss the way in which children integrate their media use with more folkloric forms of play in a rich hybrid mix.

In many ways, as I have argued here and elsewhere (Marsh, 2010), there are numerous continuities in online and offline play. Nevertheless, there are key differences. Burn (2013) notes three differences in relation to children's play on computer games and their offline play. The first relates to the perceptual distinction between them – in online play, the screen separates the player from the representations of the play world. The second difference is that in online play, children can control the avatar as a puppet, whereas in offline play, there is not such a direct relationship between intent and outcome. Third, the embodied experience is obviously different, as in online play, the avatar is bodily remote from the player, whereas in the playground, the player embodies the action. To this list, I would add three further differences, which relate to the previous discussion on friendships in online and offline spaces. First, in online play, the player is able to control the friendship group in ways which are not possible in the playground. If one does not wish to play with an avatar online, one can block them immediately and they no longer appear in the player's friendship list. This is not so easy in the playground, as children may resist attempts to reject them from a particular game, or linger at the edges once excluded to watch what is happening, which may irritate the other players. Second, judgments made about whom to play with offline are informed by knowledge of children's offline identity and practices. Whilst this knowledge does inform choices with regard to online friendships, as in the case of Carl (discussed previously in this chapter), it cannot always be the case. In these instances, children use other ways to judge whether or not they wish to play with another online user, which includes, at times, idiosyncratic judgments about the names and appearances of avatars and virtual homes (Marsh, 2012; 2013). Finally, in online play, the social relationships which often shape the nature and direction of play in offline contexts are not as discernible or able to influence play in the same way as they do in offline contexts and this can lead to children wanting to create opportunities online to thicken social friendships through ritualised play practices (Marsh, 2011).

Conclusion

From the data discussed in this chapter, it would appear that children at Monteney Primary School identified few negative consequences of not engaging in online play with their classmates. Only one child suggested that she felt excluded and the others stated either that there was no social exclusion due to this reason, or that they had not noticed any social exclusion. Children made decisions about who to play with online on the basis of their offline behaviour and generally tended to play with children online that they knew offline, that is, primarily their classmates. There appeared to be distinctions made about online and offline play, in that the children did not necessarily wish to play offline with children with whom they played online. Online social networks were more diverse than offline social networks, in that some children played online with children they did not play with in the playground and some were more likely to play with children of a different gender than themselves in an online context.

The offline and online continuum was also evident in relation to the distribution of play narratives across space and time. Children discussed playing, for example, *Club Penguin* as an online virtual world, as a Nintendo DS game on a console player, as a card collection practice and as a playground game of 'tag'. They purchased *Club Penguin* merchandise in local shops and the Disney store in an out-of-town shopping mall and some of these purchases enabled children to unlock online coins in the virtual world. This complex mix of practices effectively merged online and offline play spaces and contributed to their experience of play as a narrative-driven 'semiotic system' (Fleming, 1996).

There are numerous implications for the ongoing study of children at play. It is clear that contemporary playgrounds are shaped by children's engagement in online practices outside of school in a variety of ways and that the boundary between the online and offline is becoming more diffuse as technological developments continue to accelerate and shape the play environment. Whilst accepting Boellstorff's (2008) assertion that there are clear ontological differences between online and offline activities, I would wish to argue that there are also numerous similarities in terms of children's play. Not only are forms of play consistent across online and offline spaces (Marsh, 2010), but children talk about and engage in play in the playground which draws from their online experiences, as outlined in this chapter. Although of course it is valuable to examine children's play in specific domains, in future years it would be of interest to trace the movement of play and the circulation of discourses across online and offline spaces. In particular, there are questions raised by this study that deserve further attention. Although children's voices have been present throughout the chapter in the form of excerpts from interview transcripts, what is offered in summary are etic rather than emic perspectives; it may be the case that there are differences and tensions between children's views of online/ offline continuities and discontinuities and those of the adult researchers involved in the study. Nevertheless, I would suggest that both emic and etic viewpoints are of value and can offer different perspectives on the same phenomena (Martin, 2002:38). In addition, there are questions concerning the ways children do and can respond to the need for the 'emotionalisation of reflexivity' (Holmes, 2010) in managing friendships in online spaces. How can children who fail to develop trust in their offline relationships manage their entry into online networks? What happens when children who do not engage with particular online texts and spaces wish to participate in offline play which draws on these texts and practices? In what ways do narratives of play change across online and offline domains? These are questions that need to be explored by sociologists and anthropologists of childhood in the years ahead if we are to develop a more rounded understanding of play in the digital age.

References

Agosto D and Abba J (2010) High School Seniors' Social Network and Other ICT Use Preferences and Concerns. *ASIST Conference,* 22–27 October 2010, Pittsburgh, PA, USA. https://www.asis.org/asist2010/proceedings/proceedings/ASIST_AM10/submissions/25_Final_Submission.pdf

Bishop JC and Curtis M with Woolley H, Armitage M and Ginsborg J (2006) Participation, popular culture and playgrounds: Children's uses of media elements in peer play at school. Paper presented at the Folklore Society Conference, *Folklore, Film and Television: Convergences in Traditional Cultures and Popular Media,* 31 March–1 April 2006, London.

Blanchard J and Moore T (2010) The Digital World of Young Children: Impact on Emergent Literacy. Pearson Foundation White Paper. Retrieved from*: http//www.pearsonfoundation.org/PDF/EmergentLiteracy-WhitePaper.pdf*

Boellstorff T (2008) *Coming of Age in Second Life: An Anthropologist Explores the Virtually Human*. Princeton: Princeton University Press.

Buckingham D (2011) *The Material Child.* Oxford: Polity.

Buckingham D (1993) Children Talking Television: The Making of Television Literacy. London: Falmer Press.

Burn A (2013) Computer games on the playground: ludic systems, dramatized narrative and virtual embodiment. In Willett R, Richards C, Marsh J, Burn A and Bishop JC. *Children, Media and Playground Cultures: Ethnographic Studies of School Playtimes.* Basingstoke: Palgrave Macmillan.

Cook D (2008) The missing child in consumption theory. *Journal of Consumer Culture* 8: 219–43.

Cook D (2010) Commercial enculturation: Moving beyond consumer socialization. In Buckingham D and Tingstad V (eds) *Childhood and Consumer Culture.* Basingstoke: Palgrave Macmillan.

Davies J (2008) Online connections, collaborations, chronicles and crossings. In Willett R, Robinson M and Marsh J (eds) *Play, Creativities and Digital Cultures.* New York: Routledge.

Dowdall C (2008) The texts of me and the texts of us: Improvisation and polished performance in social networking sites. In Willett R, Robinson M and Marsh J (eds) *Play, Creativities and Digital Cultures.* New York: Routledge.

Fleming D (1996) *Powerplay: Toys as Popular Culture.* Manchester: Manchester University Press.

Gilbert B (2009) *Virtual Worlds Market Forecast 2009–2015.* Strategyanalytics, Retrieved March 2010 from http://www.strategyanalytics.com/default.aspx?m od=ReportAbstractViewer&a0=4 779

Hardey M (2008) Seriously social: making connections in the information age, Unpublished PhD Thesis, University of York.

Holland S and Harpin J (2008) '"It's only MySpace": Teenagers and social networking online'. In Holland S (ed.) *Remote Relationships in a Small World,* New York: Peter Lang.

Holmes M (2011) Emotional reflexivity in contemporary friendships: Understanding it using Elias and Facebook etiquette. *Sociological Research Online* 16. <http://www.socresonline.org.uk/16/1/11.html> 10.5153/sro.2292

Ito M, Baumer S, Bittanti M, Boyd D, Cody R, Herr-Stephenson B, Horst H A and Tripp L (2009) *Hanging Out, Messing Around and Geeking out: Kids Living and Learning with New Media.* Cambridge, MA: The MIT Press.

Kafai YB, Fields DA and Cook MS (2010) Your second selves: Player-designed avatars. *Games and Culture* 5: 23–42.

Kinder M (1991) *Playing with Power in Movies, Television, and Videogames: From Muppet Babies to Teenage Mutant Ninja Turtles.* Berkeley: University of California Press.

Lauwaert M (2009) *The Place of Play: Toys and Digital Cultures.* Amsterdam: Amsterdam University Press.

Levin DE and Rosenquest B (2001) The increasing role of electronic toys in the lives of infants and toddlers: Should we be concerned? *Contemporary Issues in Early Childhood* 2: 242–7.

Livingstone S (2009) *Children and the Internet.* Cambridge: Polity.

Luke C (2000) What next? Toddler netizens, Playstation thumb, techno-literacies. *Contemporary Issues in Early Childhood* 1: 95–100.

Malpas J (2009) On the non-autonomy of the virtual. *Convergence: The International Journal of Research into New Media Technologies* 15: 135–9.

Marsh J (2013) Breaking the ice: Play, friendships and social identities in young children's use of virtual worlds. In Burke A and Marsh J (eds) *Children's Virtual Play Worlds: Culture, Learning and Participation.* New York: Peter Lang, 59–78.

Marsh J (2012) Countering chaos in *Club Penguin:* Young children's literacy practices in a virtual world. In Merchant G, Gillen J, Marsh J and Davies J (eds) *Virtual Literacies: Interactive Spaces for Children and Young People.* New York: Routledge.

Marsh J (2011) Young children's literacy practices in a virtual world: Establishing an online interaction order. *Reading Research Quarterly* 46: 101–18.

Marsh J (2010) Young children's play in online virtual worlds. *Journal of Early Childhood Research,* 8: 23–39.

Marsh J, Brooks G, Hughes J, Ritchie L and Roberts S (2005) *Digital beginnings: Young children's use of popular culture, media and new technologies.*

Sheffield: University of Sheffield. Retrieved 18 July 2012, at http://www. digitalbeginings.shef.ac.uk/

Martin J (2002) *Organizational Culture: Mapping the Terrain.* London: Sage.

Mazur E and Richards L (2011) Adolescents' and emerging adults' social networking online: Homophily or diversity? *Journal of Applied Developmental Psychology* 32: 180–88.

McLaughlin M, Osbourne K and Smith C (1995) Standards of conduct on Usenet. In Jones S (ed.) *Cybersociety: Computer-mediated Communication and Community.* London: Sage.

Meyers E (2009) Tip of the iceberg: meaning, identity, and literacy in preteen virtual worlds. Paper presented at 2009 ALISE Conference. Retrieved 8 January 2010 from http://blogs.iis.syr.edu/alise/archives/71

Meyers EM, Nathan LP and Unsworth K (2010) Who's watching your kids? Safety and surveillance in virtual worlds for children. *Journal of Virtual Worlds Research* 3: 3–28.

Miller P and Rose N (1997) Mobilising the consumer: assembling the subject of consumption, *Theory, Culture and Society* 14: 1–36.

Nardi B (2010) *My Life as a Night Elf Priest: An Anthropological Account of 'World of Warcraft'.* Ann Arbor, MI: University of Michigan Press.

Ofcom (2011) Children and parents: media use and attitudes report. October 2011. http://stakeholders.ofcom.org.uk/binaries/research/media-literacy/oct2011/ Children_and_parents.pdf

Opie I and Opie P (1988) *The Singing Game.* Oxford: Oxford University Press.

Palmer S (2006) *Toxic Childhood.* London: Orion Press.

Pugh AJ (2009) *Longing and Belonging: Parents, Children and Consumer Culture.* Berkeley: University of California Press.

Putnam G (1997) *Dissociation in Children and Adolescents: A Developmental Perspectiv*e. New York: Guilford Press.

Rapoport A and Horvath WJ (1961) A study of a large sociogram. *Behavioural Science* 6: 279–91.

Renold E (2005) *Girls, Boys and Junior Sexualities: Exploring Childrens' Gender and Sexual Relations in the Primary School.* London: Routledge/Falmer.

Robinson V (2007) The cyberself: The self-ing project goes online, symbolic interaction in the digital age. *New Media & Society* 9: 93–110.

Shade LR and Grimes S (2005) Neopian economics of play: Children's cyberpets and online communities as immersive advertising in NeoPets.com. *International Journal of Media and Cultural Politics* 1: 181–98.

Shariff S (2008) *Cyber Bullying: Issues and Solutions for the School, the Classroom and the Home.* New York: Routledge.

Subrahmanyam K, Smahel D and Greenfield P (2006) Connecting developmental constructions to the Internet: Identity presentation and sexual exploration in online teen chatrooms. *Developmental Psychology* 42: 395–406.

Taylor TL (2006) *Play Between Worlds: Exploring Online Game Culture.* Cambridge, Mass: MIT Press.

Thomas A (2007) *Youth Online: Identity and Literacy in the Digital Age*. New York: Peter Lang.

Thorne B (1993) *Gender Play: Girls and Boys in School*. New Brunswick: Rutgers University Press.

Turkle S (2011) *Alone Together.* Cambridge, Mass: MIT Press.

Valentine G and Holloway S (2002) Cyberkids? Exploring children's identities and social networks in on-line and offline worlds. *Annals of the Association of American Geographers* 92: 302–19.

Warner M (2009) Out of an old toy chest. *Journal of Aesthetic Education* 43: 1–16.

Willett R (2013) Superheroes, naughty mums and witches: Pretend family play amongst seven to ten year-olds. In Willett R, Richards C, Marsh J, Burn A and Bishop, JC. *Children, Media and Playground Cultures: Ethnographic Studies of School Playtimes.* Basingstoke: Palgrave Macmillan.

Xu Y, Cao X, Sellen A, Herbrich R and Graepel T (2011) Sociable Killers: Understanding Social Relationships in an Online First-Person Shooter Game. Proceedings of the ACM Conference on Computer supported cooperative work, New York, 2011. http://research.microsoft.com/en-us/people/xiangc/cscw2011_sociablekillers.pdf

Chapter 6
Remixing Children's Cultures: Media-Referenced Play on the Playground

Rebekah Willett

In *Children's Games in Street and Playground* (1969) the Opies documented a variety of media-related practices: performances of advertising jingles and pop songs, passing references to public figures, guessing activities centring on film stars and advertisements and numerous pretend games involving media characters. Similarly, data from our two playgrounds reflect the dominant 'mediascapes' of UK children in 2009–2011 (Appadurai, 1996). Some games refer to specific media texts, but more often their play draws on much wider resources and includes enduring narrative themes (e.g. good versus evil, going on adventures), characters (e.g. witches, superheroes, family members) and actions (e.g. casting spells, escaping, caretaking). In our study, children often use referents broadly, drawing on current media texts as well as long-standing practices, so as to incorporate and remix referents to suit their play scenarios.

In some ways, therefore, it is misrepresentative to label games as media-referenced. The characteristics discussed by Ito (2008: 401) are more accurate as a way of discussing these games – they are remixes in which children draw on various referents including 'common cultural source material' to develop shared language and activities which fit their particular social circumstances. Drawing on Ito's description of remixes, this chapter examines data from our playgrounds which include a variety of media referents, focusing on the forms and functions of these referents in playground practices. The chapter starts with a descriptive and rough categorisation of the forms of media-referenced play we observed, based on work by Bishop et al (2006). The second part of the chapter explores different characteristics of media remixes, including performativity, proximity and originality. The chapter ends with an analysis of one episode of play, focusing on the way media referents are functioning in a specific play context.

Part One – Overview of Playground Remixes

What Did Remixing Look like on the Playgrounds?

Media references were hard to ignore on our playgrounds. In addition to branded objects such as clothing and lunchboxes, there were objects such as trading cards, books and small merchandised toys which made their way onto our playgrounds.

These objects were like a litmus test of the popularity of particular media texts. There were surges – for example, on the London playground when the World Cup football tournament was on, football trading cards (including special World Cup cards) were suddenly highly visible. Some children's media preferences were displayed through images on lunchboxes; and importantly, these often expressed their media preferences at the beginning of the school year when lunch boxes had recently been purchased. The objects reflected children's fandom, their 'mediascapes' (Appadurai, 1996) and particular social relations. Although there were overlaps in media artefacts on our two playgrounds (as one would expect with commodified objects), there were differences in consumption practices, perhaps because objects also related closely to their social contexts. For example, on the London playground, groups of friends brought 'My Littlest Pet Shop' toys to school or read a series of books together, and the Sheffield playground had a CD player which helped to create a culture of pop song singing with certain girls.

Media remixing on our playgrounds involved media texts – sometimes combining numerous media texts (for example, one nine year-old girl told us she combined *X-Men* with *Ben 10*). But more frequently and significantly, remixing involved children reading the culture of the playground and creating games that remixed media texts with a whole world of other texts and discourses present on the playground. Children remixed existing playground games with texts from a variety of sources (media, school, home), and their media-referenced play reflected the dominant discourses present in media, on the playground and in children's lives more generally. As Sutton-Smith describes:

> Play is a deconstruction of the world in which [children] live. If the world is a text, the play is a reader's response to that text. There are endless possible reader responses to the orthodox text of growing up in childhood. (1997: 166)

This chapter provides an analysis of different forms and functions of media-referenced play, taking into account the social context of these cultures and explaining remixes in terms of children's 'responses' to their playground worlds.

Beyond the highly visible objects discussed above there were many ways that media-referents were deeply embedded in children's games [see the discussion of combat narratives in Chris Richards' chapter (this volume)]. Bishop et al (2006) identified a range of practices on playgrounds which include media references during play. The four categories of practice emerging from their data are as follows:

1. *Onomastic allusion* – use of names, catchphrases, gestures, musical utterances from media used in passing in play (e.g. 'My name is Elvis Presley … Drinking Pepsi' in a clapping game)
2. *Syncretism* – text, music and/or movement incorporated into or combined with an established game [e.g. "Spiderman Tig' (touch chase) using Spiderman's name and his web-spinning gesture and the concomitant ('ssss') noise' (p.8)]

3. *Mimesis* – a range of forms of imitation and/or recreation of media content (including words, mannerisms, actions); the medium functions as a source of transmission [e.g. 'Learning a clapping rhyme from an episode of the television series *Recess*'; imitation of pop singers and their dance routines; pretending to be superheroes (p.5)]
4. *Parody* – textual, musical or gestural performance which may include elements of mimetic performance along with self-parody and 'ridicule or irony in relation to its media referent' (p.8).

Similar to Bishop et al's data, we observed numerous instances of *onomastic allusion*. The study of clapping games (Bishop and Burn, 2013) in particular, revealed references to current events such as an eruption of a volcano in Iceland and current celebrity figures/media references such as Tracy Beaker. We recorded 'musical utterances' across playground games, such as a line from a love song which was used as a way of taunting a boy during kiss-chase (see Willett, 2011). Catch phrases were also common, and often neither the children nor we could trace them. For example, at one point a group of eight to nine year-old boys surrounded one of the ethnographers, chanting 'breaking the law' possibly referencing the 1980 Judas Priest song, although none of the boys were familiar with the song. In football, we heard catch phrases which seemed to imitate sports commentators (or even parodic videogame imitations of sports commentators, e.g. 'good goal' in an electronic sounding voice) as well as references to names of teams and players. Unsurprisingly, collections from the Opies also evidence children appropriating media references in their play. For example, the Opies recorded a version of *Jesus Christ Superstar* in 1976, with the words 'Georgie Best, superstar'. They also documented various references to popular stars in children's games (e.g. Diana Dors, Shirley Temple, Marilyn Monroe, Donny Osmond) (Opie and Opie, 1985) (see also Jopson et al, Chapter 2, this volume). Our data also include examples of onomastic allusion in the form of gestures (sometimes accompanying a verbal reference). For example, a 'gangster' gesture/pose or a martial arts gesture/pose were provided by children, particularly when the camera was pointed at them. In terms of social contexts, a key element of this category is the way that onomastic allusions become embedded in a peer group, and then are taken up and transmitted. Whilst the original referent might have been a media text (e.g. Judas Priest's song 'Breaking the Law'), the social context is one of the key reasons that it survives (see Bishop, this volume). This raises questions about the meaning of the text for the players, given that the text might be far removed from the original source (e.g. 'Breaking the Law' was first recorded on heavy metal band Judas Priest's 1980 album) and also the salience of identifying playground texts as 'media references'.

In Bishop et al's second category, *syncretism*, remix culture is particularly evident – children are mixing a playground game with a media reference. Similar to Bishop et al (2006), we have examples of catching games which referenced media (numerous characters appear in catching games, according to children, including witches, zombies, queens and fairies). One group of nine to 10 year-old girls told how they played a catching game based on *Harry Potter* in which the catchers were dementors who would 'capture your soul'. In football, more extended play involved children taking on the role of a sports commentator or groups calling themselves after well-known sports teams. After the World Cup final (in which Spain beat Holland), we observed a group of six to seven year-olds playing a fantasy game of the World Cup final in which Spain was beaten by Australia. The Opies (1969) also document practices such as using media as a source for guessing games ('Film Stars' and 'Advertisements' were two such games).

Although it is difficult to measure frequency of games (e.g. one might measure time spent playing, number of children, number of incidents), we can say that syncretism and Bishop et al's third category of practice, *mimesis*, were prevalent on the playgrounds in our study. Pretend play incorporated a variety of mimetic actions, plots, characters and so on, referencing particular books, videogames, movies and TV shows; and children engaged in a range of 'performances' for real or imagined audiences in which they were imitating media (songs, musicals, comedy skits, TV programmes).[1] (Performativity in play is discussed in Part Two of this chapter.) Again, unsurprisingly, perhaps, the Opies (1969) documented a range of characters incorporated into children's play, including the Lone Ranger, Cisco Kid, Robin Hood, Ivanhoe, Man from U.N.C.L.E., Superman, Batman and Captain Marvel.

The fourth practice identified by Bishop et al (2006) is *parody*. We documented numerous parodic performances on our playgrounds including references to *The X Factor*, *Britain's Got Talent*, *The Jeremy Kyle Show*, *Who Wants to be a Millionaire*, comedy sketch shows and playground documentaries. One difficult aspect of parody is in identifying the intentions of the authors/players, which shift during performances and range from emulation through to ridicule (see Bishop et al, 2006; Willett, 2009). As Grace and Tobin (2003) describe, 'The very ambiguity of parody is the source of the power and pleasure associated with it' (p.49). I would argue that parody is a mimetic practice – children are imitating a cultural form or practice, holding it up for ridicule in its more critical form. Therefore, although parodic practice is a distinguishable form of mimeses, in Table 6.1 below I include parody as hybrid/recontextualised form of mimesis rather than as a separate practice.

The practice Bishop et al (2006) identify as *mimesis* in some cases overlaps with other categories and can be difficult to distinguish. For example, in the context of combat narratives, boys told us names of their weapons, which they had learned from particular videogames. It was difficult to know (particularly without knowledge of the specific weapons/games to which they refer) whether the naming of weapons was used simply as onomastic allusion or if during the game

---

[1]   The chapter in this volume by Chris Richards discusses one type of game in this category (combat narratives), and elsewhere we have written about pop song performances (Willett, 2011), computer game-based play, media-referenced narratives involving pretend families, and parodic performances of TV programmes (Willett et al, 2013).

Table 6.1   Practices of media-referenced play

Category	Example	Media usage
Onomastic allusion	'Britney Spears' substituted for name in a clapping game	Minimal text is used
Closely imitative	CBBC 'Green Balloon club' chant	Text (words and gestures) used in entirety; close to original text
Hybrid/recontextualised	Harry Potter catch, *Star Wars* game, 'Single Ladies' performance, *Jeremy Kyle Show* parody	Some elements of text are used (lyrics, tune, plot, characters, actions, props); original text is reference point and is altered for the playground
Ambiguously referenced	Spies, cops and robbers, pirates	Original text is general and/or ambiguous

named weapons had particular associated characteristics which then became part of the play and the narrative. Further, as documented by the Opies and many other collectors, 'war games' have a long history, and the inclusion of named weapons from a videogame could therefore be considered syncretic. Finally, the weapons might be part of a more extended example of mimesis (a game which loosely imitates a videogame and involves references to specific weapons, characters and missions).

Because of the slippery nature and the range of practices which might be identified as syncretic or mimetic, I discuss examples from our study in three subcategories of mimetic play: 1) *closely imitative*, 2) *hybrid/recontextualised* and 3) *ambiguously referenced*. Table 6.1 highlights the different ways that media referents were used in the playground practices we observed. Although the figure is necessarily reductive and ignores many complications in distinguishing children's media-referenced play, it is intended to provide an overview of some of the different practices we observed.

In our data, there were some instances of practice, particularly performances for a real or imagined audience, which we could identify on our playgrounds as *closely imitative*. For example, we recorded close imitations of words and gestures from media-based chants/rhymes (CBBC's 'The Green Balloon club', or Hi-5's 'Taekwondo') and whole pop songs (occasionally heard on the London school playground, more prevalent on the Sheffield playground where there was a CD player). Again, looking historically, the Opies documented similar practices; for example in 1967 the Eurovision song context winner Sandie Shaw who sang 'Puppet on a string' was 'faithfully copied by rows of little girls in playtime' (1985: 414). Closely imitative play was rare on the playgrounds, partly because only very particular media forms lend themselves to this practice (close imitation of a book, TV show, movie or videogame is not possible in this context), and perhaps also because closely imitative play does not suit the social context and functions of playground cultures.

More frequently, the mimetic play we observed did not represent children 'faithfully copying' the media texts to which they refer; rather the players imitated and incorporated certain elements of the text in the context of their games. We documented gestures and lyrics from pop songs, characters and plots from videogames/TV/books, pretend devices such as elaborate GPS systems and games which children referred to by the name of a media text (e.g. 'Star Wars' and 'Call of Duty'). Children improvised plots and actions, based on particular elements of the media source which they had remixed with their playground game. These games represent *hybrid/recontextualised* forms of media-referenced play.[2]

The Opies' recordings document many versions of songs and provide further evidence of *hybrid/recontextualised* practices (see Jopson et al, this volume); for example the popular song 'Sunny side up' (from 1929) was documented in various versions through the 1970s. In our study, a group of girls performed a song called 'Single Ladies (Put a ring on it)' which was originally a song performed by the pop star Beyoncé. The song also appeared in a children's movie, *Alvin and the Chipmunks*, and was performed by three chipmunks (the Chipettes). On the playground, the version of the song that was performed included two key lines from Beyoncé and the Chipettes ('All the single ladies', 'if you liked it then you should have put a ring on it') as well as three vaguely imitative gestures (putting hands in the air, turning around, pointing to their ring fingers). However, the playground song also featured new lines (e.g. 'turn around on the spot') and a host of different gestures (unsurprisingly, given the sexual nature of the Beyoncé video – e.g. women slapping their butts). In some ways the playground song can be seen as a singing game with a reference to 'Single Ladies' rather than an imitation of the entire Beyoncé song. However, the performers might have considered it to be a performance of the Beyoncé/Chipette song in some ways. Whilst the girls agreed that one of them had 'made up' the moves, they might have considered the words and some of the actions close enough to the original to mark it as a closely imitative (particularly the girls who had not heard or seen the song performed).

The third subcategory of mimetic play, *ambiguously referenced*, takes account of ambiguous and general references to cultural forms in children's play. Here we found a range of elements which might connect with children's 'mediascapes'

---

[2]   Rather than trying to distinguish between existing games which are combined with media references (syncretic) and games which are based on media references (mimetic), in Table 6.1 I combine Bishop et al's (2006) syncretic and mimesis categories and identify these practices as *hybrid/recontextualised media-referenced practices*. Whilst this allows us to discuss a broad range of mimetic play, it leaves open the risk of homogenising the cultural sources and ignoring the specificity of their forms and functions. Analysing a range of social and contextual factors, as seen in Part Three of this chapter, allows for a more in-depth and complex understanding.

(e.g. characters such as baddies, spies, witches, princesses, fairies, zombies, ghosts, cowboys; plots such as good versus evil; props such as weapons, electronic devices, magic wands; actions such as chasing, catching, fighting, spying). These forms of play are also documented by the Opies. In *Children's Games in Street and Playground* (1969), the Opies distinguish eight categories of 'pretending games' including playing horses, storybook world, war games, cops and robbers and fairies and witches. This category, therefore, includes games which are not necessarily forms of media-referenced play, rather they draw on more general and enduring cultural forms and may or may not reference media texts.

What Is Happening in Remixing? Hybrid/Recontextualised Mimesis

As indicated above, closely imitative play was relatively rare in playground games; and with general and/or ambiguously referenced play, it is problematic to assume connections with media. When considering media-referenced play, therefore, the category which demands closer attention is hybrid/recontextualised mimesis. What is being hybridised and recontextualised on our playgrounds? What are the different contexts in the process of recontextualisation? What is happening to different resources (media texts, enduring practices, surrounding discourses) in the process of hybridising and recontextualising?

A common practice in hybrid/recontextualised mimetic play is the process of adaptation – children change a resource and/or combine different resources in order to create a text or practice that is suitable for their playground contexts. Children select structures, characters, actions, rules, representations, narratives which enable them to play a game in the context of their play. These selections involve creating a hybrid text (one which includes components from an 'original' text or texts, as well as one which is combined with and adapted to the cultures of the playgrounds). (Complexities of the concept of 'originality' are discussed in Part Two of this chapter.)

In our data, creating a media hybrid text necessarily involved recontextualising the text to work on the playground. In some cases, the recontextualising was in relation to time and space, and in others it was in relation to other playground practices. In relation to time and space, recontextualising involved adapting texts and practices to the particular context of the playground. The remixed source needed to fit the physical structures available, the social context (e.g. lots of children of different ages sharing a space which is overseen by adults), prosocial rules of school spaces, the time constraints and so on. In one observation of six to seven year-old girls who were playing a game based on the narrative of *Aladdin*, there were several genies because the children had decided it was unfair for one of them to have all the magical powers, thus recontextualising *Aladdin* to fit the social group (several dominant girls) and the rules of 'fair play' on the playground. In performing parodies of *Britain's Got Talent* or *The Jeremy Kyle Show*, the recontextualisation involved adapting TV shows to become improvised skits on the playground. In the parodies we observed (primarily amongst older children ages eight to 11), part of the playground culture was to make fun of these shows, using the structure of the shows and the subject matter to create humorous and, in some senses, critical takes of the original texts (see Grace and Tobin, 2003; Marsh and Bishop, 2013).

Recontextualising media in relation to other practices involved any number of resources which constituted children's playground culture (e.g. bringing characters and actions from a media text such as *Harry Potter* into a chasing game such as 'Tig' or 'It'). Although the focus of this chapter is on media resources, another obvious source for hybridisation were enduring texts and practices, such as those documented by the Opies (amongst other researchers). In their practices of hybridising and recontextualising surrounding resources, children drew on practices which were versatile, easily transmittable and had structures which had stood the test of time. These were sometimes combined with current media resources which had more currency (amongst children's peer cultures) and seemed more interesting, exciting or new (from the children's perspectives). Basic structures from chasing games (having chasers and chased, various 'poison' touches and releases, designated safe spots or jails) were mixed with characters, actions and plots from different sources (classroom topics, books, news, TV, and so on).

Finally (and perhaps obviously), in order to understand what is happening when children produce remixes on playgrounds, the social contexts require close consideration. In creating a remix on the playground, children are using their knowledge of a wide array of practices and texts to create something that works in the very specific social space of the playground. Directly related to our study, Anne Haas Dyson analyses processes through which children produce narratives (in drama and story writing) on elementary school playgrounds and in classrooms. Drawing on Bakhtin's theories, Dyson analyses a range of social functions embedded in children's hybrid and intertextual practices connected with the production of narratives. In combining, reworking, and personalising texts, Dyson argues that 'Children can use these materials to construct their own identities as well as to establish intersubjectivity (shared worlds) with others' (1999, p. 370).

As discussed above, on our playgrounds, children adapted references from any number of sources – classrooms, homes, current events, movies, videogames, books, and so on. These sources were part of the 'shared store of cultural referents' of the playground, and more specifically, cultural referents of groups of friends (Ito, 2008). Importantly, the remixing of cultural referents functioned in particular ways, as Dyson analyses, working to define and establish particular identities and friendship groups. In our data, display of media knowledge marked social status or a niche group identity, a game such as 'cops and robbers' provided the structure needed to create a game out of a media text, numerous emotional aspects were explored through remixed cultures (acting out a scary scene from a movie, for example), and social rules were constantly being negotiated. Therefore, each example of media remixing needs to be analysed in terms of social functions as well as textual referents. Part Three of this chapter provides a case study of the social functions and different textual referents which emerged in one 18-minute play episode.

Part Two – Characteristics of Remix Cultures

Part One of this chapter provides an overview of the different practices related to children's media-referenced play on our two playgrounds. This part of the chapter analyses different characteristics of these practices, including performativity, proximity and originality.

Performativity

We documented a range of 'performances' which were enacted for a real or imagined audience: for example, comedy sketches, reality TV shows, songs, and dance routines. Sometimes the references to a media source were stylistic (a comedy sketch about the playground in which two boys talk directly to camera – similar to the style of the UK's comic sketch show presenters 'Dick and Dom'); sometimes they referenced specific programmes and elements on the programmes (for example, contestants performing on *The X Factor* and then being rated by judges). (For an extended analysis of parodic performances of reality TV shows, specifically *The Jeremy Kyle Show*, see Marsh and Bishop, 2013.)

Not all children in these performances had direct access to the media referent, and knowledge was disseminated and constructed on the playground via peers. Media-referenced performances could be embedded with power relationships, given that particular knowledge was needed in order to take part. However, in some cases we saw the relationships resemble those of a 'community of practice' in which novices started on the periphery and gradually moved toward the centre of the community as they became involved in the practices of that community (Lave and Wenger, 1991). In most cases, media-referenced play was either hybrid/ recontextualised or ambiguously referenced rather than close imitation of a media text, thus allowing for negotiation of the media text and the role of children who were unfamiliar with the text.

Other kinds of media-referenced play were less presentational (i.e. not for spectators), although in some ways all play was performative. Clapping games with media references, sociodramatic play based on families of superheroes, Harry Potter catch are examples of play in which children were performing with media texts, yet they might not call these 'performances'. Dramatic role-play is particularly complex in terms of performativity (cf. Edmiston, 2007), with children stepping in and out of roles continuously and performing with each other but not for an audience. As discussed in relation to the case study in Part Three of this chapter, the use of media in dramatic role play contributed to the pretence of the play episode. Children not only stepped in and out of roles, in the case study, they stepped in and out of an imagined TV screen.

In the context of children's performance of playground remixes, consideration must also be given to the presentation of self; and theories of identity which draw on analogies from drama are particularly salient (e.g. Butler, 1990; Goffman, 1959). Goffman analyses social interaction as a kind of theatrical performance in which people move between 'front stage' and 'back stage' performances. In this analogy, Goffman makes a distinction between behaviour which is more conformist and ritualistic ('front stage'), and that which is more honest and potentially contradictory in relation to front stage performance ('back stage'). In performing a media remix, children's identities can be seen as fluid – moving between the front and backstage. For example, a boy playing an 'army game' is clearly performing dominant masculinity in the front stage (interest in the topic, negotiating school rules about 'killing', using 'cool' catch phrases and gestures); but army games also involve physical contact, and we regularly saw boys embracing each other; armies are units of friends, and friendships are displayed and negotiated through these games; the game is taking place in school, and boys are negotiating their identities as pupils. These other types of performances might challenge the more front stage performance of masculinity. Army games can also be read through Butler's ideas concerning bodily performance (1990). Boys undertake bodily performances of dominant masculinity through army games; and importantly, through these seemingly effortless performances, they identify with this version of masculinity (see also Richards, this volume).

Children also performed peer group identity through their choice of media – groups of children displayed fandom for a range of media, positioning themselves as friends as well as fans. For example, one group of nine to 10 year-old boys created their own version of an acrobatic street dance (based on *Britain's Got Talent* winners, Diversity); a pair of 10 year-old boy friends called themselves the Diamond Brothers (based on their fandom of Anthony Horowitz's books); and groups of six to seven year-old girls performed songs from musicals (*Mamma Mia, High School Musical, Camp Rock, Sound of Music*). However, as we learned through our conversations with children, the play with these media-referents did not necessarily mean they were fans or that they even had direct access to the media source. In some cases, children knew very little about the source of the referent. Rather, media provided a platform for their game and their display of friendship. This might explain why we often heard what we might call media utterances – snippets of songs, passing references to a character – rather than more developed media references (see also Maybin, in press; Rampton, 2006).

Proximity

One of the features of media-referenced play alluded to in the discussion of the categories of practice in Part One of this chapter is proximity to a media text. We could chart a range of positions in relation to how close games are to any particular media text, with games in the closely imitative category falling on one end of a spectrum, games in the ambiguously referenced category falling at the other end and the hybrid/recontextualised games falling on many different points in between. We could also look at media objects such as books, trading cards and small toys which are part of playground cultures, charting different ways they are used. When analysing children's performances, as discussed above in reference to

Beyoncé's 'Single Ladies', it becomes apparent that an exact imitation is neither possible nor intended in this context. As Sutton-Smith (1997) states,

> There is no tabula rasa. No matter what the cultural stimuli might be (toys or television shows), they have to be mediated by children's fantasy in order to be accepted, and adjusted to their play norms and social competence in order to be assimilated into the active theatric play forms of childhood (154).

This indicates that mimetic play needs to be analysed in terms of context and mediation. For example, when we observed a group of five to six year-old children closely imitating a chant ('The Green Balloon Club') from the BBC children's TV channel, the chant was organised by one girl (a strong performer on the playground) who taught the chant to her peers and led the performance. She organised groups of children to stand facing outward on a tiered wooden platform (like a stage), and the rhythmic stamping of feet (part of the performance) resonated on the platform and brick wall behind. The children were not simply copying the chant – there was a leader and followers, the space the leader chose added to the sense of performance, there were children and/or adults watching and so on. Although the chant was as close to the 'original' text as can be expected, it was mediated through the playground performance.

On the other end of the spectrum, ambiguously referenced play (e.g. spies, cops and robbers) appears improvisational, and the play may seem only tangentially related to any particular media text. As in Barthes's (1977) assertion concerning 'the death of the author', because we are constantly borrowing our words from our surroundings, and due to the polysemic nature of any particular text, the origins of a text and the intent of the author is, in some ways, irrelevant. However, even in play there are rules associated with the referents (and, of course, there are rules on a school playground). Whilst we documented elaborate narratives, various characters, numerous imaginary props and actions in children's games of cops and robbers, all of the games follow the basic rules of the referent 'cops and robbers'. Sutton-Smith comments on this combination of rule-bound and agentive play:

> What is at first glance innovative play is found to be a highly ritualized series of events … social play has to be both innovative and ritualistic to survive … Children don't want to have to invent their play life from scratch every day, and they probably need the ritual as a kind of time and behavior marker that allows new freedoms for their fantasy life. (1997: 169–70).

Games which are close in proximity to an identifiable text may serve an important function, similar to the rule-bound and ritualistic play discussed by Sutton-Smith. 'The Green Balloon Club' performance allowed groups of children to perform together without having to start from scratch (make up words, rhythm and actions; teach other children; and so on). Pleasure in following a game or activity (such as 'The Green Balloon Club' performance) came through mastery and social inclusion on the playground. This was particularly relevant for children who learned the media text on the playground via peers rather than directly from the media source.

Keeping with Barthes's concepts, 'The Green Balloon Club' can be seen as a 'readerly text' – a text which is consumed in a straight-forward or, as he terms, 'passive' way and requires little interpretation (1975b). In contrast, remixes might be seen as 'writerly texts' – texts in which the player accepts or works with the rules whilst also producing meaning (ibid 1975b). Applying Barthes's ideas, it may be that in remix cultures, the 'pleasure of writing' is in playing with the 'magic of the signifier' (ibid: 4). Media provide resources (texts, signifiers), and part of the pleasure of remix culture is in playing with these signs within social situations. The enjoyment of remixing seems to produce a general feeling of pleasure or contentment - *le plaisir* as discussed by Barthes (1975a). Importantly, the pretence of media-referenced play may offer resources for more embodied or blissful pleasures (*jouissance*, using Barthes's term). Play in which characters die and come back to life, turn into zombies, are terrified by alien forces, and have their souls removed are all given a platform through media-referenced play. Sutton-Smith (1997) describes how play has been perceived in terms of high and low forms of play, and he argues that this division justifies certain kinds of play but neglects others. He argues that in romantic idealisations of play, games which are chaotic, nonsensical and irrational are dismissed. One of the purposes media-referenced play might fulfil is as a vehicle for more chaotic and phantasmagoric play (using Sutton-Smith's term).

Originality

Problematic to the discussion of 'mimesis' is the notion of 'media source' or 'original text'. The origin of a text may be impossible (or irrelevant) to trace, as in cops and robbers where any number of sources might be contributing to the game (TV, movies, books, news, 'real life', peer playground culture, sedimented childhood practices). Even if we focus more closely on play which references specific media texts, much of the interpretation of this play could depend on researchers' knowledge of children's media referents. Several of us have been researching children's media for most of our academic careers; and further, during the project we immersed ourselves in children's media culture (books, music, movies, television, videogames and internet sites), following up references from a whole school survey, conversations with the children, and our observations (from the playground, library, computer suite and the broader surrounding 'mediascape'). Whilst this helped us understand some aspects of the children's culture we were observing, in addition to being difficult and complex to trace, the sources frequently were not crucial to analysing the ways they were enacted on the playground. As in the example of Beyoncé's 'Single Ladies', the text of the song and video bore little relation to the performance or singing game the girls created, and more important to the analysis of how the song was performed was a knowledge of the social context (e.g. peer group, individual media access, playground rules, other singing games the girls played). When considering play which might be classified as hybrid/intertextual practice, certainly texts are structuring this play; however, the practice also references children's habitus, peer group context, school environment and a host of other factors.

Sutton-Smith (1997) also highlights problems with trying to identify an 'original' text in children's play, as in the quotation above in which he writes about the mediation involved in children's 'active theatric play forms'. Analysing popular rhetorics of play, Sutton-Smith argues that 'originality' is part of the discursive construct which frames children's play and classifies forms of play as more or less desirable or problematic. In 'the rhetoric of play as the imaginary', play is connected with the romantic movement which idealised very particular constructs of the imaginary 'characterized as an attitude of mind that glorifies freedom, originality, genius, the arts, and the innocent and uncorrupted character of the childhood vision' (Sutton-Smith, 1997: 129). Debates in which children's play is seen as increasingly less imaginative due to the impact of media draw on this romantic vision of childhood. These debates elevate some play as creative and innovative, and dismiss others as derivative and lacking in imagination. However, as discussed here, there are no games that are not derivative. Children necessarily borrow from surrounding texts and practices, refashioning them to suit their playground games (Bakhtin, 1981; Dyson, 1999). The 'originality' of the texts they create or from which they are borrowing is elusive at best, and at worst creates divisions which mark some forms of play as better than others.

Part Three – Case Study

Throughout this chapter, one of the caveats has been the importance of recognising the social context of children's media-referenced play. The context of the games includes physical spaces/objects, friendships, peer and adult surveillance, time, age, gender, ethnicity, socio-economics as well as structures children draw on from media texts and from enduring practices (see Richards, 2011, for a discussion of the ethnographic process of researching playground cultures). Analysing play as different practices of remix culture maintains the focus on the *form* of media-related games. Taking account of the context of these games allows us to consider the *function* more closely and to look at how children's agency is enacted through the structures embedded in their play. To demonstrate, the next section analyses one play episode that occurred in July 2010 on the London school playground.

3D TV

This game involved two groups of girls, with one group pretending to be actors on TV and the other group acting as an audience. There were 11 girls involved in this episode which lasted approximately 18 minutes. Five of the girls were in Year Three (ages seven to eight), four in Year Two (ages six to seven) and two in Reception (ages four to five). The episode took place in the 'brick area' – a high-arched space underneath a busy road enclosed on three sides by brick/cement walls. The area contained wooden planks, ramps and boxes designed for construction play as well as a few cushions. The area was usually dominated by younger children (ages four to six), particularly (though not always) boys (similar to gender-related construction-based play in preschool settings). On this hot day in July, the girls managed to secure the cooler brick area for their play in which they dominated both the space and the equipment (in part due to the fact that the World Cup Football was occurring and more boys were playing football in a different space). When we started observing (shortly after they had set up the scenario), the groups were facing each other, with the audience of Year Three and Reception girls sitting behind a long make-shift table, and the Year Two 'TV actors' positioned amongst a formation of wooden blocks.

The Year Two girls joined the game shortly after the other girls had set up the table (interpreted by some of the players as a dining table). In an interview, Anabel (Year Two) said she asked her sister Rachel (Year Three) if they could join the game as actors in a TV 'because normally in kitchens … you have TVs don't you'. They were first acting out a pirate movie with Anabel as the captain. In an interview, Anabel attributed her knowledge of pirates to a *Horrible Histories* TV programme (naming Blackbeard) and other programmes on the children's BBC TV channel. Soon after the action started, the girls playing pirates decided they were a '3D movie', and they started lunging at the audience with their 'guns' and 'knives' (according to Anabel). The audience responded with screams and laughter, and two girls created an imaginary remote control, pushed the 'pause' button repeatedly, and changed the channel whilst several girls requested the 3D pirate movie. The TV actors complied by 'freezing' when the pause button was pushed, and when the channel was changed they announced they were 3D grannies, using planks of wood as crutches to approach the audience, eliciting cackles of laughter (and interpreted by one audience member as 'acting drunk'). The channel changed again and the actors started to set up a musical, turning their planks of wood (formerly guns/knives) into guitars and a keyboard. (Anabel mentioned that her favourite thing to watch at home was *High School Musical*.) However, the audience was restless, screaming for more pirates, for quiet and for pauses in the action. (The screaming and laughter reverberated in this space, making the noise level very high, and one of the Reception girls put her fingers in her ears several times.) Rachel, who had been standing on the sidelines trying to direct the entire play episode, decided it was time to switch roles, and asked for and selected volunteers to become the TV actors. After switching places, similar action took place (lunging with planks of wood toward the audience), but Rachel paused the actors and announced the next TV performance. The recording is unclear, but it seems to have been a musical performance requiring some organisation. The audience announced the show was 'boring', they booed and pretended to fall asleep, and eventually the audience members turned to face each other in pairs and played a recent clapping game that had emerged on the playground, and then they vacated the seats. The 11 girls returned to their original set-up, and Anabel tried to organise the four Year Two girls into a planned performance (topic unclear), with responses of 'boring' from the audience. By unanimous agreement the play episode ended and the Year Two girls left, with Rachel announcing to the others 'we're going to do something different'.

Players who were interviewed explained the episode in different ways. There was general agreement that the Year Two girls were 'performing and pretending that it was the TV', and the Year Three and Reception girls were the audience of viewers. Different girls described the 'audience' of Year Three and Reception girls as 'queens of the forest and some kingdoms', 'queens and princesses', 'the audience' and a group 'eating dinner'. The reference to queens and princesses reflects the previous play episodes of one of the groups. The Year Three girls had a long history of playing chasing and catching games integrating characters such as fairies, witches and queens ('since Year One' according to some of the girls). However, not all 11 girls shared this history, and therefore, their interpretation of the situation varied, and the play episode evolved away from the family of queens and princesses.

In terms of the practices discussed in Part One of this chapter, the episode fits into both the hybrid/recontextualised and the ambiguously referenced categories. There were many different kinds of media referenced – TVs/DVD players, remote controls, 3D movies, musicals and books. The girls used characters, actions and props from media. At some points, the interaction between the groups of girls was similar to a TV talent contest with the judges sitting behind a table. Finally, the girls referred to the role of media in daily life – watching TV/movies whilst eating dinner and/or for entertainment and also pausing movies and switching channels. The range of 'writerly texts' children were drawing on demonstrates the difficulty of identifying an 'original' text (not least because of the variety of interpretations the girls related). Whilst individual girls may have had specific texts in their head during different points of the performance (e.g. a specific pirate visual, *High School Musical*, a TV talent contest), more likely the references were to general cultural practices and texts. If children are referring more to general cultural references, then this raises questions about classifying episodes such as this as 'media-referenced' play. Nevertheless, applying Appadurai's (1996) ideas, the general references draw on children's 'mediascapes' and incorporate the narratives that are embedded in a range of media, and therefore an analysis of these references provide insight into children's engagements within their mediascapes.

As discussed in Part One of this chapter, one question about the recontextualisation process concerns children's selection of texts which form the hybrid versions we saw on the playground. In this episode, the media which are referenced in the play are ambiguous and general enough to form an inclusive game. All of the children had experience of watching TV/movies and using a remote control; they had shared knowledge of plots involving pirates, queens and princesses; performing music was also part of their common experience provided by the school (and some of the children also watched musicals at home). Whilst the play was a hybrid/recontextualised practice (combining playground games of acting/singing, construction and pretend play with various media references), the media references were known by all the girls (e.g. DVD player with remote control, audiences watching TV) and/or ambiguous and general (e.g. pirates which may have referred to a specific portrayal of a pirate such as *Horrible History*'s Blackbeard, but more likely referred to girls' shared general knowledge about pirates), thus representing an ambiguously referenced practice.

In terms of function, the hybrid/recontextualised and ambiguously referenced play in some ways functions to create inclusivity. Anabel's suggestion of creating a scenario of an audience watching TV also allows these two different groups to play together. However, the media choices also function to position the two main year groups in opposition to each other. The Year Two group is charged with entertaining the Year Three group, first inside the confines of a television (restricting themselves to the constructed 'pirate ship'). The Year Two group then added the '3D' component to break out of the TV and 'scare' the audience, particularly through props from the pirate genre (guns and a large knife or sword). This functioned in a carnivalesque way to invert the power relationship (Bakhtin, 1984), with the formerly constrained actors on the TV literally leaving their box to dominate over the audience. In turn, the Year Three group added the remote control to attempt to pause the action and control the Year Two group. Screaming and laughing were part of the audience reaction, and the Year Two girls built on this chaotic moment of jouissance by pretending to be 3D grannies, thus taking over the control and ignoring the Year Three girls' demands to pause the action and/or return to the pirate movie. In switching roles, the Year Two girls added a critical judgment element to audience's role in the game (booing, acting bored), perhaps drawing on TV talent contests or more general references to audiences being displeased with a performance. The choices the girls made at each turn of the narrative drew on their mediascapes and served to negotiate and define their position as oppositional groups.

Finally, performativity in this episode is complex. In addition to the performances marking the different age groups, the girls are performing within discourses about gender (taking over the boys' space, performing first as dominant masculine characters and then as dominant feminine characters). Further, the episode engenders aspects of socio-dramatic role play in which the players are all taking on roles as part of a game involving an audience watching TV. However, there is a third type of performance – the theatric performance of the girls performing 'in the TV'. Across these different types of role play, the media elements created a framework which established and highlighted the pretence of the episode. The Year Two girls were not performing a pirate skit or a song for the other girls, they were performing a TV pirate skit and a TV musical, carrying the pretence further with the 3D and remote control elements. The Year Three girls pushed buttons on imaginary controls (whilst shouting 'pause'), and the Year Two actors 'froze' in their positions. If there was doubt that the Year Two girls were trying to scare or show serious aggression toward the other girls with their guns and long knives, these media elements served to highlight the pretence of the play. The media references also allowed the girls to move into a more chaotic or phantasmagoric form of play with the lunging guns, sudden 3D granny pastiche (as the TV switches to 3D and then switches channels) and the screaming/laughing audience desperate to pause and switch channels. However, when the girls added the element of judging, the pretence was less clear. Whilst parodic talent shows were performed on our playgrounds, we have no record of any of these girls involved in those performances. Further, in this episode they did not explicitly frame this segment as a TV talent show or a parody. Media could have been used to set the pretence (for example, they could have marked the change in play by saying 'let's pretend we're on *The X Factor*'). But without this pretence there was ambiguity, and perhaps this is the reason the play episode ended – because the booing was not clearly pretend and perhaps not experienced as such. As Sutton-Smith (1997) argues, 'play, like all other cultural forms, cannot be neutrally interpreted, it is impossible to keep ambiguity from creeping into the relationship between how they are perceived and how they are experienced' (216).

Conclusion

This chapter attempts to move beyond the perhaps obvious argument that media texts are being heavily mediated as they enter children's games on school playgrounds. Even with rare examples of closely imitative play, the context of the media performance is important in explaining a play episode and the role of a particular text in that episode. In some ways, there are no 'readerly texts' in children's play culture – children are always interpreting texts and practices in their play, and all texts and practices (media or otherwise) are 'writerly'. Remix culture on the playground involves selecting resources which work in the very specific context of a particular game. Playground games are thus practices of constant meaning making – children produce meaning from the variety of texts with which they engage in their remix culture. Importantly, the 'writerly texts' available to children are diverse, and include games such as cops and robbers, classroom topic work and media texts. Applying Bakhtin's theories, children select and combine elements of texts which fit their understanding of the social situation as well as their desire to act in that situation.

Throughout this chapter, I have emphasised the social functions of children's selection and recontextualisation processes. Although children draw on a variety of texts and practices, using elements which suit their games (elements which are flexible, transferrable, easy to learn and so on), some texts and practices have different currency amongst peer cultures. Games such as 'ring-a-ring a rosie' which are taught in preschool programmes are seen as 'babyish' by most of our playground children. Media provide resources for play, but they are not neutral resources; and remixing in this context involves numerous social structures. In some groups, knowledge of media might establish power relationships; in some circumstances, media might act as a way for children to perform or resist dominant subject positions. However, common knowledge of media references can act as an inclusive object of play; the pretence provided by media also provides ways of negotiating and subverting power and allowing space for moments of *jouissance* and phantasmagoria. Importantly, how media function depend on the social actors and the other structures on the playground. In our playgrounds, we saw children adapting media, creating hybrid/recontextualised and inclusive games which evolved with the players. Equally, as Chris Richards analyses in his chapter in this volume, media were acting to reinforce social divisions and questionable ideologies. Understanding children's remix play cultures, therefore, involves examining 'writerly texts' in specific social circumstances and analysing the many players and structures involved in and surrounding the play.

References

Appadurai A (1996) *Modernity at Large: Cultural Dimensions of Globalization.* Minneapolis: University of Minnesota Press.

Bakhtin MM (1981) Discourse in the novel. In Emerson C and Holquist M (eds) *The Dialogic Imagination: Four Essays by M.M. Bakhtin.* Austin: University of Texas Press, 259–422.

Bakhtin M (1984) *Rabelais and His World.* Bloomington: Indiana University Press.

Barthes R (1975a) *The Pleasure of the Text.* New York: Hill & Wang.

Barthes R (1975b) *S/Z.* London: Jonathan Cape.

Barthes R (1977) *Image-Music-Text.* London: Fontana.

Bishop JC and Burn A (2013) Reasons for rhythm: Multimodal perspectives on musical play. In Willett R, Richards C, Marsh J, Burn A and Bishop JC. *Children, Media and Playground Cultures: Ethnographic Studies of School Playtimes.* Basingstoke: Palgrave Macmillan, 89–119.

Bishop JC and Curtis M with Woolley H, Armitage M and Ginsborg J (2006) Participation, popular culture and playgrounds: Children's uses of media elements in peer play at school. Paper presented at the Folklore Society Conference, *Folklore, Film and Television: Convergences in Traditional Cultures and Popular Media*, 31 March–1 April 2006, London.

Butler J (1990) *Gender Trouble: Feminism and the Subversion of Identity.* New York: Routledge.

Dyson AH (1999) Coach Bombay's kids learn to write: Children's appropriation of media material for school literacy. *Research in the Teaching of English* 33: 367–402.

Edmiston B (2007) *Forming Ethical Identities in Early Childhood Play.* London: Routledge.

Goffman E (1959) *The Presentation of Self in Everyday Life.* New York: Anchor Books.

Grace D and Tobin J (2003) Pleasure, creativity and the carnivalesque in children's video production. In: Bresler L and Thompson C (eds) *The Arts in Children's Lives: Context, Culture, and Curriculum.* Dordrecht, The Netherlands: Kluwer Academic Publishers, 195–214.

Ito M (2008) Mobilizing the imagination in everyday play: The case of Japanese media mixes. In Livingstone S and Drotner K (eds) *The International Handbook of Children, Media, and Culture*. London: Sage, 397–412.

Lave J and Wenger E (1991) *Situated Learning: Legitimate Peripheral Participation*. Cambridge: Cambridge University Press.

Marsh J and Bishop JC (2013) Parody, homage and dramatic performances. In Willett R, Richards C, Marsh J, Burn A and Bishop JC. *Children, Media and Playground Cultures: Ethnographic Studies of School Playtimes*. Basingstoke: Palgrave Macmillan, 196–211.

Maybin J (in press) Evaluation in pre-teenagers' informal language practices around texts from popular culture. In Cekaite A, Blum-Kulka S, Grover V and Teubal E (eds) *Children's Peer Talk: Learning from Each Other*. Cambridge: Cambridge University Press.

Opie I and Opie P (1969) *Children's Games in Street and Playground*. Oxford: Clarendon Press.

Opie I and Opie P (1985) *The Singing Game*. Oxford: Oxford University Press.

Rampton B (2006) *Language in Late Modernity: Interaction in an Urban School*. Cambridge: Cambridge University Press.

Richards C (2011) In the thick of it: Interpreting children's play. *Ethnography and Education* 6: 309–24.

Sutton-Smith B (1997) *The Ambiguity of Play*. London: Harvard UP.

Willett R (2009) Parodic practices: Amateur spoofs on video sharing sites. In Buckingham D and Willett R (eds) *Video Cultures: Media Technology and Amateur Creativity*. Basingstoke: Palgrave Macmillan, 115–32.

Willett R (2011) An ethnographic study of preteen girls' play with popular music on a school playground in the UK. *Journal of Children and Media* 5: 341–57.

Willett R, Richards C, Marsh J, Burn A and Bishop JC (2013) *Children, Media and Playground Cultures: Ethnographic Studies of School Playtimes*. Basingstoke: Palgrave Macmillan.

Chapter 7
The Game Catcher:
A Computer Game and Research Tool
for Embodied Movement

Grethe Mitchell

I wish to gratefully acknowledge the work and assistance of Andy Clarke with whom I devised the *Game Catcher* application. Andy also programmed the *Game Catcher* and assisted with the technical aspects of this chapter, providing support and encouragement throughout – as well as invaluable feedback.

Introduction

Children's play inspired or influenced by popular media forms and content such as films, TV shows and pop music is described by Iona Opie in her preface to the 1984 edition of *Children's Games in Street and Playground*, and in *The People in the Playground* (1993: 211). Evidence of this from the children themselves can be heard in the original audio recordings, which provided much of the source material for the Opie publications (see Jopson et al, Chapter 2). Outdoor play influenced and inspired by videogames has been observed by Cross (2009) and was more recently observed both during the filming of *Ipidipidation My Generation*, the documentary (made by the author) as part of the project and by the researchers conducting the ethnographic study. Videogames as media culture are part of children's 'play-scape' in the twenty-first century, and it was therefore important that we engage with them in our research project, which partly aimed to update the previous research accomplished by the Opies as well as investigate children's play in the new media age.

Another aspect of our research project, also of concern to the Opies in their research, was to address the question of the transmission and transformation of playground games. The field research by the Opies was mainly conducted using audio recordings and written notes of observations. More recently, since the advent of smaller and easy-to-use cameras, ethnographic field observations and notes have been supplemented by video recordings. However, as we explain later in this chapter, both audio and video recording may lack fidelity, and transcription is generally time consuming and can potentially generate other problematic issues, such as consistency. The *Game Catcher* gave us an opportunity to also address these issues.

This chapter discusses the development of the *Game Catcher*, a combined motion tracking research tool and computer game, produced as an experimental cultural intervention with the aim of creating a new form of computer game and as a tool to assist and augment field research into children's movement, particularly the embodied movement of playground games and activities. It allows children to record movements of their clapping games (and to play against the recordings) and researchers to view these recordings from any angle and at any speed (adding, if they wish, other visualisation such as traces to show the paths of hands throughout the entire game). Like the other chapters in this book, the research described in this chapter is informed by the perspective pioneered by the Opies, of children's agency as cultural actors – creating, modifying, sustaining or discarding cultural expression and activities, including play activities.[1,2] One of our main objectives was to further this agency in the domain of computer games.

Computer games can be seen as both toys (objects for play) and media (mass representational and communicative systems). There is, as Corsaro states, no dispute about the fact that children are growing up immersed in media (2011: 126). In many (Western) households, children have their own television sets with a 2008 report[3] indicating that 79 per cent of children had a TV in their own room (33 per cent with access to multiple channels via digital transmission). Ownership of other media devices such as mobile phones, computers and game consoles are increasing amongst children, including younger age groups, with a survey conducted by Ipsos MORI for OFCOM indicating that 90 per cent of children aged 7–16 own or have use of a games console.[4] Video and computer games, played both on the web and on game consoles, have become an increasingly integral part of children's lives and leisure, in the same way that TV was for previous generations and movies before that,[5] with 5–16 year olds playing on average 1.5 hours of videogames per day.[6]

---

[1]   For example, Opie I and Opie P (1984) *Children's Games in Street and Playground.* Oxford: Oxford University Press, 16 and Opie I and Opie P (2001) *The Lore and Language of Schoolchildren.* New York: New York Review of Books, xxv–xxvi.

[2]   Later theorized as one of the tenets of the new sociology of childhood, by sociologists such as Corsaro, 2011; James, Jenks and Prout, 2010; James and James, 2004.

[3]   Children and Marketing Literature (final report), Alan France, Joanne Meredith, Graham Murdock, 2008 Available at https://www.education.gov.uk/publications/ eOrderingDownload/Appendix-H_Children-and-Marketing.pdf [Accessed 1st July 2012].

[4]   'Children's and young people's access to online content on mobile devices, games consoles and portable media players' p.2. Available at http://stakeholders.ofcom.org.uk/ binaries/research/media-literacy/online_access.pdf [Accessed 1st July 2012].

[5]   Also see Cunningham: 207 for description of cinema's importance for children in 1930s – in the UK at that time 4.5 million children went to the cinema every week.

[6]   Impact of Videogames (Houses of Parliament Parliamentary Office of Science and Technology Postnote number 405 March 2012) Available at http://www.parliament.uk/ briefing-papers/POST-PN-405.pdf [Accessed 1st July 2012].

Children's consumption of television, videogames and the Internet have provoked criticism and anxiety (for example, Postman, 1996 and Palmer, 2007), though the phenomenon of perceiving new technologies as having a negative influence is not new, with similar anxieties expressed in response to the arrival of film in the early twentieth century, television in the mid-twentieth century and video in the 1970s.[7] It would therefore seem that, rather than a particular technology being 'toxic', it is more a case that the arrival of any new form of technology causes adult anxiety about its effect on children, with videogames and the Internet being merely the latest examples of this. Paradoxically, and as Buckingham (2008: 41–57) outlines, there is also, at least in relation to recent media (television and computers), a countervailing utopian view that presents new technology as a positive development – though, as Buckingham points out, this is mainly in relation to their potential for education. In these arguments, one can perceive Sutton-Smith's 'rhetoric of progress' at work (2001: 35–40), with the developmental value of technologies – rather than their play or entertainment value – being foregrounded.

Computer games are a media and play phenomenon of the late twentieth and the twenty-first centuries. Away from the more adult environment of arcades, they were first introduced for domestic consumption in the 1970s[8] and have increased in popularity ever since. Videogame hardware (for example the Xbox, Wii, DS and Playstation) is both a technological and cultural artefact. Videogames are also complex cultural texts which combine narratives, characters, general game mechanics and conventions specific to video or computer games, as well as player agency or interaction – which influences the progression and outcome of the game. In addition, most computer games are also mass and popular culture commercial products – designed, produced and manufactured under the umbrella of large publishing or media content companies. Computer games are also often in a transmedial relationship with films, books and Internet content.[9] Henry Jenkins (2003) defines transmedia storytelling:

> [...] each medium does what it does best – so that a story might be introduced in a film, expanded through television, novels, and comics, and its world might be explored and experienced through game play. Each franchise entry needs to be self-contained enough to enable autonomous consumption. That is, you don't need to have seen the film to enjoy the game and vice-versa. As *Pokémon* does so well, any given product is a point of entry into the franchise as a whole.

---

[7]   Also see Cunningham: 206–7 on the alleged harmful effects of the picture house and the music hall in early 1900s.

[8]   The first domestic videogame, *Pong,* was released by Atari in 1975.

[9]   For example the Harry Potter series which traverses book, film and videogame; The Matrix brand which expanded across three films, comic books, videogames and short animations; or the *Pokĕmon* franchise whose properties include anime, manga, trading cards, toys, books, videogames and other media.

Computer games are now embedded in children's lives, both as a form of play and as a popular form of children's entertainment. As a form of mass culture, computer game play mechanics, content and characters have also become a further resource, along with films, popular music, television and books, upon which children draw (Curtis, 2001: 69; Burn, 2013) for the construction of identities, social grouping and status in the playground, to incorporate into their imaginative play (Cross, 2009), or to meld with other forms of more traditional playground activity such as racing games.[10] In video interviews with children from the two schools in our study,[11] videogame titles are mentioned as featuring in playground games (for example *Mario Kart, Pokémon, Call of Duty, Tekken*) along with other media such as films and TV shows.

Although prior to starting the project we did not know exactly to what extent computer or videogames would be part of the playground environment being studied, we nonetheless knew that, given the consumption statistics on computer games mentioned previously[12] and our acknowledgement of children's agency as participants and cultural actors within society, it was essential, as mentioned above, that a project engaging with children's playground games and culture also engaged with this increasingly important aspect of play in the lives of contemporary children.

Game Catcher: One Project, Two Aims

Aim One: Computer Game

The Circuit of Culture model outlined by Du Gay et al (1997) identifies the ways in which cultural artefacts and texts are embedded into the wider social and economic contexts through an analysis of the representation, identity, production, consumption and regulation of the artefact or text (e.g. the Sony Walkman). In our project, it may be more accurate for concepts such as *appropriation* and *play* to replace consumption, whilst retaining the same characteristics of a dynamically active relationship between production, appropriation/play and the wider socio-economic environment. This relationship also contributes to the production of meaning, with the player as an active and influential participant, rather than just a passive receiver of, for example, advertising or marketing messages. At the level

---

[10]   The racing videogame *Mario Kart* (Nintendo 2008) was popular amongst Y1 and Y2 children in the Sheffield school (participating in our research), who then used this as a resource for a playground racing game.

[11]   Interviews conducted by the author for the documentary film she made, on children's play and games (*Ipidipidation My Generation*, 2011).

[12]   Impact of Videogames (Houses of Parliament Parliamentary Office of Science and Technology Postnote number 405 March 2012) Available at http://www.parliament.uk/briefing-papers/POST-PN-405.pdf [Accessed 1st July 2012].

of the playground, this also means that children as players/appropriators exercise agency and choice over which texts are used and whether or how they are modified.

Of course, some videogames disallow or discourage forms of intervention, co-creation or misuse/alternative use. This contrasts with the myriad ways in which a child will use their physical toys – allowing a toy train, for example, to act variously as the barrel of a pretend gun, or part of a wall of a fort. Videogames, as a digital medium allowing interaction, should in theory be more flexible than the physical toy, but most are constrained in their use. So, for instance, in *Mario Kart* (Nintendo, 2008), there is no way for the player to design their own car or character, or modify the characteristics or behaviour of the car, or change the car into something else. They can only use those already defined in the game, and although they can drive off the track, the conventions of the game (that in a racing game there are checkpoints and time limits) and the constraints of this game (which limit how far one can drive off the track) both conspire to make such actions pointless. Some videogames – such as first person shooter (FPS) games like *Half Life 2* (Valve/Sierra, 2004) with its Valve Hammer Editor (Valve, 2003) – provide level and character editing tools, but these typically require a level of competence with computers beyond that of a young child of primary school age. One should be wary, however, of regarding this as an inevitability and seeing the lack of simple tools to create content for a computer game as being a direct and necessary result of the resources and skill needed to create the computer game in the first place.[13] After all, digital cameras and video camcorders are complex technology, yet are easy for a young child to use to produce their own content.[14]

One of the main research questions of the 'Playground Games and Songs in the New Media Age' project as a whole was 'what is the relationship between children's playground culture and their media culture?'. While acknowledging the extent and reach of commercial videogames in children's play, both as a play activity and as a cultural resource for other games and imaginary play, the team producing the *Game Catcher* nonetheless saw the opportunity to highlight, through this development, that while the content of commercial videogames feeds into children's play outside the domain of the game itself (see Cross 2009), the broader content of children's play doesn't feed, and indeed, because of the design of the games, deliberately cannot feed, into the videogame. The *Game Catcher* therefore gave the project an opportunity to investigate, through a process of research by practice, the possibilities of other forms of embodied computer game play, distinct from the available commercial genres. It also gave us the opportunity to investigate reversing the trajectory of videogame to playground – by bringing playground action into the domain of computer game play. It was described in Mitchell (2010) as:

---

[13]   See for example Burn (2007) and Jewitt (2008: 36).

[14]   See, for example The *Guardian* article: http://www.guardian.co.uk/lifeandstyle/2008/jan/19/familyandrelationships.zdontuseshopping [Accessed 1st July 2012].

an attempt to blur the boundaries between the computer game application as a play 'tool' for emerging game agency/activity generated by the players themselves, and the current role of the computer game as a vessel for received and pre-determined game content where agency and activity is defined and regulated by the pre-programmed application.

In specifying the aim of the *Game Catcher* project to formulate and build an alternative computer game for embodied movement that would provide opportunities for creating, recording, modifying and sharing game content, we acknowledged the current (successful) forms of commercial computer games, and did not intend to replace them. However, this was nonetheless an opportunity to investigate whether a more open-ended game system was possible, one that would enable them to 'capture', 're-play' and potentially share with others, the responsiveness, creativity, agency and re-fashioning that children bring to bear on all their embodied play (even rule-based and structured games). In essence, what we aimed to do was not to invent another form of game or game play on behalf of children, but to provide a form of open system which children could modify according to their own play imperatives, in the same way that a corner of empty park space or a piece of waste ground becomes, when they play there, whatever children want it to be.

Aim Two: Research Tool

In parallel with our first aim, the *Game Catcher* development team also wanted to engage with and address one of the supplementary research questions of the project as a whole, which was concerned with understanding the processes of transformation and transmission of playground games (particularly, though not exclusively, games combining routines of movement and song or rhyme, such as clapping games) and with tracking the evolution/mutation in the form and the content of games occurring over time. We aimed to do this by investigating possibilities for augmenting existing research methods.

The task of understanding processes of transformation and transmission – which necessarily involves a process of comparison, and is therefore distinct from that of documenting the format of a single game, in a single location, at a single moment in time – presents a number of practical difficulties. The first lies in identifying similarities between recordings in order to identify possible variants of a single game; the second arises in identifying the differences between games once two, or more, candidate variants have been shortlisted. Video is often used in folklore or ethnographic research (this was also the case with the research conducted for our project), and while this provides a convenient format for the initial recording of material in the field, the footage is not directly searchable and making it so typically involves manual transcription and indexing. In the case of clapping games, this indexing would need to cover both the words of the rhyme and the moves of the game as each would have to be independently searchable. This is because each can evolve independently of one another and it is possible for the same rhyme to be used with different moves, or for the same moves to be used with a different rhyme.

Transcribing the words of a clapping rhyme is time-consuming, but produces a searchable text, and a free-text search for a word or phrase (and alternate spellings) brings up matching songs. Textual comparison is also relatively straightforward as differing sections can be spotted by eye once the songs are put side by side.

Transcribing the movements of the clapping game is more difficult. Searching and shortlisting relies upon the movement being transcribed and indexed in a consistent, comprehensive and unambiguous form (which may be different to that in which it was captured) and a failure to do this could result in both false positives (wrongly identifying two games as being similar when they are not) and in false negatives (not identifying similarities). The latter is both more likely and more serious – more serious because it could exclude recordings from further analysis whereas the false positives, if they are wrongly included, can still be eliminated at a later stage. As Ann Hutchinson Guest says in her introduction to *Labanotation*:

> The handing down of detailed knowledge in any field requires a system of notation for recording pertinent facts in an unambiguous way. Comparisons can then be made, difference evaluated, new ground broken ... [T]he student of movement requires a method of notation in order to compare variations of the same movement pattern and reach conclusions that would not otherwise be possible. (Hutchinson Guest, 2005: 7)

The problem is that to be consistent, comprehensive and unambiguous, formal movement notation systems[15] require an extensive vocabulary of descriptors applicable or adaptable to every (significant) movement. This suggests two further issues. Firstly, the descriptors have to be learned, both by those transcribing the data and those accessing it, otherwise the system is unusable. Secondly, the need to be comprehensive (both in terms of what is described and the detail in which it is described) increases the time taken to transcribe the movement, and the verbosity of the description, once produced.

Folklore or ethnographic research typically relies on written notes made in the field or by using video, photo, sound recordings and so on, which are then subsequently transcribed to a less-formal textual description and as Elizabeth Grugeon says in relation to games featuring verbal and movement routines 'The written transcript can only be a pale reflection of a vibrant, three-dimensional performance' (2001: 101). To avoid the issues with formal notation systems, these descriptions may range from being 'semi-structured' (e.g. using an internally consistent terminology) to being completely free text, but even these raise their own problems. For example, Bishop in her paper for the project's Interim Conference (2010: 3–5), refers to one gesture as a 'three way clap' and while this term is used consistently within her article, and may be fully understood by other

---

[15]   Although this paper refers to Labanotation, the same issues apply to other dance/ movement notation systems, such as Benesh notation.

specialists, there is no guarantee that researchers outside of this domain would necessarily use the same descriptor, or even regard it as one gesture, rather than three separate moves. One could therefore imagine that a search across articles by different authors in different domains, for example for the purposes of comparing versions of a clapping game, would not uncover all instances of where this move had been described.

In addition to the issues related to transcribing and searching, there were also those of how to identify the differences between games. If, as in the project ethnographic study, video has been used to record the games (such as the different versions of 'Eeny Meeny Dessameeny' recorded by Bishop 2010), then the two recordings could be viewed side by side, but this process could be complicated by the fact that the pace (or tempo) of the two games might often be different – sometimes also using different rhymes, or the same rhyme sung at a different pace or the addition of different movement elements (as was the case in Bishop's paper) – and this will cause the two recordings to constantly go out of sync. If some other transcription or notation format is used – such as Labanotation or textual descriptions – then difficulties may arise owing to the degree of accuracy with which the original movement was documented and/or can be reconstructed.

One could regard this as being the trade-off between existing systems for documenting movement, but the development of the Game Catcher provided us with an opportunity to overcome such a trade-off. Thus our second aim was to develop the Game Catcher as a research tool to augment these systems, by introducing motion capture as a complementary method for capturing and analysing movement. For instance, using a motion capture system to record an original movement directly would minimise the loss in fidelity involved in each layer of translation – bearing in mind that even video loses fidelity as it just records the image of the movement, rather than the actual movement, whereas a motion capture system numerically records the position in space (in three dimensions or axes) of allocated parts of the body, such as head, shoulders, torso, hips, arms, hands, legs, feet and so on. As we later demonstrated,[16] the recorded numerical data of the sequence could then be attached to a 3D model to allow visualisation and animation of the recorded movement in 'real time' or at different speeds (for instance paused, slowed down or speeded up). The visualisation can be seen in three dimensions, thus allowing for viewing the movement from all angles including from directly overhead or from beneath the 'floor' on which the movement takes place. Movement viewed from this selection of angles can provide useful data not otherwise available. The captured 3D data can be used to animate any type of model – from a stick figure to a photo-realistically rendered human figure. This can be useful where it is necessary to preserve the anonymity of the subjects –

---

[16]   At the Project Final Conference held at the British Library in March 2010, the Movement Capture in the Arts and Humanities Symposium held at the London Knowledge Lab in January 2012 and the ESRC/NCRM-funded MODE seminar at Newcastle University in May 2012.

for instance when working with children where video and photography may be disallowed – but could also be relevant to other situations or purposes (for instance in the production of fictional narratives or artworks). The animation is an accurate reconstruction of the original movement unlike, say, Labanotation, where there may be some degree of interpretation involved in both directions (going both from the movement to the written form and from the written notation back to movement).

The process of transcription can also be automated with a motion capture system such as the *Game Catcher*, with significant poses, gestures or sequences (e.g. hand claps) being identified by the speed at which limbs are moving (or moments when they are stationary), the relative position of body parts or the extension of limbs, the frequency with which similar poses are adopted (see, for instance, Hachimura 2006). Simpler analysis (the identification of hand claps) was later implemented as part of the *Game Catcher* proof of concept prototype and included in our demonstrations of the application.[17] Similar processes could also, in theory, be used to automate the comparison of captured sequences, thus assisting manual processes of comparison, such as those performed by Bishop (2010). Such analysis or comparison in body positions is easier with motion capture data than with video recorded data, as extracting information on the body position from an arbitrary frame of video is a non-trivial task in itself (bearing in mind the potential for occlusion of one body part by another or problems with interpretation due to focus or lighting, for instance). Furthermore, unlike video, motion capture data can be compared or analysed numerically, thus allowing for automated computational analysis which in this case is both more accurate and less time-consuming than manual comparison or analysis by eye.

It is worth repeating that the *Game Catcher* was not designed to replace other methods of data recording, transcription or analysis. It is acknowledged that writing and visual recording (in still or moving images) can provide information that cannot be furnished by motion capture alone. For instance, motion capture cannot provide a description of the context in which movement takes place, unlike video, photography or the written word, nor can it provide interpretation. Motion capture also has some technical constraints, although these are being minimised as the technology improves. However, as described above and as we have demonstrated, motion capture systems provide an excellent means for *augmenting* (rather than replacing) other methods of recording, transcribing and analysing movement.

Game Catcher: Design Issues

As outlined briefly in our introduction and discussed in more detail above, our intention with the *Game Catcher* was to produce a combined motion tracking research tool and computer game. As already discussed (Mitchell and Clarke, 2011b), there were synergies between these two aims of the *Game Catcher* as a

---

[17]   See footnote 16 above.

videogame and as a motion capture/analysis tool, and they were, at a very deep level, closely related. The two functions of computer game and research tool formed a virtuous circle with the products of one feeding into the content of the other (e.g. the motion capture data from the computer game potentially becoming data for the researchers using it as a visualisation/analysis tool), but other more subtle interrelationships and overlaps also existed. Combining the two functions meant, for example, that for the *Game Catcher* to be useful as a research tool, it also had – in its function and implementation *as a game environment* – to enable free-form embodied play as there would be little benefit, in its function *as a research tool*, in capturing the movements of a tightly constrained game. For example, a 'bemani' videogame like *Dance Dance Revolution* (Konami, 1998) – which has a set of pre-determined and unmodifiable dance routines – features plenty of foot movement on the part of the player, but as the sequences are pre-defined the player (using their feet to hit touchpads on the floor and match patterns on the screen) only has a limited set of movements to accomplish. This means that, although such a (fixed) game could be created in the *Game Catcher*[18] or recorded with it, there is little benefit (from a research point of view) in tracking the movements of the players during such games, as they will only be minor variations on a pre-defined set of moves in which both the foot positions and the timing of the moves are constrained by the structure of the game.

For the initial iterations of the *Game Catcher*, we decided to adopt a clapping game format. This was useful for a number of reasons: clapping games were a popular feature of the two playgrounds in our participant schools (played mainly by girls, but also, particularly in the London school, by some boys); they provide a recognisable structure with a clear beginning and end; they are commonly modified and varied by children; they are easily repeatable. Clapping games were also, we felt, adaptable for the game hardware we were using at this initial stage of development (the Nintendo Wii). In addition, selecting a clapping game for the *Game Catcher* had useful synergies with the other aspects of the project which also featured research into these games (e.g. Bishop, 2010), as well as with previous research by the Opies (e.g. 1985: 440–77) and others (e.g. Arleo, 2001: 115–32; Grugeon, 2001: 99–114; Roud, 2010: 296–333).

In considering which game to select, we also had to consider other important issues: for instance, which elements of the playground game could be carried across to the computer game and which could not (or did not need to be). In addition, we had to think very consciously about the formal and implicit structures, forms and conventions of the selected playground game and which could be dropped, substituted or translated to the computer game environment. This included thinking about the particularities of virtual worlds and virtual play, and how these would affect or influence the transfer of the physical, embodied game into a virtual environment, where the player is effectively 'disembodied'.

---

[18]   There were requests for this type of game from children in our testing sessions (which we discuss later in this chapter) and although our timescale prohibited its implementation at that time, this could be enabled in a future iteration.

Multimodality and Transduction

Multimodality theory was useful to us in thinking through these issues. We consider both playground games and computer games to be multimodal forms (Kress and Van Leeuwen, 2010: 2–7), meaning that they each combine more than one semiotic 'mode' or system, in the making of meaning. As Kress and Jewitt state:

> *mode* is used to refer to a regularised organised set of resources for meaning making, including image, gaze, gesture, movement, music, speech and sound-effect (Kress and Jewitt, 2008: 1, author's italics)

Modes are the 'material stuff of signs' and 'central in giving form to meaning' (Kress 2010: 155). I would add that they are also central to imparting meaning, as different modes have inherently different material and cultural properties for meaning making. Kress' description of the 'translation' of a text (in our case, the clapping game) from one combination of modes (or multimodal form) to another, is defined as 'transduction': 'the shift of semiotic material […] across modes' (2009: 36) – a concept we found very useful in theorizing this aspect of our development. Unlike the concept of 'transformation' (which in multimodality terms is the remaking of a sign in the same mode as the original sign, for example remaking a typed text into a handwritten text or vice versa – both using the writing mode), *transduction* is the remaking of a sign or collection of signs in a mode other than the mode in which the original was made (such as playground game to computer game). However, like literary translation or film adaptation, transduction is *not* a transparent process. Each mode carries with it both culturally determined and inherent significations and assumptions – the many different (culturally determined and understood) conventions (for example, grammars) of the modes, and inherent differences in the 'materiality' of the modes (for example that film has frames, computers are digital, speech and music are sound). These therefore imply that transduction has an accompanying and often profound 'transformative effect' on the (transducted) text. It can therefore be seen that our aim of moving a game from a physical to a virtual environment and from an embodied to a disembodied form of play was likely to be highly transformative of our selected clapping game.

An early indication of transformation was the realisation of the importance of touch in the embodied physical version of the clapping game. Clapping games rely on a combination of touch and sound (e.g. the rhyme or song and the sound of the claps) for establishing harmony and synchronicity between the two players. For example, if the first player in the physical version is slightly off the beat, or slow – then a combination of touch (or a lack of touch), sound (or lack of) from the other player will provide feedback, which can then be used to make a correction. Whilst the computer game could provide sound and visual feedback at the point of clap (and this was implemented for the *Game Catcher*) it could not provide touch, and therefore an important part of this complex combination of physical modalities would not be available for the player using the computer version of the clapping game. The above discussion highlights one big difference between physical and virtual environments: the presence and absence of embodiment. Embodiment is an important issue in the design of any human computer interaction, including computer games. Firstly both our sensory perception and our cognition is embodied – the body is the site of reception, interpretation and comprehension of stimuli (whether purely sensory or symbolic). Secondly, computer game systems are essentially simulations in a virtual environment that is devoid of the constraints of physics or of the flesh, and where the results of sensory input from the physical world via the body need to be simulated. Thus we have a situation in computer games, where the human player interacts with a system that is required to simulate experiences that make phenomenological sense to the players, in order for interaction to be both comprehensible and enjoyable. Interaction design is therefore the design of the relationship between embodied and disembodied experience.

Affordance

These differences in embodied experience can also be seen to be a result of the difference in 'affordance' between the environments and modes of the physical and virtual clapping games. The term 'affordance' was invented by the perceptual psychologist J.J. Gibson (Norman, 1999) and refers to the actionable properties between the world and an actor (a person or animal). In multimodality theory, the term 'affordance' defines the inherent qualities of the range of materials for making meaning (Kress and Jewitt 2008: 13–15). Affordances also pertain to modes:

> Modal affordance has a physical, material side (the material features of a mode) and it has a social, cultural, historical side (what has been done in the past with this material, and how the meanings made in the past affect what can be done with a mode). (Kress and Jewitt, 2008: 15)

Although conceptually similar, affordances applied to a virtual world system (such as a computer game simulation) are somewhat different to those of the physical world. For instance, if one considers a virtual game world (leaving aside emergent or deliberate modifications), the potential agency of one's avatar (the player's in-game character or presence) is only governed by the rules of the game (built into the system) and by what Norman (1999) calls 'perceived affordances' (in this case, the *virtual* actionable behaviours and properties designed into the game world). There is no actual embodiment, physical ability or gravitational force to affect or constrain actionable relationships between the virtual world and the player's avatar and all 'game' constraints and actionable behaviours (affordances) are designed (leaving aside the constraints inherent in the computer system such as the software and/or hardware). In the physical world, actionable relationships are governed by all manner of properties both of the world and of the actors, such as the laws of physics, materials, configuration, size, shape, age and physical ability. For example, one of the affordances of hands, is that they can be used to clap.

The concept of affordance was therefore useful to us in addressing the differences between the physical and virtual clapping games, including the particularities of the physical and virtual worlds, and of the clapping game pertaining to each, such as the issue of embodiment/disembodiment. It was also useful in making choices about which elements of the playground game could, or could not, be carried over to the computer game, and deciding how much of the physical world (and its affordances) could or should become part of the virtual world of the clapping game. For example, for the *Game Catcher* we agreed that, to facilitate comprehension and ease-of-use, certain features of the physical game would need to be reproduced, such as hands, whereas others such as arms and faces, could be omitted.

Of course there are also other issues to consider in relation to the difference in affordances between the environments and modes of the physical and virtual clapping games – such as how the properties of the physical world environment (in which the physical game takes place) affects or influences the game, and therefore also the design of the virtual environment, as well as the game play within it. In general terms, these considerations might include the affordances of seasons and weather (for example does rain afford a certain type of game and sunshine another; are some games only played in winter) or the affordances of certain objects or props such as the texture and hardness of a wall; the bounce-ability of a ball and as we have already discussed – the affordances of hands (for example that they can be clapped together).

Props are not necessary in a physical clapping game; it requires only players and the game can take place in most physical environments. As discussed above, the environment of a virtual game can be whatever is selected as appropriate (for whatever reason) – as the virtual environment does not have to obey any physical laws. However, considerations such as comprehensibility, ease-of-use and importantly, *playability*, will in effect, provide affordances for the virtual game environment. For example, given the performative nature of clapping games their game mechanics lie mostly in achieving harmony and synchronicity between players whilst performing movement and song or rhyme. Clapping games therefore do not rely on complex visual or behavioural structures or representations to make them playable and enjoyable in a virtual world. In designing the virtual environment for the clapping game, we needed to provide a means for the player(s) to see and hear the effect of their clapping, but for instance, we did not have to provide a complex 2D or 3D world or complex game objects. In fact the visual environment of the computer game could be relatively simple and sparse, as the important aspects of the clapping game lie in the action of clapping, accompanied by song and rhyme. To ensure optimum playability, we did however, have to ensure that the on-screen visualisation of clapping did not have 'lag' in relation to the clapping of the physical players. We also had to ensure that the visualisation of the hands could replicate the type of individual hand orientations found in most clapping games (see Figure 7.1) as well as ensuring that the movements linked together in sequence (as happens in the physical game).

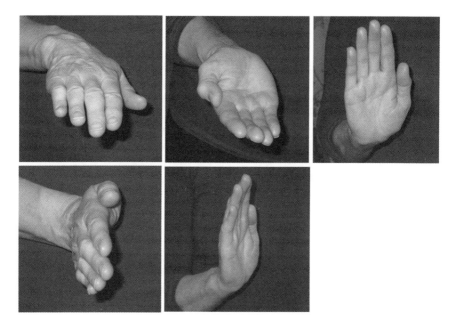

Fig. 7.1   Individual hand orientations for clapping games

Also, in designing a virtual clapping game there has to be consideration and evaluation of the physical affordances of game consoles, input devices, screens and other peripherals – as well as their positioning, portability and accessibility. For example, the *Game Catcher* clapping game was initially developed using two Wiimotes (one for each hand) which children had to hold. Effectively, the children used the Wiimotes as 'proxy' hands – in that they held the console devices to perform the clapping routine, standing in front of a screen, on which the users saw images of two hands. The Wiimotes (proxy hands) functioned as input devices to the game system – signalling when a clap occurred (this being when the two Wiimotes came together within a certain range of speed and axis) which was then represented aurally (as a clap sound) and visually (two cartoon hands clapping) on a screen, in real time (as the movement occurred). Although the use of the Wiimotes fulfilled some of the clapping functions very well such as providing the orientation of the hands, we did have problems with the size of the devices relative to the size of some children's hands and the movements we required from them, so for some children it was difficult to perform the clapping movements whilst holding the Wiimotes. Here the physical affordances of small hands constrained certain movements and one of the physical affordances of the Wiimotes – their size – made them unsuitable for certain children. Our solution to this problem, which we did not have time to implement, was to design small wearable replacements for the Wiimotes which would provide the required orientation-sensing functionality, but would not require holding, as they could be worn on the hands.

Conventions

Finally and in order for the physical clapping game to make sense as a virtual clapping game, we needed to consider and evaluate the 'real world' conventions and contexts of the selected game and how these might translate from a physical to virtual environment (which also has its own conventions). For the design expert Donald Norman (1999), conventions are constraints that encourage some activities and prohibit others, they require a community of practice, they evolve slowly, are slow to be adopted and once adopted, are slow to disappear – multimodality theory has a similar definition for conventions in relation to modes discussed in Kress and Jewitt (2008: 13–14). In relation to interaction design and virtual environments, Norman sees cultural conventions as 'cultural constraints' – defined as learned conventions shared by a cultural group. For instance, the choice of actions involved in scrolling (moving the mouse towards the right hand side of a graphic, clicking and holding, and dragging the mouse downwards) are arbitrary in the sense that alternative actions that fit equally well to human cognition could be used and there is therefore nothing inherent in the device or design that requires the system to act in this way, other than an established cultural convention. For the *Game Catcher*, this meant identifying the conventions of the clapping game, so that these aspects of the physical playground game would be recognisable and coherent in the virtual environment. One way of doing this involves creating visual similarities between physical and virtual; however this is not necessarily required and even if done, may not be sufficient. For instance, the set of hands for the virtual clapping game did not have to be 'realistic' so long as the players understood that the on-screen objects were doing what hands in the physical world do. Likewise, the game would not be comprehensible if, even where the hands were rendered photo-realistically, the conventions of the clapping game were ignored. A *coherent* (as opposed to realistic) match from physical to virtual also acts as a means of implementing a short-cut to comprehension (on the part of the player) of how the game works and what actions are required – and therefore lessens the steepness of the initial learning curve for the game (this also relates to our previously discussed objective of ensuring that the game we created had sufficient points of reference to be familiar to the children without excessive explanation). Of course, conventions also exist in computer games and human-computer interaction generally and it would therefore be necessary for the design of our system to also make sense in terms of these conventions.

In order to comply with our stated aim of wanting to minimise creating a totally new set of conventions that children would have to learn, the interaction design of the *Game Catcher* complied with a number of existing conventions. For example, we provided a pair of hands which, although cartoon-like (and therefore not realistic), were sufficiently recognisable in look and behaviour to provide coherence in terms of the conventions of clapping game action. We also complied with conventions of interaction design by providing a menu from which players or users could select a number of options by means of clicking on the 'button' or option label (for example record, playback, analyse). Other commands (such as start, stop) used the buttons on the Wiimotes (game controllers), another convention with which children are mostly familiar. Also, in the initial iteration we had a scoring system which counted the number of claps and presented the total at the end of the game, and thus introduced into the game play a familiar convention of computer games which was recognised and referred to by numerous children in the interviews conducted after one of the testing sessions.

Game Catcher: Implementation

Our aim in developing a videogame adapted from or inspired by children's playground games, (coupled with the second aim of developing a research tool for capturing movement) led us to consider motion-sensitive videogame hardware such as the Nintendo Wiimote, as this approach, possibly combined with video tracking[19] would allow us to reduce – though not entirely eliminate – the adaptations needed to transfer the physical game to the virtual. In addition, using motion tracking also allowed us to more easily explore issues of physicality and embodiment in the playground game and the videogame, and because of this, had advantages over a game using a keyboard/mouse or a conventional, hand-held, 'D pad' gaming controller. The use of motion tracking also enhanced the synergies with the other research questions on transmission, particularly if transmission is understood as a multimodal process involving multiple modes of communication, such as speech, music/rhythm, movement and gesture.[20]

Existing motion capture solutions such as those by Vicon[21] and Animazoo[22] were available. These were, however, expensive and required a substantial degree of skill to set up and operate properly and whilst they would (if one ignores the expense and degree of skill) be very suitable for capturing and visualising movement – they would not have been suitable for our aim of creating a computer game system that could be used and modified by children.

Methodology

Our development methods consisted of a combination of strategies from computer application development and the social sciences (particularly childhood studies) in relation to research with children. Methods involving children were child-centred (James et al, 2010: 188–91; Punch, 2002) and included the use of drawings,

---

[19]   The Kinect was not available at the start of the project, but once released, it replaced the video tracking.

[20]   See for example, Kress and Jewitt, 2008; Kress, 2009; Kress and Van Leeuwen, 2010; Kress, 2010.

[21]   Vicon, http://www.vicon.com/products/system.html. [Accessed 7th April 2012].

[22]   Animazoo. Available from http://www.animazoo.com/products. [Accessed 7th April 2012].

observations, video-recorded group interviews and discussions, video recording of user-testing and group feedback sessions. This approach to research with children accords with other work involving young people, such as Punch (2002); Lundy and McEvoy (2012); White et al (2010).

The methods for the computer application followed an iterative 'agile' model of prototype development. This is in contrast to a more formal model of software development in which a large proportion of the development cycle is given to designing the specification prior to development. An iterative model of software development entails rapid prototyping and testing of the application in a continual cycle of development and testing, the results of which are then fed back into the next iteration and so on. The term 'agile' implies a development cycle that is responsive to feedback from users, rather than following a strict pre-determined plan, and where the development is emergent.[23] This method suited the innovative and experimental *Game Catcher* development, as we were, to some extent, venturing into uncharted waters.

Drawing on the new sociology of childhood,[24] children were seen as active participants in the research. The children involved in the study were either members of the school council (selected by their peers and teachers) or were selected for participation by teachers. A rigorous ethical procedure ensured a system of informed consent and an unconditional right of withdrawal by children and their parents or guardians, as well as by school staff. Children in the study were invited to have a view on and actively participate in research (if they wished to). For instance children from both schools participated in workshops to determine the classification of games for the British Library website of the project (*Playtimes: A Century of Children's Games and Rhymes*)[25] as well as contributing to the content. Children also participated in collecting data for the project by, for instance, videoing their play and games (with easy to use Flip cameras) for the ethnographic study. For the *Game Catcher* section of the project, children were invited to contribute comments and suggestions on the development of the computer game application. They were also invited to test sessions where they had a chance to try out the development. This was followed by workshop sessions where they could provide feedback on aspects of the game design and experience if they wished. During these sessions children contributed suggestions on which games could be added to the *Game Catcher* repertoire, both in group video interviews and in drawings.

[23] For more information on the 'Agile Movement', see www.agilemanifesto.org and www.agilealliance.org. [Accessed 4th April 2012].

[24] See for example, Corsaro, 2011; James, Jenks and Prout, 2010; James and James 2004.

[25] Available from http://www.bl.uk/playtimes [Accessed 4th April 2012].

Development

As discussed above, the *Game Catcher* was produced through an iterative process and we developed a number of versions, experimenting with various alternative technical solutions. Though this is not a technical paper, it is nonetheless useful to outline, in the briefest possible terms, some of these practicalities. (Those interested in the technical aspects of the project are directed towards Mitchell and Clarke, 2011; 2012; 2013 which focus more on these areas.)

Concentrating development of the *Game Catcher* (at least during its initial stage) on clapping games was a relatively straightforward decision, for the reasons explained earlier in this chapter. It was, however, also appropriate from a technical point of view, as it uses a relatively small, static, play space and has conventions regarding the type of movements used. This is not to say that the *Game Catcher* was free of technical difficulties as the fast pace of the movements and the potential for occlusion (one body part being obscured by another) are both examples of issues presented by this type of game.

We originally envisioned the project using Nintendo Wiimote controllers for the clapping game and we produced a number of versions using this technology alone. However, the release of the Microsoft Kinect controller later on in the period of the project meant that we eventually switched to a 'hybrid' solution which used technology from these two rival games companies: the Wiimote (for the Nintendo Wii console) and the Kinect controller (for the Microsoft Xbox). The reason for this was that the Kinect is motion *tracking*, whereas the Wiimotes are just motion *sensitive*. In other words, the Kinect can tell the position of the user's hand in 3D space, whereas the Wiimote can only tell that the hand is moving and give an indication of its direction and orientation. This made it easier to design the detection of when hands were clapping – something which had been problematic using the Wiimotes alone.

In addition to improving the clapping game; the release of the Kinect also gave us options to develop a full body motion capture version of the *Game Catcher* – which could function both as game and a more free-form play space in which movement of the entire body (and not just the hands) could be recorded and played back (in addition to its second function as a research tool).

By the end of the project we were able to develop two versions of the *Game Catcher* prototype, both using the Kinect and (one or more) Wiimotes. The first is a single-player version, optimised for clapping games, that uses the Kinect to track the player's hands in space and a Wiimote controller held in each hand to track their orientation. The captured movement is seen in 'real time' as it occurs, by means of an on-screen stick figure with oversized hands (see Figure 7.2). Both the movement and the audio are captured and can be played back in sync. The second version is optimised for free-play and allows 'whole body' movements of up to four players to be tracked and captured in real time over an area of around 6 square metres, the maximum range for the Kinect (this area is represented on-screen as a simple virtual 'play-space' that subtly references the playgrounds of

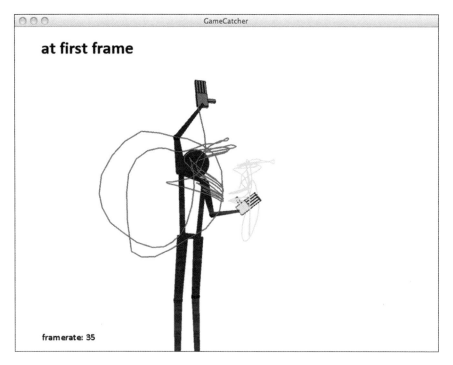

Fig. 7.2　　Trace visualisation using the Kinect for the full body skeleton and Wiimotes for hand orientation

the participating schools). As with the single-player, the movement data and audio is captured and can be played back. A single Wiimote is used, but only to navigate the menus for selecting different modes (record, playback, etc.). This is because a number of issues make it difficult to do the hand orientation tracking with multiple users – these include the quantity of data produced and the issue of knowing which hand orientation data corresponds to which on-screen user. Both versions allow the recording (both movement and audio) of any previous game to be played back. With the single player version, this playback is also 'mirrored' and in close up, allowing the user (or anyone else) to play the clapping game against their recording, if they wish (this mode can also detect when the player claps hands with their recording). It also offers other visualisation and analysis facilities, such as allowing the playback to be rotated and viewed from any angle or adding overlay lines tracing the path of the hands throughout the whole game. The multiplayer version also allows playback of any previous recording, which can likewise be rotated to any angle and zoomed in/out. The analysis options (traces of hands, etc.) were not implemented during the course of the project, owing to the added complexity of doing this for multiple on-screen figures, but this has been added subsequently. The 'mirrored' playback was likewise not implemented during the project (due to the lesser focus on clapping games in this version), but is being added as part of the process of merging the functionality and underlying code of the two versions. This process has been started in the AHRC-funded *Beyond Text* follow-on project 'The Theory, Practice and Art of Movement Capture and Preservation: An Interdisciplinary Investigation'[26] which focuses more specifically on movement capture and it is hoped that funding to develop this further will become available at a later stage.

Testing and Findings

Testing

Testing of initial iterations took place with children from both schools. These were recorded on two video cameras running continuously throughout the test session. One camera focused on the child doing the user-testing and the second camera was focused on the screen. This allowed comparison to be made between the actions on the screen and those of the child (for example using video editing software to present the information from both cameras, synchronised together on one screen). After testing, children participated in group interview sessions where they provided feedback on a number of aspects, including the quality and difficulty of the game play, the ease-of-use of the controllers and their feelings on the overall experience. Children also participated in group sessions where they made drawings about the game including suggestions of alternative or additional games, suggestions for the screen (interface) design and suggestions about the overall experience (see Figure 7.3).

Children's interviews and drawings demonstrated a high level of familiarity with the conventions of videogame and computer game interaction. All the children appeared to enjoy making the hands clap together, and also enjoyed the contest of getting more claps than their companion (see Huizinga's definition of play as 'tense' due to competition (1955: 11); and Caillois's inclusion (2001: 14) of competition (agôn) in his classification of the basic attitudes of play. During the interviews, when asked for improvements, one boy suggested the controllers be turned into 'sensors' to be placed on various parts of the body (knees, elbows etc.) so that these would trigger interaction. A number of children asked for the controllers to be made smaller so that they could hold them more easily (see our discussion of this aspect in the section on design issues). Overall, children appeared to be very confident about how screen interfaces worked, and did not find it difficult to follow their actions on screen. Most children seemed to find it easy adapting to the requirements of the virtual clapping game, even though technical issues at

---

[26] For more information on the project see: http://projects.beyondtext.ac.uk/playground-games-fol/index.php [Accessed 1st July 2012] and Mitchell G (2014 forthcoming).

Fig. 7.3   Children's drawings of suggested additional games

the time of these initial tests made the clapping quite difficult to achieve. Some children even perceived this as a challenge, treating it as if it was a difficult level in a conventional computer game, rather than a technical problem – see for instance, the discussion on opposition and antithesis even in solitary games by Avedon and Sutton-Smith 1971: 7 or the discussion by Juul (2005: 92) on quality videogame play as the provision of challenging choices. Nevertheless, despite the children's enthusiasm, the test session highlighted the difficulties with the technology used in that particular iteration, and spurred us on to a better solution for achieving more user-friendly movement tracking.

Although the participating schools were exceedingly helpful in providing time, access and assistance, arranging the availability of groups of children within busy school time-tables was a difficult task and this impacted to some extent on the type and quantity of testing that could be done. Overall a total of around 90 children took part in four user testing sessions (two in London and two in Sheffield), with most sessions lasting about four hours, and individual testing lasting approximately 15 minutes per child.

The testing session for the multiplayer *Game Catcher* took place in Sheffield (in February 2011), at the Children's Conference for the project as a whole. Three main activities were scheduled for the children during the day. About 50 children in total were present at the conference from both schools in the project, although there were fewer children from the London school than from the Sheffield school. The children were divided into three groups of about 15 to 20 children, with each group rotated in turn through three activity sessions, one of which was the *Game Catcher*. Because of the scheduling of this event, and the relatively short amount of time allocated to each workshop session, it was necessary to run the user tests in a 'tag team' format, with two children using it at a time and swapping for another pair after a few minutes. We felt that it was most useful to us – and enjoyable for the children – to allow each one to have a go on the *Game Catcher*, even if this was only for a brief period, rather than to just do a demonstration of the system or only allow a few of the children to use it.

This session was not, however, only a user test to see how much the children liked the *Game Catcher*. At the time, it was still under very active development, with the pace being driven not only by our desire to improve it and make it as complete and engaging as possible before the test, but also by the rapid evolution of the open source Kinect libraries that the *Game Catcher* development was using at that time. As a result, we were using this session to also test technical aspects of the project. At the time, we were not even sure that the Kinect would be able to reliably recognise and track the smaller children. Another concern was whether the children would be able to adopt the so-called 'psi' pose (a 'hands up' calibration position that the Kinect uses to allow it to recognise the player and start tracking them as a skeleton, rather than a silhouette). A further concern, specific to the format required for this user testing session, was whether the *Game Catcher* would handle the throughput of users, with so many swapping in and out so quickly.

Because the pace of this testing session meant that we could not perform a formal structured interview with the participants nor question them beforehand to ascertain their current baseline familiarity with videogames, we adopted a more rapid, lightweight and informal process for gathering feedback. The participants were invited to give their feedback on extra large 6×4 'Post-it' notes, which they then stuck to the wall (see Figure 7.5). This technique allowed us to gain a wide range of feedback very quickly and with little intervention. It also meant that the feedback was direct from the source and was also relatively free from influence – either from us as organisers and figures of authority or due to peer pressure from one participant to another. The children were free to add whatever comments they wished, but we encouraged feedback in a number of distinct areas:

1. Their views on, and rating of, the *Game Catcher*
2. Their suggestions on the *Game Catcher* (improvements, etc.)
3. Ideas for games to play in or with the *Game Catcher*

The test area itself was a large room (normally used as a café area) in the children's conference venue, an arts cinema complex in central Sheffield. Space (about 10 square metres) had been made in the centre of the room by clearing tables from this area, although tables remained in the surrounding space on either side. We were able to use a light coloured wall as a screen on which to project a large image showing the virtual game area for the *Game Catcher*. Children were ushered into the space and they lined up along one side of the room to await their turn to have a go. This meant that (unlike in other sessions) the children performing the tests were also observed by the other children in the room who were waiting their turn. Children mainly performed the test alongside their friends or peers; however

Fig. 7.4   Testing the full body multiplayer version of the *Game Catcher*.
             Photograph by Chris Richards

at times children volunteered to perform with other children they did not know
or hadn't met until the conference. It is perhaps a measure of their interest in
the project that most children overcame any shyness from performing alongside
someone they hadn't met before.

The layout and organisation of the space had both positive and negative
aspects. On the positive side, the layout of the space was useful, as those waiting to
use the *Game Catcher* could watch the other participants using it, and this reduced
the need to explain aspects of the game – such as the calibration pose – to the later
users in the group. The downside was, however, that some children were nervous
about using the *Game Catcher*. From speaking to participants at the time, concerns
about the openness of the space – and consequently about performing in front of
peers – were a factor in this nervousness. It is possible, however, that in at least
some of the cases, it was an anxiety about technology (or possibly an aversion
to it learnt from parents etc.), rather than a nervousness about the space or about
performing in front of strangers, but many factors – including the pace of the testing
sessions, the structure of the groups, a lack of knowledge of each child's previous
experience with videogame technology and an inability to question participants
systematically and in depth at the time – prevented us exploring this issue further.
It is possible, in retrospect, that a better layout for further testing sessions may be

one like that for the virtual reality artwork *Osmose* by Char Davies (exhibited at the Barbican in London in 1997). This provided a silhouette of the (in this case, single) participant to be seen by those waiting to experience the artwork, and may therefore strike a suitable balance between pre-familiarising participants-to-be and providing them with anonymity whilst they are actually using it. However, despite the issues described above, the user testing session was, according to feedback, enjoyed by most children, and it provided very useful data for further development of the *Game Catcher.*

During this session, the children were free to make any moves in front of the *Game Catcher*. Examples included:

- Traditional playground activities (skipping, hula hoop, etc. with props that were provided).
- Simplified or constrained versions of other playground games. These are games which could not be played in their normal form due to a lack of space and/or participants, but where the children tried an 'analogue' of the game. For instance, at one point two of the participants played 'tag', but the person being chased didn't run, and instead just dodged out of the way on the spot (and the chaser likewise constrained their movements to 'make a game of it').
- Dancing
- 'Kung Fu' style play fighting.
- Random movement (which doesn't fit into any of the above recognisable categories)

Most children were keen to test the space and see how their on-screen avatar (the skeleton figure) behaved in response to their off-screen moves, and, as indicated above, a wide variety of movement took place, even in a relatively short space of time. If possible, it would be interesting to conduct future tests to see whether the amount of time with the game changed the type of movement and play that occurred.

A total of 89 feedback 'Post-its' were filled in. These ranged from single word comments to full sentences and lists (of objects to put into the game, for example). A few children drew images, either on their own or as an adjunct to their written comments. A selection of typical comments is shown in Figure 7.5.

Overall, the response to the *Game Catcher* was positive. Few negative comments were recorded and most of these related to the graphics. Interestingly, most of the comments about the graphics related to the background (for example: 'very plain and simple') rather than to the stick figure used as the avatar. Comments on the avatar mainly remarked that it should be more customisable, with the ability to dress it up and choose its clothes. One comment even suggested that not only should the figure be customisable with the face of the player, but that players should also be able to choose its hairdo. These comments could be an indication of children's familiarity with avatars such as the Nintendo Mii avatar (featured

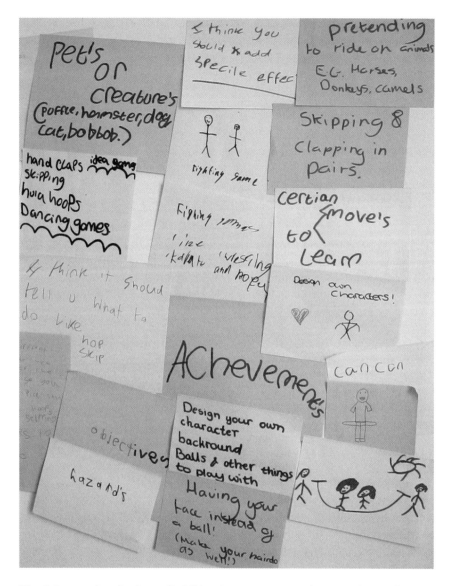

Fig. 7.5   A selection of children's comments and suggestions after user-testing the *Game Catcher*

in Nintendo Wii games) which can be modified, within limits, by selecting from amongst a number of hair styles, clothes and colours. Alternatively (or in addition), this comment indicates a desire to modify, to have (creative) control over the game.

We wanted, in the multiplayer version, to provide for more 'open ended' play, and in essence, provide a tool which allowed the children to adapt it to their own play (and ideally to use it without any conscious adaptation), rather than making them adapt their play to the application, or to only be able to play certain forms of game. To ascertain what type of play would occur in this relatively unstructured space, we did *not* introduce the more conventional videogame structures, such as specified goals, scoring levels and progressive levels of difficulty. It was therefore interesting to us that much of the feedback from this test of the multiplayer *Game Catcher* application proposed in one way or another that we introduce elements of this type of structure. It is useful to divide this particular type of feedback into two subcategories and to consider each one individually. On one hand, there were those which suggested that the *Game Catcher* should replicate or imitate real-life games already known to the children – such as basketball, football, rugby and so on – which have their own scoring, structure and rules (and of course, some sports are also popular videogames). On the other hand, there were those which sought to imitate more videogame-based gaming structures – achievements, levels and so on. Many children suggested 'special moves', 'special features' or 'certain moves to learn'. The first two suggest the type of 'hidden feature' or 'combo' found primarily in fighting games, but also in other genres – while the latter, seems (at face value) to be more along the lines of a game where one follows the moves of the computer. Some comments were specific about introducing this type of 'bemani' format, saying 'Needs more sport like you have to follow sports moves'.

These comments, like the ones made during interviews at the earlier testing sessions, indicate substantial knowledge of, and familiarity with, conventional videogames – as well as indicating a substantial level of literacy in relation to this medium; leading us to observe that contemporary children, even very young ones (aged 5 and above) are conversant with videogame conventions, structures and game play.

There was a similar distinction in the type of suggestions that the children made about the type of play. We provided some physical props such as hoops and skipping ropes during the testing session – in part, because we were interested to see how accurately and realistically the system could track and replicate the type of movement produced when playing with them. Some of the feedback suggestions proposed other realistic, familiar, playground objects such as balls, basketball hoops or other play objects such as a swing, trampoline, see saw or bicycle. Others suggested more fantastical objects, behaviours and actions. Animals were suggested in a variety of forms/contexts. These included animals to pet such as dogs, cats, hamsters and 'puffles' (a creature from the Disney *Club Penguin* online world for children[27]), as well as animals to ride (including horses and camels). Some children also mentioned the ability to pretend to be an animal (lions and tigers were mentioned in this context) and this tied in with the imaginary play activities which we had observed in the playground and been told about in interviews with children. Vehicles were also mentioned as objects to be included in the game.

---

[27] See http://www.clubpenguin.com [Accessed 1st July 2012].

A surprising number of users suggested fighting games and/or forms of fighting such as karate, kung fu and wrestling. One even mentioned 'weapons' as an object to be included in the *Game Catcher*. Fighting is a common form of 'contest-play' in videogames and weapons are part of this genre, but fighting – even play fighting – is an activity generally banned in schools and was, to varying degrees, disapproved of at both schools participating in this project (see for instance Richards, Chapter 4, this volume). The request for fighting games from the children in our testing session should not automatically be seen as an indication that children enjoy fighting 'for real'. Rather this type of 'fantasy fighting' could be requested precisely because children understand that it is not real fighting and therefore appropriate for the videogame space as opposed to the playground space. Making the request in relation to the *Game Catcher* also possibly underlines the fact that children understand it as a videogame space, rather than a school or playground space.

The multiplayer version of the *Game Catcher* that we tested was an early one, which used a different Kinect library to the one that we finally settled upon. Nonetheless, it performed well under most circumstances, although there were occasional glitches. This occurred, for example, when one child passed rapidly in front of another and the system temporarily assigned a limb to the wrong user. Another example is when the children went too close to the Kinect and their feet went out of its angle of view. When this occurred, their avatar's feet would appear stuck to the floor while their body was free to move, causing their legs to be extended. Although the children recognised this as a 'bug', most did not, as players, regard it as an undesirable feature – and in fact were amused by it when it occurred and tried to re-trigger the effect. Only one comment referred to it, saying '[n]ot get tangled up all the time'.

In relation to the function as a research tool, the *Game Catcher* performed well on the test day, recording movement data which could be replayed and/or analysed subsequently. As mentioned above, there were some visual glitches caused by certain movements of the children, but these were eliminated in later iterations of the application.

Two minor technical issues were identified during the day's test session. We originally wanted to present a seamless experience to the users and to minimise the distractions onscreen. As a result, we chose to use a verbal cue (of the computer speaking) when a new user enters the frame and calibration starts. We found, however, that this caused the animation of the other person to judder. This was subsequently rectified by replacing it with a visual cue: a thumbnail image of what the Kinect camera sees. This thumbnail image also solved the other technical issue we discovered in the course of the day – because the Kinect was angled low to spot the children, it was easy for it to cut off the heads or arms of adults when they were doing the 'psi' calibration pose, thereby preventing them being spotted and tracked. By providing the thumbnail, we can now spot when this happens and provide feedback which enables the adult to move back to a position where they can be seen in full.

Findings

We feel that that the feedback obtained was sufficiently coherent and decisive for us to at least start to draw some tentative conclusions from the day and to identify areas for further exploration and development.

With regard to the *Game Catcher* as a game, our conclusions are divided into two broad areas: (a) the performance of the *Game Catcher*; and (b) the children's use of it. I will discuss each of these in turn before exploring how they have together informed (and continue to inform) further development of the *Game Catcher* as a research tool. The *Game Catcher* performed well on the day, with the throughput of participants being sufficient for all of the children to have the opportunity to use it. We were pleased with the ease with which the children were able to relate with their avatar on the screen, even though this was deliberately kept as a relatively simple stick figure. There was a genuine sense of delight on the part of the children when, after holding the 'psi' pose for a second or two, they were successfully recognised and their avatar appeared on the screen reproducing their movements. In a sense, this validated a number of the design decisions that we had made in producing the *Game Catcher* – to concentrate on the speed of responsiveness (the lack of 'lag') as a way of engaging the user, rather than sacrificing speed for visual gloss – and we are currently investigating whether a move to a different, lower-level, programming language would allow us to improve the improve the look while maintaining speed.

Development of the *Game Catcher* has continued[28] and we are hoping to develop it further. One of the main aims of recent development was to combine the code from the single player and multiplayer versions of the *Game Catcher* and provide a system which allows both types of game play – and potentially any other form of movement – to be tracked, recorded, replayed and analysed within a single application. This involves a significant amount of work however, and is not yet complete, but was felt to be desirable for a number of reasons. Firstly, we felt that it was essential for us to provide this flexibility so as not to constrain either the researcher using the *Game Catcher* or the participant(s) whose movements are being recorded. For instance, children's play is notable for the fluidity with which it switches – often without conscious interruption or negotiation – from one form of play to another. These changes are typically triggered by the children becoming bored with their current play or tired by it, by being distracted by children nearby or disrupted by others passing through the space of their game and disrupting it temporarily or by the arrival or departure of players in the middle of a game. Secondly, we felt (and this was validated by the follow-on Movement

---

[28]   The latest version was demonstrated 'live' at the symposium for the AHRC *Beyond Text* funded follow-on Movement Capture project: 'The Theory, Practice and Art of Movement Capture in the Arts and Humanities'. For more information on the project see: http://projects.beyondtext.ac.uk/playground-games-fo1/index.php.

Capture project[29]) that there were also substantial benefits in making the *Game Catcher* a general-purpose, low-cost, motion analysis capture tool that would have multiple applications (including outside the domain of children's play), rather than constraining its use to a particular form of movement or any particular form of analysis. During the development of the initial 'proof of concept' version of the *Game Catcher*, it was necessary to restrict the scope of its functionality to ensure that its goals were feasible within the timescale of the project. It likewise made sense, given that our wider project included a focus on clapping games, that the *Game Catcher* should also explore the same area. Having developed the initial proof of concept for the clapping game – and proven in the other version that multiplayer tracking was both possible and useful – it did, however, seem a somewhat artificial constraint to limit ourselves to this one form of play and we look forward to the opportunity for widening both the game play and the research tool aspects of this innovative prototype, in addition to its application in other domains.

Our overall long-term goal in relation to the *Game Catcher* was, and still is, to produce a 'solution in a suitcase' for both children and researchers, and the version produced during the 'Playground Games and Songs in the New Media Age' project was the first proof-of-concept of this idea. We envision that the level of technical knowledge and skill required to use this 'solution in a suitcase' would be equivalent to (and, ideally, also very much like) switching on a laptop and setting up a video camera and involve little or no specialist configuration (ideally, it would be self-configuring and self-calibrating). It is to this end that we hope to direct the next iteration of the *Game Catcher* development.

Conclusion

As we described in this chapter, we had a number of primary and secondary aims and objectives in developing the *Game Catcher*. An overarching aim of the project as a whole was to enquire into the nature of children's play in the new media age.

We recognised the importance of computer games – both as a form of play, and as a wider cultural phenomenon which is recycled in children's non-digital play away from the computer – and therefore sought to engage directly and actively with them in the course of the project. We did this by investigating – through a process of research by practice – the possibilities of other forms of embodied computer game play, distinct from the available commercial genres, thereby helping to further the playground agency of children in the domain of computer games and re-setting the circuit of culture to also include a cultural and ludic trajectory from playground to videogame (and not just from videogame to playground).

In addition we also aimed to address the question of the transmission and transformation of playground games (the other overarching aim of the project as a

---

[29] See the footnote above.

whole) through adding to and augmenting conventional methods of field research into children's movement, particularly the embodied movement of playground games, by introducing motion capture as a complementary method for capturing and analysing movement (alongside existing techniques such as photography, video, written descriptions and so on).

In attempting to succeed in these aims, we realised that we were, like explorers, travelling through unmapped territory. Nevertheless, the journey of this development has been exciting and enlightening, not least because we have been accompanied by the children of the participating schools, whose perceptive feedback and open-minded enthusiasm has been inspiring. We have built and implemented a proof-of-concept prototype computer game that allows children to record clapping games (with synchronised sound) and play them back either as recordings, or when in 'mirrored' mode, as a game which they or other players can then play ('against' the computer). We have therefore succeeded in our aim of providing a more open-ended computer game environment in which children can 'capture' and then 're-play' or modify and change, and re-capture some of their playground games.

We have also built and implemented a second computer game environment which can capture and record the embodied movements of children's free-form play visualised in real time and in 3D space, as a full-body figure. Using this environment, full-body movement of up to four players can be captured and played back. We believe the possibilities for embodied play using this environment will be many and we look forward to our further development and implementation of capabilities and functions for this system (including the addition of a 'mirrored' game mode).

The lessons learned in the design and implementation of the prototype *Game Catcher* as a whole, and from the comments made by the children on 'Post-its', in interviews and in drawing sessions during and after the user tests, will inform the future development of the *Game Catcher* (from the user point of view) and help us to widen the choice of games and movements in the next iteration. We are conscious of a tension between introducing conventional gaming structures (rules, points, props, etc.) and allowing free-form play (without this being 'steered' in any direction by the designer of the game) whilst remaining excited by the possibilities engendered by the development of this project.

Another important aspect of our *Game Catcher* development, particularly given the overall focus of the project on games in the 'new media age' was what it revealed about the relationship between physical and virtual play, and also about the relationship of the children to videogames and their knowledge and literacy of this medium. For instance, we observed playground activity which referenced and used aspects of videogames, but the ease with which the children (including the youngest ones) entered and navigated the (deliberately different) virtual environment of the *Game Catcher*, as well as the perceptiveness of their comments (both on 'Post-its' in the final user test and in earlier discussions) demonstrates that this is not just a superficial appropriation of game iconography in the playground game, but comes from actual experience of the games and a much deeper familiarity with and understanding of the sometimes complex structures, mechanics and conventions of videogames and virtual environments which has been acquired as users of these games/environments.

With regard to the *Game Catcher* as an analysis tool, both versions enable researchers to use them for capturing, visualising and analysing the movements of play, but the multiplayer version, as it allows more free-form activity, could also be used for the analysis of other forms of movement, such as dance (dance routines, and other play inspired by TV talent shows such as *Britain's Got Talent* and *X Factor*, were also popular playground activities during the course of our project). We believe that the *Game Catcher* (described in detail in this chapter) will therefore greatly benefit the collection and analysis of embodied movement both indoors and outside, and will be useful to researchers from a wide variety of disciplines engaged in the study of movement. To assist in this aim, an unstated yet nonetheless important set of aims in the development of the *Game Catcher* was to make it easy to use and inexpensive, thus making it accessible to researchers, performers, schools and other organisations and individuals for whom professional motion capture solutions are both too expensive and too complex.

References

Arleo A (2001) The saga of Susie: the dynamics of an international handclapping game. In Bishop JC and Curtis M (eds) *Play Today in the Primary School Playground*. Buckingham: Open University Press.

Avedon EM and Sutton-Smith B (1971) *The Study of Games*. London: John Wiley & Sons Inc.

Bishop JC (2010) 'Eeny Meeny Dessameeny': Continuity and Change in the 'Backstory' of a Children's Playground Rhyme. Paper presented at *Children's Playground Games in the New Media Age Interim Conference*, London Knowledge Lab, The Institute of Education, London University. February 2010. Available from http://projects.beyondtext.ac.uk/research_workshops. php?i=35&p=Children%27s%20Playground%20Games%20and%20 Songs%20in%20the%20New%20Media%20Age [Accessed 3rd April 2012.]

Buckingham D (2008) *After the Death of Childhood*. Cambridge, UK: Polity.

Burn, A. (2007). 'Writing' computer games: Game literacy and new-old narratives. L1 – Educational Studies in Language and Literature, 7 (4), p. 45–67.

Burn A (2013) Computer games on the playground: Ludic systems, dramatized narrative and virtual embodiment. In Willett R, Richards C, Marsh J, Bishop JC and Burn A. *Children, Media And Playground Cultures: Ethnographic Studies of School Playtimes*. Basingstoke: Palgrave Macmillan.

Caillois R (2001) *Man, Play and Games*. Chicago: University of Illinois Press.

Corsaro WA (2011) *The Sociology of Childhood*. London: Sage.

Cross B (2009) Mimesis and the spatial economy of children's play. In Willett et al (eds) *Play, Creativity and Digital Cultures*. Abingdon, UK: Routledge.

Cunningham H (2006) *The Invention of Childhood*. London: BBC Books.

Curtis M (2001) Counting in and counting out: Who knows what in the playground. In Bishop JC and Curtis M (eds) *Play Today in the Primary School Playground*. Buckingham: Open University Press.

Du Gay P, Hall S, Janes L, Mackay H and Negus K (1997) *Doing Cultural Studies: The Story of the Sony Walkman*. London: Sage (in association with the Open University).

Grugeon E (2001) 'We like singing the Spice Girl songs…and we like Tig and Stuck in the Mud': girls' traditional games on two playgrounds. In Bishop J and Curtis M (eds) *Play Today in the Primary School Playground*. Buckingham: Open University Press.

Hachimura K (2006) *Digital Archiving of Dancing*. Available from http://elib. mi.sanu.ac.rs/files/journals/ncd/8/ncd08051.pdf [Accessed 23rd April 2012].

Huizinga J (1955) *Homo Ludens*. Boston: Beacon Press.

Hutchinson Guest A (2005) *Labanotation: The System of Analyzing and Recording Movement*. London: Routledge.

James A and James A (2004) *Constructing Childhood*. Basingstoke, Palgrave Macmillan.

James A, Jenks C and Prout A (2010) *Theorizing Childhood*. Cambridge: Polity Press.

Jenkins H (2003) Transmedia Storytelling in *Tech Review*, Cambridge: MIT. Published online: http://www.technologyreview.com/news/401760/ transmedia-storytelling/ [Accessed 6th April 2012].

Jewitt C (2008) Computer-mediated learning: The multimodal construction of mathematical entities on screen. In Jewitt C and Kress G (2008) *Multimodal Literacy*. New York: Peter Lang.

Jewitt C and Kress G (2008) *Multimodal Literacy*. New York: Peter Lang.

Jopson L (2010) The Opie Recordings: What's Left to be Heard? Paper presented at *Children's Playground Games in the New Media Age Interim Conference*, London Knowledge Lab, The Institute of Education, London University. February 2010. Available from http://projects.beyondtext.ac.uk/research_ workshops.php?i=35&p=Children%27s%20Playground%20Games%20 and%20Songs%20in%20the%20New%20Media%20Age [Accessed 3rd April 2012].

Juul J (2005) *Half-real: Video Games between Real Rules and Fictional Worlds*. Cambridge: The MIT Press.

Kress G (2009) *Literacy in the New Media Age*. London: Routledge.

Kress G (2010) *Multimodality: A Social Semiotic Approach to Contemporary Communication*. Abingdon: Routledge.

Kress G and Jewitt C (2008) Introduction. In Jewitt C and Kress G (2008) *Multimodal Literacy*. New York: Peter Lang.

Kress G and Van Leeuwen T (2010) *Multimodal Discourse*. London: Bloomsbury Academic.

Lundy L and McEvoy L (2012) Children's rights and research processes: Assisting children to (in)formed views. *Childhood* 19: 129–44. Sage Publications.

Mitchell G (2010) Porting Playground Games Into a Computer Game Environment: Game Catcher concepts, aims and issues. Paper presented at *Children's Playground Games and Songs in the New Media Age Interim Conference*, London Knowledge Lab, The Institute of Education, London University. February 2010. http://projects.beyondtext.ac.uk/research_ workshops.php?i=35&p=Children%27s%20Playground%20Games%20 and%20Songs%20in%20the%20New%20Media%20Age

Mitchell G and Clarke A (2011) Game catcher: Recording and archiving playground games in Beale K (ed.) *Museums at Play: Games, Interaction and Learning*. Edinburgh: Museums Etc.

Mitchell G and Clarke A (2011b) Playground Gaming with Wii, Kinect and Processing in *ISEA2011 Istanbul Conference Proceedings:* http://isea2011. sabanciuniv.edu/paper/playground-gaming-wii-kinect-and-processing [Accessed 23rd April 2012].

Mitchell G and Clarke A (2013) Visualising and preserving ephemeral movement for research and analysis in Bowen J, Keene S, Ng K *Electronic Visualisation In Art And Culture*. London: Springer-Verlag London Ltd (Cultural Computing Series).

Mitchell G (2014, forthcoming) Introduction in Mitchell G (ed.) *The Theory Practice and Art of Movement Capture*. Newcastle Upon Tyne: Cambridge Scholars Publishing.

Norman D (1999) Affordance, design and convention (Pt 2). Originally published as Affordance, conventions, and design in *Interactions*: 38–43. Available from: http://www.jnd.org/dn.mss/affordance_conv.html [Accessed 13th October 2008].

Opie I and Opie P (1984) *Children's Games in Street and Playground*. Oxford: Oxford University Press.

Opie I (1993) *The People in the Playground*. Oxford: Oxford University Press.

Opie I and Opie P (1985) *The Singing Game*. Oxford: Oxford University Press.

Opie I and Opie P (2001) *The Lore and Language of Schoolchildren*. New York: New York Review of Books.

Palmer S (2007) *Toxic Childhood: How the Modern World Is Damaging Our Children and What We Can Do about It*. London: Orion

Postman N (1996) *The Disappearance of Childhood*. London: Vintage.

Punch S (2002) Research with children: The same or different from research with adults? *Childhood* 9: 321–41. Sage Publications. Available from http://chd. sagepub.com [Accessed 23rd April 2012].

Roud S (2010) *The Language and Lore of the Playground*. London: Random House Books.

Sutton-Smith B (2001) *The Ambiguity of Play*. Cambridge: Harvard University Press.

White A et al (2010) Using visual methodologies to explore contemporary Irish childhoods. *Qualitative Research* 10: 143–58. Sage. Available from http://qrj. sagepub.com [Accessed 23rd April 2012].

Chapter 8
Co-Curating Children's Play Cultures

John Potter

One of the key publicly accessible representations of the playground games research after its completion was a website which was produced collaboratively by the British Library and some of the children who participated in the project. It is important to note at the outset that not all the children were involved in this process and that, for those who were, their agency was constrained by both time pressures and issues of hierarchy. This was, after all, the main outward facing online portal of a major cultural institution and, in the context of Foucault's reflections on heterotopia, libraries and museums are among those institutions producing an immobility which contrasts starkly with the children's dynamic and participatory play cultures (Foucault, 1984). Nevertheless, there was a willingness on the part of the library to generate and engage with design and navigation ideas from representative groups of children; it is these which this chapter will examine and situate within appropriate theories of design, of authoring in new media forms, and in relation to the concept of 'heterotopian games', adapted from Foucault (see Chapter 1).

Based within the 'Language and Literacy' section of the 'Learning' pathway on the main library pages, the site *Playtimes: A century of children's games and rhyme*s (British Library, 2010) offers the visitor two parallel means of negotiating a selection of resources from the playground games archive. One of these is the 'Browse Games' portal, represented across half the screen by a black and white image of children skipping. On the other half of the screen, in colour, is the 'Kids' Zone', represented by a cartoon-like depiction of a playground, commissioned for the project, from Danish artist Bjorn Rune Lie, (2011). The former leads to a set of thumbnails, arranged by game category, behind which short video clips play as a series of adult experts recount directly to camera and/or as voiceover, the main elements of a particular playground game or games and show some examples of them. The latter set of links in the 'Kids' zone' leads to an area introduced and co-curated by some of the children which features their own scripts, drawings and designs for a set of accompanying animations. These links are made accessible by users hovering and clicking on cartoon figures, behind which are the categories of play in the games, arranged non-hierarchically across the screen space. In this section, the voiceovers were provided by the children themselves.

Panels of children from both of the primary schools involved in the playground games project made significant contributions to the design of the 'Kids' Zone' on the website as well as to the curatorial choices and interpretation of the material. This chapter looks in some detail at the authoring processes involved and the eventual outcome as realised on the site itself. It draws on examples of the children's designs and videos of their pitches and presentations during the site-building process in order to say something about the nature of new media production and its relationship to the lived experience of digital culture.

In order to understand and contextualise this aspect of the project, there are a number of potentially useful theoretical traditions as well as emergent ways of thinking about children's productive engagement with new literacies and new technologies. These include ideas ranging from participatory design (Druin, 1999; Kafai, Ching and Marshall, 1997) through to conceptions of learner voice and participatory research with children (Fielding, 2004; Selwyn, Potter and Cranmer, 2010) and on into the conception of curatorship itself as a new literacy practice in the lived experience of culture (Potter, 2010). The last of these locates some of its evidence base in younger learners' experience of co-design and co-authoring in new media and provides a corollary to the process of discussion and design within the creation of the playground games website.

The chapter will draw on records of the children's work during the development of the website – their concept drawings, presentations to the design team and animations made to add to the website, to introduce categories of play. It will look at how this evidence connects with thinking about how younger learners become productive and engaged in new media more widely, in order to raise further questions. Did these activities make possible a child's-eye view of the history and contemporary culture of children's games? How did the children think about the transition from the secret places of play to the public world of museum website exhibition? What did this process reveal about their productive engagement with authoring in new media and their conceptions about how knowledge is owned, accessed and distributed?

Firstly, though, it is important to elaborate on the assertion that new media production can be conceived as a form of self-curatorship in which children are seen as having their own agentive dispositions (Potter, 2012). The aspects of 'curatorship' of experience which suggest themselves as new literacy practices entail the merging of many skills and attributes into one, all of which involve being literate and productive with new media authoring. In fact, there is frequent and growing use of the word 'curated' to describe what the creators and editors of online spaces actually do. Whereas, in earlier media forms, the apposite verbs which were used to credit an author would have been simply 'written', 'edited' or even 'created', it is clear that they don't capture all the self-representational activities or *practices* in new media authoring which the verb 'curated' does. This is because *curating* a site is not only about writing or creating within it but also collecting, interpreting, distributing, assembling, disassembling and moving it across different spaces and forms. In other words, it is an active practice which is larger in its reach, scope and nature than the others but which contains and subsumes them. The meaning in the eventual exhibited form of video, visual art, music or other text, is made from the previously selected resources by knowing how the resources and forms work together across the many available modes of communication. In digital culture, *curating* is, in its most sophisticated form, about organising how these different resources work *intertextually* to make meaning; this is a new process, resulting from human agency in the changed *social arrangements, practices* and *artefacts* of new media (Lievrouw and Livingstone, 2006: 2).

Curating, as a verb, incorporates many sub-components and actions; it suggests at least the following: *collecting, interpreting, cataloguing, arranging and assembling for exhibition* and *displaying*. From the outset, the children were aware that they would be helping in some way to construct a website about the games which they had been helping to collect and record throughout the project. For some of the children the website design offered the possibility of extending the reach of the project by making some of the previously hidden aspects of their playground culture accessible to a potentially vast audience.

Whether or not younger learners are full users of social media, and increasing numbers are, children are aware that online spaces are under specific kinds of authorial control which are designed for either private or public consumption. They involve the previously noted characteristics of *collecting, cataloguing, arranging and assembling for exhibition, displaying* and it is worth commenting further on how they apply in this case.

Collecting in this context refers to gathering found resources, such as video clips, sound files, still images and more and placing them inside or alongside self-created media texts. In earlier research into digital video production, with children of the same age as the playground project, analysis of their authoring practices revealed sophisticated and appropriated re-enactments of habitual play which were subsequently collected, played with and incorporated into new intertextual forms (Potter, 2012). In this project, the resources were collected in order to be accessed through specific categories by a wider audience. The children consulted in the design process needed to make such categories stand for them and for their own experiences when they were not personally present, by investing effort in *cataloguing* as an essential part of the authoring process.

Arranging and assembling were further key aspects of curatorship in the project. Each of these skills requires knowledge of how elements can be in dialogue with one another, to suggest specific meanings by their location and juxtaposition in the space onscreen and in the navigational metaphor chosen. This is an active process of working with navigability and intertextuality. Of course, the ultimate editing and assembly of the website was out of the hands of the children in the project, but ideas presented by the children consulted were important contributions to the overall look and feel of the pages.

Miller wrote how digital media create their own 'sensual field' which respects 'the larger integrity of connections between the media it incorporates' (2008: 71). This 'integrity of connections' is an important concept because it suggests a set of organising principles located, not least, in the *displaying* aspect of curatorship. The particular kind of production in new media dictates this to an extent so that, in the examples of new media in these studies, the navigable site has its own conventions, the breaking of which results in incoherence and lack of a viable representational form for a collection. Where it works, however, it allows users to control, select and publish aspects of their performed, recorded self in new media; and we can see here an essential life skill; the management of resources and assets made for, by and about us in a range of media, as posited in recent work which focuses specifically on the digitisation of personal memories in media assets (Garde-Hansen, Hoskins and Reading, 2009; Williams, Leighton-John and Rowland, 2009). Of course, for the children in this project there was the added concern to represent the project itself to an outside world in the clearest way possible using media forms and genres close to their cultural experience.

From the design process it was possible to draw on evidence from collected interviews and a planning paper trail to understand children's perceptions of the project as it formed. Their recorded actions during the briefing and during the construction of the website revealed evidence of the children's understanding of museum and library curatorship as a communicative process. As the original project proposal stated, the aim was to explore the 'kinds of description, classification and interpretation which (the children) propose for the public display of childlore'. It was simultaneously important to identify ways in which this connected with their understanding of how a website attracts visitors and represents information.

The choice of methods in the analysis was designed to look carefully at the various kinds of texts produced by the children for the way information was organised and for evidence of authorial intent in the finished product. Children in the project were involved in the overall look and feel of the website, its design elements and content right from the start and workshops were held with both sets of children in the two research sites. They knew that their work would be used to design access to the material. So, for the purposes of answering questions about their input, amongst the evidence collected were drawings made by the children, as well as videos of them presenting to the group about the proposed design they had made, along with designs for character sets playing games to be animated by the library's chosen animation company, alongside their scripts for the narratives of those animations.

In order to examine the project as a piece of participant-design it was useful to begin at the top level of navigation, proceed through some of the available original designs for the site, record how the children presented them during the workshops (by means of some videos made at the time) and finish by examining some of the drawings for the animations and how these were rendered on the site at the end of the process.

Earlier in the chapter there was a description of how the site displays the navigational options to a visitor and the gateway to the 'Kids' Zone' as it appears on the British Library website. Onscreen, a school playground provides the metaphorical navigational elements with each of the game categories accessible by means of clicking on a single cartoon character or character set. These nine categories emerged from earlier discussions between the researchers and the

Fig. 8.1   The Kids' zone interface from the Playtimes pages on the site, by
                Danish artist Bjorn Rune Lie (2011)

children's panels in the schools and became the accepted way of collecting and
organising the games. They became central to the way in which navigation was
organised in the final design for the website. In the adult zone the onwards links to
the resources for visitors were provided by the standard horizontal menu system,
with site users encouraged to click links below thumbnails of talking heads. In the
'Kids' Zone' however, a more playful element was introduced with the cartoon
character sets playing the games on a playground square orientated corner to
corner and seen from above (see Figure 8.1).

The visitor to the site peers into a school playground from above, a neighbouring
window perhaps, and selects the character or character set of choice. As the mouse
hovers over each one of these, the categories are revealed. A click takes the visitor
through to the children's own scripted narratives and designed – if not fully
authored – animation sequences.

Onscreen in the final website design for the Kids' Zone the categories were
associated with cartoon characters and set out as follows:

> *Ball Games* (top of the screen, top corner of the playground, three figures, two
> children, one rabbit, playing with a ball);

Playing with Things (left-hand side, two figures, one girl and one duck playing with a spinning top and a hula hoop respectively);

Clapping Games (a sailor figure, disproportionately tall and possibly on stilts, walking across the space, playing 'I'm a long-legged sailor');

Pretend Play (far right, a group of three characters, a superhero, a cowboy and a girl with a pram);

Running around Games (centre left, a giant policeman figure chasing two smaller figures right to left across the playground, playing 'cops and robbers');

Singing and Dancing (two girls, one singing into a microphone and one dancing);

Jokes and Rude Rhymes (three figures at the foot of the screen, disappearing off at the bottom, two giggling girls facing each other and one embarrassed male figure with a moustache and glasses looking back at the visitor);

Skipping Games (bottom centre left, two female figures, one is in the game as 'Cinderella dressed in yellow' and the other in what appears to be Spanish dance costume turn the rope for a figure of a bear to jump over);

Counting out Rhymes (bottom right under the tree, three smaller figures surround and count out a larger cat figure who looks unhappy and appears to have a thermometer in its mouth from 'cat's got the flu/out goes you').

The playground as designed for the site looks like an urban one but clearly it could represent many different places and times, with some archaic clothing and traditional characters suggesting a historical element to the links which could be followed by a visitor. Imaginary characters play with children who, in turn, play with each other. The page contains elements which suggest life, movement and playfulness before any choices are made as wind 'blows across' the screen suggested by animated leaves moving. Birds are drawn on the ground by the chalked in hopscotch squares.

Starting with the navigational metaphor which represents the 'Kids' Zone' on the site then, what evidence is there from the workshops that the children had input into this? What was the nature of the input? And what can we infer from this evidence about their knowledge of how websites work as well as how their knowledge of how the curatorial process works in this case?

Drawings and videos provide useful examples on which to draw to help with these questions. As for similar research conducted with children's drawings in another project (Selwyn, Potter and Cranmer, 2010; Selwyn, Boraschi and Ozkula, 2009) researchers were looking for key markers of purpose and motivation alongside consistency of message and purpose. In this project, the drawings were made by children aged between eight and 11.

Methods derived from visual analysis at the level of design provided a useful set of criteria as a starting point for looking at these drawings, namely

Fig. 8.2   'Games from now and then'

a consideration of *Information value* – the placement of elements with specific values attached to the zones in an image and in relation to an audience; *Salience* – elements which attract the attention of an audience member with their placement and relation; *Framing* – the presence or absence of connectives between elements that suggest they belong together (drawn from Kress and Van Leeuwen, 2006). The central two-part question being asked was: What in each image was criterial to the children and what did it allow us to say about their knowledge of, and engagement with, the design process?

Other drawings are useful counterpoints. Figure 8.2 shows 'Games from now and then'. Here, applying the *information value, salience* and *framing* criteria (Kress and Van Leeuwen, 2006) we see designers (two children created this one) approaching this in an organised manner. First of all, both the adult and child areas are represented side-by-side. The title is prominent, and yet this doesn't appear to be a children's playground in a school so much as an outdoor play area. A swing, a slide and some hills to play on are joined by a skipping rope. The menu on the right-hand side is demarcated from the rest of the screen by a red line. Titles as 'adults for teaching', the menu follows beneath with three further sub-categories: 'Playing games', 'make a game' and 'watch a game'. Below this are the skipping rope and the slide alongside the children's names. Criterial to these children are simple, easily demarcated zones which allow elements to be presented discretely from one another. To an audience there is high information value from the placement of the different elements but not quite so much an overriding sense of a whole unified set of elements. Interestingly, on this page, the designers suggest it is possible to design and make your own game, suggesting a sophisticated and productive level of engagement and an awareness of the active and engaging nature of many such websites. The title of this piece 'Games from now and then' shows an emergent sense of the historical perspective on the project. Researchers, both in this project and elsewhere, report that children are disinclined to acknowledge that their games have a history, often claiming to have made them up (see chapters 2 and 3). Creating the web resource, at least for some of the children, seems to have helped to develop more of a sense of the past, following on from earlier sessions at the library in which samples from the Opie archive were played (see Chapter 2). This is further developed in the voiceover commentaries for the animations. This engagement with history forms one aspect of what we have described as 'heterotopian games'. Foucault's contention that the library is a heterotopian institution, arresting time in the very attempt to document and exhibit it, may seem a bleak assertion. But children at play, on the other hand, as Burn argues in Chapter 1, are historical amnesiacs, their habitus exhibiting a daily forgetting of its own history, to paraphrase Bourdieu (1986). While Bourdieu's proposal applies to adults and children and adults alike, the repeated denial of history and provenance in children's interviews about their play suggests a particular case.

In the act of curating their own games and the histories behind them, they achieve two things. On the one hand, they unfix, at least a little, the immobility Foucault perceives in the archive, adding dynamic representations of the moment of contemporary play which they inhabit. On the other hand, reaching back into the histories of play their parents recalled, they dissolve something of the amnesia of the habitus. They saw this as a kind of time travel: one child described the historian of folklore, Steve Roud, who helped them with the history, as Dr Who, taking them back in time in his Tardis. Too celebratory an account of this process, however, would be misplaced. Rather, the historicizing of play here is an educational intervention, which attempts to balance a proper regard for the children's cultural knowledge with a move from tacit knowledge to explicit knowledge, not only of their own play but of how it connects with the play of previous generations.

In Figure 8.3, by contrast, we learn more about the designer than about how the resource could be navigated or the historical perspective of the resource as a whole. 'Playground activities' is the main title of this piece displayed top left. Four games follow, dispersed across the page with no unifying element such as an enclosing shape and neither are there dividing lines and neat menus and markers. It seems to have taken a long time for the football to be drawn. It has been very neatly coloured in and shaded in such a way as to create a 3D effect. So, catching games, football, clapping games, trading cards and, finally, on the left-hand side the giving up game, with the word mercy written across somebody's raised right hand, probably a truce term used to 'gain respite' in a game, as the Opies put it

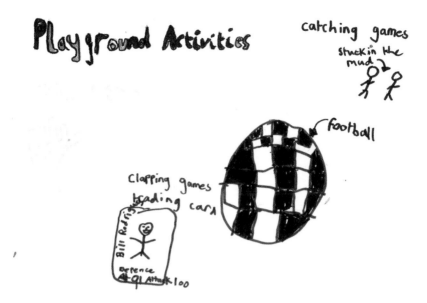

Fig. 8.3   Some favourite games suggested for the web page by one of the children in the project

(Opie and Opie, 1959).[1] We learn, in other words, about this particular child's favourite playground activities.

Clearly, as we would expect, there is a difference between how the different children engaged in the task and reflected their own dispositions. Some were understandably motivated to prioritise their own favourite games on the site. Others wanted to provide an experience for visitors to the site which led to them engaging directly with playful activity. For example, the child who designed Figure 8.4 was principally concerned with adding a facility to the site which allowed people to enjoy the experience of waiting for images to build and load by becoming active and playing a game. This awareness of the nature of browsing practices around both entertainment and information gathering is sophisticated and fully realised in the design. You can see the bar drawn centrally with the word 'Loading' and the number '100' at the extreme right. Beneath that and drawn fairly sizeably in relation to the whole screen is the game. Asked in a videotaped interview about this design during the workshop, the boy says: 'After you've pressed something, say skipping rope, and it's loading and you're waiting and it goes up to 100% you press on this game … you go through the maze collecting things … running shoes

---

[1]   'Mercy' is not referenced by the Opies as a truce term, but is referred to in one online source describing expatriate English children in Turkey playing arm-wrestling: http://steepholm.livejournal.com/15548.html?thread=67516, accessed 11.7.12

Fig. 8.4   Proposed waiting game for visitors to the site

…'. The engagement with this aspect of the site is a holistic experience of having fun, taking part in pastimes whilst waiting for the information about pastimes to load.

One of the other proposals for the site produced by one of the girls in the workshop survived almost intact in the official design. It ended up providing a set of visual metaphors and a navigation system which was very close to the one eventually adopted.

In this design, shown in Figure 8.5 and entitled 'Games of the past and present', you can see clearly see areas of high information value. There are a number of words onscreen, most prominently of all, the word 'Games' written in high colour bottom left. Balancing each other on the left-hand side, and on the right-hand side, are two key elements of web navigation. Written on the left-hand side is the word 'help' and directly opposite 'tour of sight' (sic). These are balanced at the top and bottom of the design by 'photos' and 'videos'. The design is clearly informed by a high level of awareness of classic elements of information based web pages. There is a unifying metaphor in terms of both place and outdoor and climatic conditions. This is recognisably a playground, containing swings, slide and climbing frame. But there is a strong unifying connected theme of weather in the presence of bright sunshine, rain and even night sky elements. Trading card games, clapping games (drawn inside the circle of the sun), ball games and more are all available as per the brief to represent the games categories established in the project. Through it

Fig. 8 5   Games of the past and present

all a river flows, sometimes used as a wider key signifier of a London location; though in fact this London playground space was built and designed during the project to incorporate a painted blue river running through painted green fields and hills. This mixture of purposeful content, imaginative content and locative content is consistent with the purpose of the site, to be engaging and accessible to children when they visit and select the 'Kids' Zone'. More than that, there is an attempt to be faithful to the aims of the project, namely that of curating the experience of playground games for a visitor. This designer wishes to render the experience in different media forms for the end user, realising both video and still images need to be considered.

This is one level of analysis of one design but we are also fortunate enough to have a video of the girl concerned, presenting the pitch for how it might work to an audience from the British Library and the playground games researchers. In the video, as she talks through the design with the workshop audience, we see the use of many modes of expression in one performed explanation of the navigation of the site. She brings the process to life by means of gesture and performance and, with this in mind, we can employ a means of reading these modes together through time as the video plays derived from the multimodal analysis of moving image texts (after Burn and Parker, 2003). Combining a traditional transcription with an examination of other salient modes in her performance helps us to draw some conclusions about the nature of the engagement in the process as a whole:

00–10 seconds:
It's called games of the past and present
And look all round if you can find different places

(she waves her hand round and round the page/screen/ attempting to lift it while she speaks; she is a performer of the website as well as a viewer. She expresses agency in the gesture, she chooses not to abstract herself from the performance and hold it out front, looking at it from above. Her finger traces the route of a mouse arrow across the page …)

10–22 seconds:
Here's a puddle that's splashed out of the river if you scroll over it then it says video games (text revealed from under objects)

22–30 seconds:
… if you carry on go over this hill it says trading cards – (again she performs with the hand sweeping left up the hill to the right, the movement through the screen space)

30–37 seconds:
… And then there's lots of different places (this time stabbing at the picture to show the different jumping off points)
… if you scroll over different things will pop up …

37–45 seconds:
… so there's photos, games, video games, trading games, clapping games (she has internalised the typography and categorization made during the project) and now she wants to see it represented prominently in the design …

45–58 seconds:
(A researcher asks about when you click on the ball games what will you see …)
… you'll go er er … it will zap you to the ball area where there's different things to watch, the background is the ball area with balls flying around … and then there's … there's video of board games

This child knows about web design and what happens when you click on elements and things happen, resources are displayed and presented in different media; you travel through the pages by being 'zapped' to different places. This much is an obvious and even prosaic finding in the digital age when we would expect the experiences of viewing sites to have been habitualised among children with regular web access. What is new and revealed by taking a closer look at both the drawn and performed elements which are essential to the site for her, in both the still image and in the video, is the embodied and aesthetic response to the activity. She wishes to perform the site as it would be encountered by a visitor and, at the same time, she wishes to meet the demands of the brief and to make the collection accessible to a viewer. This level of construction of the site from the raw material of the collection shows a concern for content as well as process, for production as well as consumption. It illustrates a high level of personal engagement and investment in the process.

I would further argue that the presentation of this design and its associated meaning making resources across the available modes is evidence of an agentive awareness of two kinds of curatorial processes. Firstly, there is an awareness of the responsibility in the outward facing and specific initial task of representing a curated exhibition of a collection to an audience. Secondly, there is a developed sense of what it is to place and connect resources in new media authoring and to know how they work in an ensemble of meaning making. I have argued elsewhere that this represents a new literacy and cultural practice of curatorship (Potter, 2012).

A further element of design for which the children were responsible, though at a lower level of personal agency, was the construction of the animated resources inside the 'Kids' Zone' itself. Once this branch of the collection has been accessed by an end user, they find themselves navigating the school playground and clicking on categories which lead to short animated sequences. As the sequences play, children's voices provide a commentary about the game or games in question. For these sections of the site, children had control over the elements which were to be animated as well as the spoken sequences. In one of the modes, that of movement through time, they had very low levels of agency; in others, that of the drawn elements they had much higher agency and awareness of the final purpose to which their work would be put. In most cases, their drawings frequently represented the possibility of movement in the way they were constructed. The animation company in question largely pursued these aspects which were present as visual cues in the drawings. The children provided commentaries which were used as voiceovers for the animations and these were self-authored. The process leading to their composition involved forms of research such as interviewing parents and interviewing the historian of folklore Steve Roud, a consultant on the project (Roud, 2010). In this sense, aspects of their play culture usually confined to tacit knowledge (Polanyi, 1983) were developed as explicit knowledge through the research process. Two members of the research team have considered elsewhere how the children in this project were encouraged to become researchers (Marsh and Richards, 2013). In this case, one aspect of such knowledge was an awareness of the history of the games, commonly disowned in interviews with children who claim to have 'just made it up' (Opie and Opie, 1959; Beresin, 2010; Jopson, Burn and Robinson, this volume). One example is transcribed below from the 'Running around games' pathway off the main 'Kids' Zone' site:

> There are loads of different versions of Tig, sometimes it is called Touch or Tig. Hundreds of years ago it was called He. You run around and if you touch someone they're 'It'. We also play 'Chain Tag'. One person is 'It' when he catches someone they hold hands until they become a long chain. Bulldog is a hundred years old. Back then when they tagged someone they had to lift them up for five seconds or pin them down ... Today we play star wars droids chasing Darth Vader.

These pieces of writing were composed and narrated by the children and the compilations are brief, lasting in the region of 30–40 seconds, and accompanied by moving image sequences created by the animators from the character sets and

Fig. 8 6   Skipping games as drawn for the animated sequences

backgrounds designed by the children. In the example quoted above, a concern for the task at hand, representing the games of the past, is accompanied by a wish to see contemporary cultural affiliations and interests represented in the designs. Thus, whilst Tig and Bulldog, as popular examples of lived playground experience, have a place in representing 'Running around games' to the outside world on the site, so too do the appropriations into fantasy play of the Star Wars characters. The sense of the past is never far away, as in the interjections about games played 'hundreds of years ago'. This constant reminder of the overall purpose of the site and its relationship to the past suggests a full engagement with the need to relate the histories of these practices. They are aware of their responsibilities, as researchers and as curators.

But what of the drawings which were created for this part of the resource? In the examples shown below, you can see how the original drawings contained the possibility of movement. In Figure 8.6 the skipping ropes twist away from the viewer, and the weather plays a part with rain blowing in with a cloud on the left. Criterial to the children here, as in the earlier website designs are the influence of the weather, the fact of being outside, represented by the tree on the extreme right, and, the proximity of other skippers. Activity and movement are highly salient in the overall design of this space as suggested by the drawn character sets produced by the children. Interestingly, four female figures are represented and one male, a fairly accurate representation of the gender balance in skipping games on this playground. The commentary on the site refers to gender and to changes over time with boys joining in '50 years ago', but then mainly being an activity in which girls dominate.

In the conker games drawing in Figure 8.7, the close-up and overhead view shows the detail of the ties to the fingers and the movement of the string. Each nail

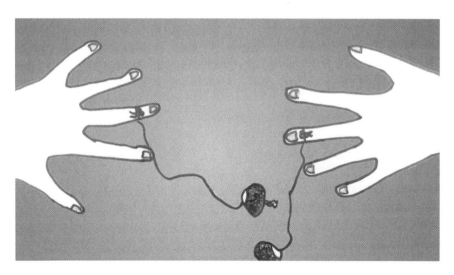

Fig. 8 7   Conker game drawn for the animated sequences

is carefully drawn and the key purpose here seems to be to provide a plan view of the action with the kinks and ties of the string faithfully recorded. Conkers was not recorded on either playground during the project. However, this image can only be read as a committed imaginative effort to recreate the game from the description of others, perhaps parents.

In another drawing, the sailor at sea (a character in the widely-played A Sailor Went to Sea, Sea, Sea clapping game; see Bishop and Burn, 2013) is travelling through large waves, with the clouds scudding along behind him as the boat tips slightly and he balances on the prow (see Figure 8.8). The image of the sailor himself suggests that Popeye is a reference point, albeit a somewhat surprising one for contemporary children, with his pipe and smoke rising towards the sky. But again, movement is salient in the picture and the detail of the waves and clouds all make sense in the overall scheme.

The visitors to the 'Kids' Zone' and the *Playtimes* site as a whole comprise an unseen and unknown audience for whom the children are engaged in acts of preservation of memory and artefact. Curating here means preservation and memory, as we have seen; but it also means descriptive commentary, interpretation, the extension of their own memory into family memory and the recovery of history in their accounts of the games. In the site design, using drawings for animation and short, recorded commentary the children co-curate this space with varying degrees of ownership of the process, bounded as they are by the demands of the cultural institution, the researchers and their peers in the project as a whole.

Nevertheless, we have seen how their agency in the process of representation remains high, with significant personal investment by them in written elements and designs which they knew would be viewed by large numbers of people beyond their playgrounds. It is possible that the preservation of their own lived experience in

Fig. 8.8   Sailor on the sea drawn for the animated sequences

this way finds an affinity with wider processes of self-representation and reflexive authoring of the lived experience in new media. This is a potentially powerful means of giving voice to experience which is part of young people's everyday, wider cultural experience as they grow and use social media for themselves. In this process, of course, they will curate other aspects of their lives. This is not to say that this self-reflexive and agentive authoring can't happen with younger learners, including those of the same age as the children in the primary school project. This has been seen at the time of writing in the blog, NeverSeconds, by a nine year-old girl in Scotland who provides a daily photograph and commentary on her school dinners, rating them for 'health' and 'mouthfuls' (how many to finish it) amongst other things (Payne, 2012). Her awareness of impact, and developed sense of her own curatorship of her experience, have won her a large following worldwide and created an impact beyond her immediate situation (BBC News, 2012).

As we have seen earlier in the chapter, reviewing the videos of the web designers in the playground games research reveals a heightened understanding, on their part, of the behaviours and activity of audiences on websites beyond simply the organisational and navigational issues. The exploration of the website as *performance* is engendered in the descriptions of the designs. But what of their relationship to the mission of cultural curatorship, to the stated purposes of the site, which was to preserve and exhibit the playground game as a fact of previously lived and, indeed, ongoing living experience?

The aspects of 'curatorship' of experience which suggest themselves as new literacy practices in this work entail the merging of many skills and attributes into one, all of which involve being literate and functioning in new media as readers as well as producers and authors. They also imply a means of being able to work and assemble assets *intertextually*, to know how they speak or relate to one another in the meanings which are made. For some, the interest here lies in the design for social action, how meaning is made from the resources *multimodally* (Kress and Van Leeuwen, 2001). For others, this is a partial understanding of the processes of engagement and affect and it means adding embodied and aesthetic responses to our interpretation of how meaning is made in social media (Leander and Frank, 2006). In all cases, the whole composition is being made from the accumulated assets of experience and habitus (Bourdieu, 1986), and from those selected aspects which are both 'transient' and 'anchored' affiliations and markers of identity (Merchant, 2005).

As we saw at the beginning of the chapter, 'curating' is a word which captures this as an essentially agentive process, applied in this instance to online spaces. It incorporates and suggests at least the following: *collecting, cataloguing, arranging and assembling for exhibition, displaying, interpreting*. The children in the playground games research were aware of *collecting* on many levels, from their engagement with a project involving archiving in partnership with a famous cultural institution, through to the deep ethnographic documentation of their own present day games and pastimes which they knew was occurring throughout the project. Each textual resource or recorded artefact, the collected item, whether self-produced or not, comes to be allocated its place in the overall collection for the project and their witnessing of this process and their eventual involvement in a key public outcome may have made the children more aware retrospectively of their participation in a curatorial project.

As the children knew from the outset, it was important to develop a common language for talking about the games and for arranging them and the project attempted to engage them fully through the pupil councils in both settings. Naming, tagging, sorting, as discussed earlier, have all been noted as areas for potential development as both skill sets and resources in educational settings, developing learners' capacity for working with user-generated tagging systems or 'folksonomies' (see Davies and Merchant, 2007). As we have seen, the children exploited the game categories in their web designs and operationalised these in their navigational metaphors and menus.

The *arranging* and *assembling* aspects of curatorship are those of planning for elements to be in dialogue with one another, to suggest specific meanings by their location and juxtaposition on the screen, in the design when it is complete. This is an active process of working with intertextuality, using the tools in the software to assemble a coherent whole in a design, exploiting salience, information-handling and framing (Kress and Van Leeuwen, 2006). Miller's (2008) 'integrity of connections' is an important related concept because it suggests a set of organising principles, albeit one dictated by the form of new media production under consideration. For a digital video production, the resources are gathered and mixed multimodally to make meaning through a time-based text – in the kineikonic mode (Burn and Parker, 2003). In the case of the co-curated webspace, the design of the screen has its own conventions, the breaking of which results in incoherence and lack of a viable representational form. In many cases, the children's designs reveal a concern that the experience for visitors should be coherent and navigable through their sophisticated use of metaphor and movement.

At the same time, there was a sense throughout of the locus of control in these processes not always being located wholly with the children but rather negotiated and reinterpreted in the context of the wider adult-led research team, British Library staff, web designers and other collaborators. They knew, for example, that they were – to an extent – guardians of people's recorded experience of an aspect of their cultural life, in a space for which they were only partially responsible, for a very wide audience of unseen and unknown visitors. Having been invited to help organise the public representational spaces for these games, they had to negotiate their relationship to the playground games as *historically* handed down. It's possible that this initiated an awareness of the place of their own games in the contested and curated spaces of recorded culture for the future. In this, of course, they were aided and abetted by the library staff and researchers to whom they offered their own nascent ability as curators in new media in the designs which they produced.

References

BBC News (2012) *NeverSeconds blogger Martha Payne school dinner photo ban lifted.* BBC. Available from http://www.bbc.co.uk/news/uk-scotland-glasgow-west-18454800 [Access date 16.6.12].

Beresin A (2010) *Recess Battles: Playing, Fighting and Storytelling.* Jackson, MS: University Press of Mississippi.

Bishop JC and Burn A (2013) Reasons for rhythm: Multimodal perspectives on musical play. In Willett R, Richards C, Marsh J, Burn A and Bishop JC. *Children, Media and Playground Cultures: Ethnographic Studies of School Playtimes.* Basingstoke: Palgrave Macmillan, 89–119.

Bourdieu P (1986) *Distinction: A Social Critique of the Judgement of Taste.* London: Routledge.

Bourdieu P (1990) *The Logic of Practice.* Stanford, CA: Stanford University Press.

British Library (2011) *Playtimes: A century of children's games and rhymes* 2010 [cited 3.6.11]. Available from http://www.bl.uk/playtimes

Burn A and Parker D (2003) *Analysing Media Texts.* London: Continuum.

Davies J and Merchant G (2007) Looking from the inside out: Academic blogging as new literacy. In: Knobel M and Lankshear C (eds) *A New Literacies Sampler.* New York: Peter Lang.

Druin A (1999) Cooperative inquiry: Developing new technologies for children with children. *Human Factors in Computing Systems: CHI 99*: 223–30.

Fielding M (2004) Transformative approaches to student voice: Theoretical underpinnings, recalcitrant realities. *British Educational Research Journal* 30: 295–311.

Foucault M (1984) Of other spaces, heterotopias. In *Architecture, Mouvement, Continuité* 5: 46–9.

Garde-Hansen J, Hoskins A and Reading A (2009) *Save as ... Digital Memories.* London: Palgrave.

Kafai Y, Ching C and Marshall S (1997) Children as designers of educational multimedia software. *Computers in Education* 29: 117–26.

Kress G and Van Leeuwen T (2001) *Multimodal Discourse: The Modes and Media of Contemporary Communication.* London: Arnold.

Kress G and Van Leeuwen T (2006) *Reading Images The Grammar of Visual Design* (Second Edition). London: Routledge.

Leander K and Frank A (2006) The aesthetic production and distribution of image/subjects among online youth. *E-Learning* 3: 185–206.

Lie B (2011) *The History of Children's Playground Games.* Available at http://bjornrunelie.blogspot.co.uk/2011/02/history-of-childrens-playground-games.html

Lievrouw L and Livingstone S (2006) *The Handbook of New Media (updated student edition).* London: Sage.

Marsh J and Richards C (2013) Children as researchers. In Willett R, Richards C, Marsh J, Burn A and Bishop JC. *Children, Media and Playground Cultures: Ethnographic Studies of School Playtimes.* Basingstoke: Palgrave Macmillan, 51–67.

Merchant G (2005) Electric involvement: Identity performance in children's informal digital writing. *Discourse: Studies in the cultural politics of education* 26: 301–14.

Miller D (2008) *The Comfort of Things.* Cambridge: Polity.

Opie I and Opie P (1959). *The Lore and Language of Schoolchildren.* Oxford: Oxford University Press.

Payne M (2012) In NeverSeconds: One primary school pupil's daily dose of school dinners Available at http://neverseconds.blogspot.com

Polanyi M (1983) *The Tacit Dimension.* Gloucester MA: Peter Smith.

Potter J (2010) Embodied memory and curatorship in children's digital video production. *Journal of English Teaching: Practice and Critique* 9 (1): 22–35.

Potter J (2012) *Digital Media and Learner Identity: The New Curatorship, Digital Education.* New York: Palgrave MacMillan.

Roud S (2010) *The Lore of the Playground.* London: Random House

Selwyn N, Boraschi D and Ozkula S (2009) Drawing digital pictures: An investigation of primary pupils' representations of ICT and schools. *British Educational Research Journal* 35: 909–28.

Selwyn N, Potter J and Cranmer S (2010) *Primary ICT: Learning from Learner Perspectives.* London: Continuum.

Williams P, Leighton-John J and Rowland I (2009) The personal curation of digital objects: A lifecycle approach. *Aslib Proceedings: New Information Perspectives* 61: 340–63.

Postscript:
The People in the Playground

Chris Richards and Andrew Burn

Centuries of Play

Our research took place between April 2009 and May 2011. As Burn notes in Chapter 1, the British Library website representing both the work of the project and material from other archives eventually took the title *Playtimes: A Century of Children's Games and Rhymes,* thus inviting comparisons along a diachronic axis, between 'then' and 'now'. That axis, figured as the 'century', or 'one hundred years', had already surfaced, from time to time, in our project – as an imaginary time line offering a vantage point from which the 'now' of life in the playground might be viewed. Iona Opie, in her preface to *The People in the Playground* (1993), wrote:

> I tried to explain to the people in the playground why I turned up every week and wrote down whatever was happening … 'I think it will be interesting in 100 years' time,' I said. 'I wish somebody had done the same 100 years ago, then we would know what it was like.' (Opie, 1993: vii)

Attempting to explain her presence and her interest, she suggested a position that neither she nor any of the children could ever expect to take up. In part, this seems to imply that the distance, and perhaps the unfamiliarity, that others might experience in reading her account could enable them to 'see' or perhaps to 'know' something more than was available at the time. But it is also, more broadly, a recognition of the importance of documenting the present in a longer historical perspective and an attribution of value to the record of the apparently mundane.

In the playground at Christopher Hatton Primary School (Richards, field notes, 25 March 2010) a Year Five teacher, commented on the issue of play fighting and remarked that in computer games, 'you can just re-set and cease to be dead'. He also suggested that it might be 'a hundred years before we know if this generation has been significantly affected by the computer game scene', and he cited *Call of Duty* as a currently popular example (see Richards, chapter 8, and Burn, chapter 6, in Willett et al, 2013). Like Iona Opie, he projected the imaginary standpoint into a future from which mortality excludes us all. For that teacher, even more than for Iona Opie, the attainment of reliable knowledge lay beyond currently living generations. Of course, we might imagine ourselves 100 years hence, looking back, but such strategies are not likely to be taken seriously in academic research. Nevertheless, this 'impossible' vantage point does suggest an important question – how long does it take to 'know' anything at all about the play we observed and documented?

We had two years. Iona Opie, following the publication of *The Lore and Language of Schoolchildren* (Opie and Opie, 1959), began a series of visits to a school playground maintained for more than two decades:

> I started going down to the playground in the spring of 1960, and in January 1970 began the regular weekly visits that continued until November 1983. My notes gradually became less note-like, and more like a narrative account of what one person could see and overhear and be told directly during the fifteen eventful minutes of morning playtime. I learned to submerge myself as far as possible in the milling throng. (Opie, 1993: vii)

Slow research of this kind, building on long-term familiarity with a particular site, is usually conducted outside the frameworks required for funded research. Nevertheless, such approaches, taking years to carry out an enquiry, have their advocates. In her preface to *Recess Battles,* Anna Beresin (2010) notes that 'I began this research project carrying my one-year-old on my back: he now shaves, giving new meaning to the phrase *longitudinal study*'. (Beresin, 2010: xi). Shirley Brice Heath (1983) researched *Ways with Words* 'between 1969 and 1978' when she 'lived, worked and played with the children and their families and friends in Roadville and Trackton' (Heath, 1983: 5). Les Back has explored some of the tensions between the urgency of political engagement and the value of slow, reflective, research but he also endorses cautiously considered studies, if not those that might take a decade or more to reach publication (Back, 2007: 20–21). Reflecting on the studies gathered in his *The Art of Listening*, he remarks: 'The lives described in this book are now out of date and my attempts to apprehend them sociologically are like relics of a world that has already passed' (Back, 2007: 25). In this context, we should say that our study was a modest one but that it nevertheless identified important *new* tendencies in children's play and recorded the state of play in two primary school playgrounds at a particular time, now passed. With numerous Flip video recordings, a documentary film and the enquiries that fed into the *Game Catcher* development, we had a mix of strongly visual records of the children's play in those two years. More optimistically than the teacher quoted above, we have not waited for 100 years to further, clarify and confirm our findings. We have tentatively named these new forms of play, in Chapter 1, as three 'types'. Briefly, the first is *cultural rehearsal* – iterative, performative play drawing on forms of repetition in new media (see Chapter 3). The second is *ludic bricolage* – the adaptive creation of game systems by children, influenced in particular by computer games, and including not only the game systems and rules devised by the children on the playground, but also the interplay of player and machine in the *Game Catcher* (see Chapter 7). The third is *heterotopian games* – play in liminal spaces, including, in our project, the virtual worlds of playgrounds and new media, but also the ambiguous spaces of the library archive and website (see Chapter 8). In framing these types, we hope to have captured something distinctive, traced in the broad contrast between early twenty-first century play and the media-rich play of the Opies' research. At the same time, we hope to have proposed ideas about play which will be salient to the developing relationship between play and media in the future that we, like the Opies, can only guess at.

Ways of Knowing

A further question, also addressed by Iona Opie, is that of how, and sometimes how slowly, a research site becomes a coherent social world (see Richards, 2011). Commenting that 'boredom is the bane of humankind' she recalled 'the sensation of being surrounded by the kaleidoscopic vitality of the eager, laughing, shouting, devil-may-care people in the playground' (Opie, 1993: ix). In her further introductory reflections, under the heading 'The Intruder', she adds to this with emphasis on her early perceptions of the frenetic scenes she encountered:

> At first the playground seemed uncontrolled confusion. Balls whizzed by my head, bodies hurtled across my path, some boys were on the ground pummelling each other, and a dense black mob rushed across, apparently taking no notice of anyone else. Gradually, often with the aid of an interpreter, it became possible to sort out the intermingled games; the chasing game, for instance, which was superimposed upon a diffuse game of Germans and English, both games being intersected by boys competing in running races. (Opie, 1993: 2)

Though Iona Opie probably did not have the wider problems of social science methodology in mind, it is striking how similar her account is to that offered in *After Method: Mess in Social Science Research* by John Law (2004):

> If much of the world is vague, diffuse or unspecific, slippery, emotional, ephemeral, elusive or indistinct, changes like a kaleidoscope, or doesn't really have much of a pattern at all, then where does this leave social science? How might we catch some of the realities we are currently missing? Can we know them well? *Should* we know them? Is 'knowing' the metaphor we need? And if it isn't, then how might we relate to them? (Law, 2004: 2)

Like Back, Beresin and Brice Heath, cited earlier, Law too turns towards an argument in which the *time* that it takes to produce understanding is a key theme:

> ... method, in the reincarnation that I am proposing, will often be slow and uncertain. A risky and troubling process, it will take time and effort to make realities and hold them steady for a moment against a background of flux and indeterminacy. (Law, 2004: 10)

In this slow work, 'catching' realities may well also require a mix of perhaps 'unorthodox' methods.

Though his field is science and technology, Law's suggestions are remarkably apposite for playground research and recall some of the lived experience of our project (for the detail of Law's account see 2004: 108–16). He suggests, for example, that we might know the realities we encounter:

> ... through the hungers, tastes, discomforts, or pains of our bodies. These would be forms of knowing as embodiment. Perhaps we will need to know them through 'private' emotions that open us to worlds of sensibilities, passions, intuitions, fears and betrayals. These would be forms of knowing as emotionality or apprehension. (Law, 2004: 2–3)

As adult researchers we entered play spaces of a kind we had had relatively little opportunity to inhabit for any extended time since our own childhoods. Sometimes it was very cold, wet and uncomfortable and also overwhelmingly noisy. At times, such discomforts were also compounded by the anxiety that nothing was happening – nothing, that is, that made any sense for us at that time (Law, 2004: 104–5). Together, these experiences, recorded in field notes, could be re-articulated as resources for understanding how, as Iona Opie remarks, boredom had to be countered – for the children around us, for ourselves as researchers and, in memory, for ourselves as children in the playgrounds we once inhabited – see Burn on 'embodied histories' in Chapter 1. Such an 'emotive and embodied' (Law, 2004: 3) route to interpretation is apparent, for example, in the enquiries into clapping games (chapters 2 and 3), into media-referenced and pretend play (Chapter 6) and into play fighting offered in this book. In the case of play fighting, Richards (in Chapter 4) draws explicitly on autobiographically recovered experiences, partly because they intersect with the Opies' research in the 1950s but also because they connected with the troubled uncertainties apparent in the negotiation of play fighting between staff and students at Christopher Hatton Primary School. Back (2007), cautioning against allowing 'self-reflection' to 'inhibit or pre-empt the need for dialogue and deep listening to others' goes on to specify the value of 'autobiographical or experiential knowledge' as 'an interpretive device'. He adds, 'subjectivity becomes a means to try to shuttle across the boundary between the writer and those about whom s/he is writing' (Back, 2007: 159). In this respect, interpretation was also a matter of 'shuttling' from the present moment to another – perhaps decades before – but to further explore the present 'moments' that were the main focus of analysis in our research.

In *The People in the Playground* Iona Opie wrote that 'By now, folklorists are familiar with the circulation of folklore into and out of the media, and are reconciled to it' (Opie, 1993: 14). 'By now' – the present moment is contrasted with an unspecified moment in the past of folklore studies when such 'circulation' was both surprising and, it is implied, regretted. But, more particularly, she also recalls the moment when *The Lore and Language of Schoolchildren* (1959) was published and was met with dismay from the 'intelligentsia' (Review, *Evening Standard* 5 Nov. 1959, 14, headlined 'A mother of six looks at a book that will "horrify the nation".' cited by Opie, 1993: 12). This movement back and forth between moments in a career separated by, at that point, more than 30 years, further illustrates the processes of recursive interpretation, the revisiting of debates and instances in the shifting contexts of contemporary re-evaluation. She concludes her introduction to *The People in the Playground* with a calm ambivalence. She comments:

> Defecation, urination, nudity, the private parts, the sex organs, and the sex act, which in a civilized society, are kept private, have a fearful fascination for children. The growth of permissiveness has meant that fathers and older brothers now share sexy stories with the younger boys, and children stay up late to watch extremely 'adult' programmes on television. (Opie, 1993: 15)

This is laced with the vocabulary of lament – for a loss of privacy and civilization. Yet when she cites examples in her daily narrative – see for example the story of the three fleas and the big bad hairy long juicy thing (Opie, 1993: 75) – she records them with dispassionate precision and little comment – 'After that I had to leave'. Her stance is that of sympathetic allegiance to 'the people in the playground':

> Children already seem to know that 'human kind cannot bear very much reality'. Childhood is a time more full of fears and anxieties than many adults care to remember, and play is the way of escape. (Opie, 1993: 15)

John Law alludes to the same line from Eliot in considering his own encounters with 'realities' (as an ethnographer):

> Too many realities – and representations of realities – were being enacted. In short … the balance between the manifestation of entities, the real, on the one hand and the enactment of the non-real, of silence, of Otherness on the other, was wrong. Allegory is about enacting, and knowing multiple realities. But … allegory is also about the movement between realities. In particular, it is about holding them together. To misquote T.S. Eliot, there was too much reality to bear. (Law, 2004: 108)

Allegory and play both allow 'movement between realities' and, in Iona Opie's account, such activities are pursued, in part, in response to excess, to a thickening of the real in the lives of children. As Sutton-Smith has also argued, play includes strategies for coping with the emotional vicissitudes of the real. It is an unexpected parallel but, like the children in the playground, we, as researchers, also had to 'move between realities', to engage, sometimes almost through immersion, and to withdraw, to think and reflect, to take 'time out'. 'Making sense', in play and in research, entails both this movement between realities and the habit of thinking of one thing in terms of another (Lakoff and Johnson, 1980), thus exercising a degree of control either playful or analytical.

Iona Opie wrote *The People in the Playground* with little overt reflection on the work of interpretation and analysis. But her account is an extended rhetorical claim about children-as-people, their status as interpreters of their own social worlds and the pre-eminence of speech in their lives. By contrast with Father Damian Webb, discussed in Chapter 2, her priority, to represent the complex flow of 'intertextual' talk sustained by the children in her local primary school (in Liss, Hampshire) locates meaning in language more often than in physical action. We have attempted, within our relatively brief period of research, to represent children's play by a wider variety of means – especially giving greater emphasis to visual documents – but also to present our accounts in an analytical language well removed from that of the children themselves. So, on the one hand we produced records (short Flip videos, animations made by the children on the British Library website and the documentary film) the children could easily engage with, and on the other, academic analyses often grounded in claims about the longer histories of play – shifting the play event from the immediacy of its enactment into the long time frames of adult, or more particularly, academic thinking. Such time frames were often of little apparent interest to the children themselves other than within the context of a pedagogically conceived exercise (see Chapter 8). Of course, in the wider corpus of the Opies' work (see Chapter 2), the centrality accorded children's voices in *The People in the Playground* is balanced by a great deal of scholarly historical and folkloric endeavour but Iona Opie's argument, without very obviously making it one, implies that interpretations – and the analyses built on interpretations – are negotiations with children as knowing social actors (see Clifford, 1988). John B. Thompson makes this explicit:

> ... in social inquiry *the object of our investigations is itself a pre-interpreted domain*. The social-historical world is not just an object domain which is there to be observed; it is also a *subject domain* which is made up, in part, of subjects who, in the routine course of their everyday lives, are constantly involved in understanding themselves and others, and in interpreting the actions, utterances and events which take place around them ... The analysts are offering an interpretation of an interpretation, they are re-interpreting a pre-interpreted domain; and it may be important to consider ... just how this re-interpretation is related to, and how it may be informed by, the pre-interpretations which exist (or existed) among the subjects who make up the social-historical world. (Thompson 1990: 275)

In this view, the process of re-presenting play in this book is a lengthy, and (always) unfinished, transaction with the children who participated in the project (and with those other generations represented in the archival material discussed in Chapter 2). Our work of interpretation and analysis does not replace the children's own situated interpretive activity but it re-inflects such activity, re-articulates it through metaphorical strategies other than those of the children themselves, to engage debates around the status and meaning of play largely conducted between adults without the involvement of children.

The 'Ludic Century'?

When the Opies looked back at the work of earlier collectors of children's folklore, they found startling similarities with the cultures they charted as well as striking differences. They noted that of the chants recorded by Norman Douglas in 1916, more than 78 per cent were still sung by the children they studied in 1959 (1959: vi). At the same time, they observed changes in the sources and mechanisms of transmission which seemed to be new, and which anticipated the media cultures of the present day. The best example of accelerated global transmission, perhaps, is their account of the ballad of Davy Crockett, launched on the radio in 1956, and subjected to a near-identical parody within months in sites as far apart as London and Sydney (1959: 7).

We have had a similar experience. When we set our data against the recordings in the Opie Collection, we noted extensive similarities, especially in the genre of musical play; but also in the ways in which children rework, revoice and rehearse material from media sources. At the same time, we observed the differences: the diminishing echoes of long lost cultures; the changing fashions, crazes and preoccupations; the material and economic changes in 'mediascapes' and commercial toys from the 1970s to the present day.

As our categories of cultural rehearsal, ludic bricolage and heterotopian games suggest, then, the age of new media does bring novel affordances and cultural emphases. The forms of participatory creation and critique and near instantaneous distribution characteristic of online culture have extended the 'transworld couriers' employed by the 'schoolchild underground' noted by the Opies (1959: 7). Meanwhile, the ubiquitous culture of the computer game, with its procedural versions of imaginary worlds and its programmed rule systems, feeds back productively into the playground. Unlike other media (which may provide content, imagery, character sets and narratives), games provide ludic systems for exploitation in the playground. Henry Jenkins has suggested that play is a component of the kind of literacy needed for the new media age (2007); while game designer Eric Zimmerman has gone so far as to claim that the twenty-first century is the 'Ludic Century', characterised by playful attitudes to the conventional authorities of language, politics and education (2014). But we should sound a cautionary note: older media forms such as television and film are still dominant in children's cultures; and as we have argued, there are as many continuities with older, even archaic, forms of play as there are innovative departures. Yet it may be true that this is a century less inclined to infantilise play; to recognise that it is not only a preparation for adulthood but a continuing condition of adult culture (Sutton-Smith, 1997); and to see that it has lessons for educators beyond the scope of this volume.[1] We can conclude that in the games, choreographies, music and drama of the playground, the resources for the arts and humanities curriculum are explored and shared, and their complexity challenges us to rethink our inadequate educational templates in a continuing engagement with the cultures of play.

---

[1]   A follow-up project, funded by the Arts and Humanities Research Council, and led by Rebekah Willett, has considered this. Entitled 'Talkin' 'Bout My Generation', the project developed a resource pack of teaching materials for primary schools in collaboration with the Centre for Literacy in Primary Education in London. The pack is available as a downloadable pdf from the Playtimes website: www.bl.uk/playtimes.

References

Back L (2007) *The Art of Listening.* Oxford: Berg.

Beresin AR (2010) *Recess Battles: Playing, Fighting, and Storytelling.* Jackson, MS: University Press of Mississippi.

Burn A (2013) Computer games on the playground: Ludic systems, dramatized narrative and virtual embodiment. In Willett, R, Richards C, Marsh J, Burn A and Bishop JC *Children, Media and Playground Cultures: Ethnographic Studies of School Playtimes.* Basingstoke: Palgrave Macmillan, 120–44.

Clifford J (1988) *The Predicament of Culture: Twentieth-Century Ethnography, Literature, and Art.* Cambridge, MA: Harvard University Press.

Heath SB (1983/1996) *Ways with Words: Language, Life, and Work in Communities and Classrooms.* Cambridge: Cambridge University Press.

Lakoff G and Johnson M (1980) *Metaphors We Live By.* Chicago: University of Chicago Press.

Law J (2004) *After Method: Mess in Social Science Research.* London: Routledge.

Opie I (1993) *The People in the Playground.* Oxford: Oxford University Press.

Opie I and Opie P (1959) *The Lore and Language of Schoolchildren.* Oxford: Oxford University Press.

Richards C (2011) In the thick of it: interpreting children's play. *Ethnography and Education* 6: 309–24.

Richards C (2013) Agonistic scenarios. In Willett R, Richards C, Marsh J, Burn A and Bishop JC *Children, Media and Playground Cultures: Ethnographic Studies of School Playtimes.* Basingstoke: Palgrave Macmillan, 170–95.

Thompson J (1990) *Ideology and Modern Culture: Critical Social Theory in the Era of Mass Communication.* Cambridge: Polity.

Zimmerman E (2014) Manifesto for a ludic century. In Walz, S and Deterding S (eds) *The Gameful World. Approaches, Issues, Applications.* Cambridge, MA: The MIT Press.

Index

'A Sailor Went to Sea, Sea, Sea' 36, 45, 201
Abba 10, 39
actors 96, 145–6, 148
    cultural 154, 156
    social 4, 150, 212
adaptation 139
adolescence 45, 47, 124
adults 9, 19, 20, 22, 65, 88, 90, 93, 99
adversaries 101, 102, 103
advertising 2, 40, 133
affiliations 39, 200, 203
affordances 164–6
age; *see* adolescence; childhood
Age of War 2 111
agency 10, 42
aggression 88
agonistic play 22, 25, 85, 88, 93–103
agonistic scenarios 85, 86, 96–8, 99, 104
Aladdin 139
aliens 144
allegory 211
Alvin and the Chipmunks 15, 138
ambiguity 91
ambiguously referenced play 137, 138–9, 147
America 3, 33, 45, 58, 73, 86, 88
animals 14, 97, 178
animation 7, 17, 23, 40, 160–61, 187, 188, 190, 199, 201
Animazoo 168
anthropology 17, 33
anxieties 4, 10, 12, 92–3, 104–105, 155
Appadurai, Arjun 147
appropriation 156
archives 1, 5, 7, 17, 23–4, 31–35, 36, 37, 39, 48, 49, 187, 194, 203, 207
arranging 189, 203
artefacts 112, 114, 134, 156, 189
assemblies 90, 94
assembling 188, 189, 203

audiences 16–17, 136, 137, 141, 145–9, 201, 202
authority 56, 102
autobiography 86–9, 210
Avatar 125
avatars 23, 164, 176
Avedon, Elliott M 173

babies 109
Back, Les 208, 209, 210
Bakhtin, Mikhail M 48, 55, 56, 57, 78, 149
Bakugan 102
ball games 4, 191
Barbie 111
BarbieGirls 112
Barter, Christine 89n
Barthes, Roland 143, 144
Batman 88, 136
Bauman, Richard 55–6, 79
Bay City Rollers, The 10, 37, 39
Beaker, Tracey 15, 135
Bebo 23
bedrooms 12
Ben 10: Alien Force 96, 134
Ben Hur 88
Bennett, Andy 45
Beresin, Anna 208, 209
Berridge, David 89n
Beyoncé 15, 138, 143, 144
Beyond Text 172
Bin Weevils 112, 113
biography 85–6
Bishop, Julia 2, 4, 14, 16, 17, 18, 19, 23, 38, 45, 53, 59n, 62, 125, 126, 133, 134–5, 135, 136, 159
Blackbeard 98, 146
Blank, Trevor J 17
bodies 7, 115, 160, 161, 164, 170; *see also* embodiment
Bodleian Libraries 5, 31
body moves 62

Boellstorff, Tom 20, 115, 127
books 18, 125, 133, 136, 138, 140, 144,
    147, 155, 156
boredom 210
boundaries 9, 41, 46, 97, 99, 109, 114, 127,
    158, 210
Bourdieu, Pierre 13, 23, 194
boys 12, 19, 20, 22, 88–9, 94, 99–103, 116,
    142
Brice Heath, Shirley 208, 209
bricolage, ludic 17–20, 125, 208
Briggs, Charles L 55–6, 80
Britain's Got Talent 136, 139, 142, 183
British Film Institute 5
British Library 23, 31, 32, 46, 197; *see also*
    Playtimes: A Century of Children's
    Games and Rhymes
  Digital Archive 3
  Sound Archive 1
Buckingham, David 114, 155
buildings, school 89n
bullying 89
Burn, Andrew 1, 31, 62, 92, 114, 125, 126,
    194, 207

Caillois, Roger 18, 25, 172
Call of Duty: Modern Warfare 2 19, 20, 21,
    22, 125, 156, 207
Camp Rock 142
Captain Marvel 136
capturing play 153, 158, 160–61; *see also*
    Game Catcher, The
cartoons 18, 59, 111
cataloguing 189, 203
causality 105
change, continuity and 2, 4, 17, 53, 54–7
chants; *see* clapping games; rhymes;
    singing games
chaos 93n, 144
characters 18, 20, 22, 41, 96, 114, 125,
    133, 135, 136, 137, 138, 139, 140,
    142, 143, 147
chasing games 4, 14, 100, 102, 103, 135,
    140
childhood
  and agency 10, 42
  as generational unit 12
  migrant 11
  and structure 13, 24

temporalities of 13
toxic 10
tribal 10, 34, 47
childlore 10, 190
Christopher Hatton Primary School 4, 111,
    125, 126, 207
Circuit of Culture 156
Cisco Kid 136
clapping games 4, 7, 14, 15, 16, 17, 18, 41,
    43, 53–84, 135, 141, 162, 192; *see*
    also rhymes
  'Eeny Meeny Dessameeny' 53, 59,
    60–80, 83–4, 160
  'When Susie Was a Baby' 15, 41
class, social 11–12
closely imitative play 137–8
Club Penguin 23, 111, 112, 113, 114, 124,
    125, 127
collecting 113, 188, 189, 203
combat 88, 95, 96, 99, 100, 101–103, 136
commercial enculturation 113
commercialism 9, 57, 65, 113–14, 213
common sense 91, 92
community of practice 91, 167
computer games 2, 4, 8, 16, 18, 20,
    99, 104, 110, 125, 126, 154–6,
    207, 208, 213; *see also Game*
    Catcher, The; videogames; specific
    computer games
conduct 90, 91
conflict 90, 96, 100, 101–102, 104
Conkers 4, 200–201
consumption 113, 134, 155–6
continuity, change and 2, 4, 17, 53, 54–7
control 9, 45–6, 58, 76, 91, 93, 102, 126,
    177, 189, 204, 211
controversy 85
conviviality 102
Cook, Daniel 113
cooperation 90
Cops and Robbers 140, 144
Coram's Fields, London 25, 33, 35, 38
Corsaro, William 18, 22, 154
counting-out rhymes 4
cowboys 139
'Crackerjack, Crackerjack' 35
creativity 14, 18, 42, 45, 56, 57, 158; *see*
    also imagination
crime 94

Cross, Beth 153
cultural rehearsal 14–17, 39, 54, 66, 208
cultural studies 2, 18, 33, 47
curation 17, 23, 187–204
    as arranging 189, 203
    as assembling 188, 189, 203
    as cataloguing 189, 203
    as collecting 188, 189, 203
    as design 187–8, 189, 199, 201
    as exhibition 189–90
    as heterotopian 194
    as historicizing 194, 199, 200, 204
    as interpretation 189
    as intertextual 189, 203
    as literacy 188, 199, 202
    as memory 201
    as multimodal 203
    as preservation 201
    self-curatorship 188
Curtis, Mavis 16, 42–3, 126

Daily Express, The 10
damage 91, 94
Dance Dance Revolution 162
danger 12, 93, 94, 99, 100, 103
Davies, Char 176
Davy Crockett: King of the Wild Frontier
    86–8, 213
death 20, 97
Deleuze, Gilles 15
dialogism 55
digital culture 188, 189
discipline 89
discourses 7, 11, 55–6, 113, 114, 127, 134,
    148
dispositions 13, 23, 88, 188, 195
dissonance 85
Dixon, Shanly 20
Doctor Who 111, 194
documentary 1, 8–9, 153
domains 45, 97, 109, 127, 157, 160, 181,
    212
domestic play 4, 97
domination 148
Douglas, Norman 213
drama 2, 20, 100, 213; *see also*
    sociodramatic play
Du Gay, Paul 156
Dungeons and Dragons 18

Dusty Bluebells, The 8
Dyson, Anne Haas 140

East Asia 98
Edmiston, Brian 96
'Eeny Meeny Dessameeny' 53, 59, 60–80,
    83–4, 160
    learning 60–68
    as mimetic dance 75–6
    movement changes to 73–5
    musical changes to 76–8
    teaching 60–68
    textual changes to 68–73
    variation in 68–75, 76–80
eighteenth century 57
embodied history 13
embodiment 21, 126, 154, 158, 164, 182,
    183
emotion 103, 118, 128, 210
energy 90
England 3, 33, 58
entrainment 62
ethical procedures 169
ethnicities 11
ethnography 3–4, 9
Evony 111
exclusion
    and friendship 109–28
    social 48, 117, 119, 120, 127
exhibition 5, 17, 23, 189, 199, 203

Facebook 23
fairies 135, 139, 147
families 4, 9, 21, 93, 109, 133
fantasy 4, 14, 85, 86, 94, 97, 98, 100, 104,
    112, 124
fantasy engagement 104
Farmville 111
femininity 148
fiction; *see* books
fighting 12, 22, 85–105, 104
film 4, 11, 16, 17, 37, 40, 57, 62, 63,
    68–70, 99, 100, 104, 111, 125, 136,
    140, 144, 146, 147, 153, 154, 155,
    156, 213; *see also* specific films
first person shooter (FPS) 157
folklore 2, 14, 16, 54–7
folklore studies 2, 10, 14, 15, 33, 35, 53,
    54, 158, 159

folksongs 10, 18, 45
football 91, 101, 102, 134, 135, 136
forms 20, 53, 55, 85, 89, 104, 133, 134,
  135, 136, 138–9, 145, 156, 189
Foucault, Michel 20, 22, 23, 24, 92, 187, 194
framing 193
French skipping 4
friendship
  and exclusion 109–28
  offline 115–24
  online 115–24
function 41, 47, 55, 133, 134, 140, 143,
  145, 148

Game Catcher, The 7–8, 153–83
  aims of 156–61
  design issues 161–68
  development 170–72
  findings 180–81
  implementation of 168–72
  methodology 168–9
  testing 172–9
games; *see* clapping games; computer
  games; rhymes; singing games;
  skipping games; specific games
  ball 4
  catching 135
  chasing 4, 14, 100, 102, 103, 135, 140
  fighting 22
  guessing 136
  heterotopian 20–24, 125
  kiss-chase 14, 135
  running around 192
  street 1, 8, 10
  with things 192
gangs 33, 93, 94
Geertz, Clifford 103
gender 99–103, 104, 116, 148, 200; *see
  also* boys; girls
genies 139
gestures 21, 35, 60, 62, 65, 73, 74, 76, 78,
  134, 135, 137, 138, 159–60, 168
ghosts 19, 139
Gibson, J. J. 164
Gilbert, Barry 113
Gilroy, Paul 85–6, 88, 104
girls 38, 53, 59–64, 68, 76, 97, 102–103,
  116, 138, 145–9
Glitter, Gary 10, 39, 40

Goffman, Erving 141–2
Gogo's Crazy Bones 111
Grace, Donna 136
Grand Theft Auto 20
Grayson, Larry 37
'The Green Balloon Club' 137, 143, 144
Grugeon, Elizabeth 159
guessing games 136
Guest, Ann Hutchinson 159
Guitar Hero 19
guns 19, 86, 94, 95, 97, 98, 100, 103, 146,
  148

Habbo Hotel 23, 112, 124
habitus 13, 23
Half Life 2 157
Hammond, David 8
handshake, personal 62
Hannah Montana 111
happiness 93
Harry Potter 15, 18, 136, 140, 141
Hebdige, Dick 18
heterotopian games 20–24, 187, 194, 208
heterotopias 92
hide-and-seek 124
hiding 99
High School Musical 142, 146, 147
histories 2, 5, 9, 12–13, 14, 23, 24, 35, 86,
  137, 147, 194, 199, 200, 204, 212
Hobsbawm, Eric 24
Holland, Patricia 92–4
Holland, Penny 95
Holmes, Mary 118, 123
homophily 124
homosocial 102
Honko, Lauri 14, 54–5, 73
Hopscotch 4, 16
Horrible Histories 98, 146, 148
Horvath, William J 115
Hotel Management 126
Huizinga, Johan 19, 172
Hurd, Michael 34, 36, 42n, 43
hybrid/recontextualized mimesis 136, 137,
  138, 139–40, 142, 147
hybridity 15, 22, 40, 126, 144; *see also*
  hybrid/recontextualized mimesis

idealization 48, 90, 101
identity 2, 25, 126, 141

Imaginary Tennis 18–19
imagination 24, 45, 145; *see also* creativity
inclusivity 147–8
information value 193
innovation 17
Internet 62, 109–12, 113, 118, 119, 121,
    155; *see also Playtimes: A Century
    of Children's Games and Rhymes*;
    YouTube
interpretation 7, 8, 47, 144, 146, 147, 149,
    161, 164, 188, 189, 190, 201, 203,
    210, 212
intertextual gap 55–7, 68, 71, 72, 76, 78, 79
intertextuality 189, 203, 212
interviews 4, 7, 8, 19, 33, 37, 59, 94, 97,
    98–9, 100, 115, 117, 120, 121,
    146, 147, 156, 168, 169, 172, 194,
    195, 199
intrusion 98, 103
Ipi-dipi-dation, My Generation
    (documentary film) 8–9, 153
It; *see* Tig
iterative models 169
Ito, Mizuko 133
Ivanhoe 136

Jackson, Michael 16, 25, 39, 40
James, Allison 10, 13, 15, 34, 47
Japanese 95
Jenkins, Henry 17, 155, 213
Jenks, Chris 10, 13, 15, 34, 47
Jeremy Kyle Show, The 136, 139, 141
Jesus Christ Superstar 135
Jewitt, Carey 163, 167
jokes 192
Jopson, Laura 14, 16, 22, 31
jouissance 144
Juul, Jesper 173

karate 22, 98, 179
Kelly-Byrne, Diana 48, 90–91, 92, 93,
    101, 103
Kinect 21–22, 170, 174, 179
kineikonic 203
kiss-chase 14, 135
knives 98, 146, 148
Knock-Down Ginger 12
knowing 209–12
knowledge, tacit 17, 95, 194, 199

Kress, Gunther 163, 167
kung fu 179
Kung Fu 37–8

language 12, 14, 16, 18, 24, 35, 133, 203, 212
    native 4, 11
    variation in 17, 42, 49, 69–73
laughter 48, 146
Lauwaert, Maaike 114
Law, John 209–10, 211
Leach, Edmund 33
learner voice 188
learning 16, 54, 56, 59, 60–69, 76, 80, 89,
    90, 167
Leman, Marc 65
libraries 22, 187, 194; *see also* British
    Library
    Bodleian 5, 31
Lie, Bjorn Rune 187
literacy 23, 178, 182, 188, 199, 202, 213
literature 14; *see also* books
Lone Ranger, The 136
longitudinal study 208
ludic bricolage 17–20, 125, 208
'The Ludic Century' 212–13
Lundy, Laura 169

magic circle 19
Malpas, Jeff 115
Mamma Mia 39, 142
Man from U.N.C.L.E., The 88, 136
Mario Brothers 111
Mario Kart 156, 157
Marsh, Jackie 4, 11, 21, 109
Marsh, Kathryn 2, 3, 15, 38, 57–8, 63,
    64–5, 66, 69, 76, 79
martial arts 16, 98, 102, 179
masculinity 142, 148
Massively Multiplayer Online Games
    (MMOGs) 110, 111, 112, 124
Match Attax 102
Matrix, The 155n
Maybin, Janet 55, 62
McEvoy, Lesley 169
McNamee, Sara 20
meaning 12, 18, 34, 55, 85, 135, 144, 149,
    156, 163, 164, 189, 199, 203, 212
media; *see* computer games; film; Internet;
    television

cultures 37–42, 57–60
    effects of 155
    fears of 109, 118, 155
    remixes 18, 133–50
media source 144
mediascapes 133, 134, 138, 147
memory 201
merchandise 86, 88, 127, 133
Merleau-Ponty, Maurice 14
metaphor 7, 17, 20–21, 22–3, 56, 212
Meyers, Eric 112
'Michelle, Michelle' 35
micro-histories 13
Miller, Daniel 189
mimesis 19, 38, 135, 136, 137–9, 144
mimetic dances 75–6
Mister Maker 111
Mitchell, Grethe 7, 8, 21, 153, 157–8
MMOGs; *see* Massively Multiplayer
    Online Games (MMOGs)
modal affordance 164
modal transduction 163
modality 24, 91, 95, 97, 99
modes 163
monitoring 88, 90
Monroe, Marilyn 135
monsters 16, 24
Monteney Primary School 3–4, 58, 109,
    110, 124, 125, 126, 127
moral panic 105, 113
Moshi Monsters 111, 112, 113
motion capture 160–61, 170–72
motion tracking 168, 170
movement 17, 21, 24, 36, 134; *see also*
    clapping games; gestures
    -based activities 7–8, 21
    embodied 21, 154, 158, 159–61, 162,
        165, 170–71, 182, 183
    between realities 211
movies; *see* film
multimodality 16, 41, 53, 163–4, 167
mundane 207
museums 22, 187
music 17, 18, 24, 53, 147, 163, 213; *see*
        also clapping games; musicals; pop
        music; rhymes; singing games; songs
    change in 76–8
    media culture interaction with 57–8,
        76–8, 134

mimesis in 38, 135, 137–8
musical chairs 124
musicals 4, 39, 136, 142, 146, 147

narratives 14, 16, 49, 86, 96, 99, 101, 125,
    127, 133, 136–7, 139, 140
nature 24
Neopet 112
new media 2, 16, 17, 25, 66, 188–190, 199,
    202, 208, 213
Newkirk, Thomas 101
nineteenth century 10, 11, 43
noise 100, 134, 146; *see also* music
Norman, David 164, 167
nursery rhymes 10, 45

objects of play 9, 14, 16, 24, 45, 114,
    133–4, 142, 145, 165, 178
offline
    friendships 116, 117, 121, 127
    play 65–6, 80, 114–15, 124–6, 127
offline transmission 53, 60, 65–6, 67–8, 80
One Potato, Two Potato 8
Ong, Walter 15–16, 17
online activities; *see* computer games;
        virtual worlds
    children involvement with 109–11
online transmission 60–64; *see also*
        YouTube
onomastic allusion 18, 41, 125, 134, 135,
    137
Opie, Peter and Iona 1, 2, 5, 9, 11, 15, 16,
    23, 25, 31, 34, 35, 46–7, 48, 56, 57,
    75, 86, 88, 111, 135, 136, 138, 140,
    194–5, 209, 210, 213
    'Children's Calendar' 13
    and multimodality 35
    and pop songs 38–40
    research collaborations 32, 34, 36
    research process 32–6
    and slow research 208
    surveys 32
    and television 37–8, 40
    works
        *Children's Games in Street and
            Playground* 133, 139, 153
        *Lore and Language of
            Schoolchildren, The* 24, 32, 33,
            35, 208, 210

Opie Collection of Children's Games and Songs, The 3, 9, 10, 31

People in the Playground, The 32, 153, 207, 210–12

Singing Game, The 4, 14, 25, 31, 32, 34, 35, 36, 37, 39, 40, 42, 43, 46, 49

Opportunity Knocks 38

oral formulaic composition 15, 57

oral tradition 37–42

oral transmission 15–16, 17, 37, 43, 54

order 93, 96

organic variation 14, 54

original text 144, 145, 147

originality 144–5

Østberg, Berit 32, 34

Oxford, University of 5

paidea 18

paradox 12, 15, 101

parody 135, 136, 139

participants 91, 96

participatory design 188

participatory performance 17

participatory research 188

participatory web 55

Pelletier, Caroline 102n

performance 14, 15, 16–17, 38–41, 45, 46, 55, 58, 60–64, 66, 68–74, 78–9, 96, 136, 137, 138, 139, 141–3, 144, 146–7, 148–9, 202

performativity 1, 136, 141–2, 148, 208

photographs 5, 8, 11, 23, 32, 182

physicality 168

Pimkin 20

pirates 98, 146, 148

Pirates of the Caribbean 98

Pitt Rivers Museum 5, 32

Pixie Hollow 114

plaisir 144

play
  agonistic 22, 25, 85, 88, 93–103
  ambiguous 14, 137, 138–9, 147
  deep 103
  domestic 4, 97
  embodied 21, 126, 144, 158, 162, 163–5, 182
  fantasy 4, 14, 85, 86, 94, 97, 98, 100, 104, 112, 124

-fighting 12, 85–105, 94–9, 104

folkloric 39, 126

and gender 99–103

geography of 114

idealization of 48, 90, 101

as ludic 17–20, 21–22, 47, 125, 213

media-referenced 133–50, 210

mimetic 19, 38, 75–6, 135, 136, 137–9, 144

musical; *see* clapping games; music; songs

narrative 14, 16, 86, 96, 99, 101, 125, 127, 133, 136–7, 139, 140

offline 65–6, 80, 114–15, 124–6, 127

online 109–11; *see also* computer games; virtual worlds

as paidea 18

performative 16

phantasmagoric 25, 144, 148

pretend 2, 4, 91, 95–100, 104, 126, 136, 139, 145–9, 178, 192, 210

progressive 178

role 141

rough 12, 85–105

with rules 124

scatological 46–9

sexual 22, 35, 46–9, 211

sociodramatic 21, 46, 112, 124, 141, 148

street 9, 12

transgressive 11–12, 22, 31, 37–8, 47, 48

virtual 21, 162, 163–8, 182–3

playability 165

playgrounds 12, 24, 89–92

Playtimes: A Century of Children's Games and Rhymes 5–7, 169, 187–204, 207

  Browse Games 187

  Kids' Zone 187, 190–201

pleasure 21–22, 25, 46, 92, 99, 109, 136, 143–4

points of view 65, 182

Pokéman 102, 155n, 156

policy, school 95

Pong 155n

pop music 2, 4, 37–41, 43, 57, 75, 134, 135, 137–8, 142, 156

portals 24, 187

positions 78, 102, 103, 104

Potter, John 7, 17, 23, 187
power 8, 48, 90–91, 101, 104, 136, 141,
        148, 149, 150
Power Rangers 94, 99
practices 2, 9, 10, 14, 16, 17, 18, 23, 39,
        66, 73, 80, 109, 113–14, 123, 124,
        125, 126, 127, 133, 134, 136–42,
        144–5, 147–9, 188, 199, 200, 202
presentational performance 17
Presley, Elvis 15
pretence 96, 99, 141, 144, 148–9
pretend play 2, 4, 91, 95–100, 104, 126,
        136, 139, 145–9, 178, 192, 210
princesses 139, 147
Prout, Alan 10, 13, 15, 34, 47
provocation 88, 103
proximity 142–4
Pugh, Allison J 68, 72, 113–14
Punch, Samantha 169

queens 135, 147

race 85
Rapoport, Anatol 115
Rawhide 88
readerly texts 144, 149
reading 134
reality 24, 91, 96, 211
reality television 4, 141
reflexivity 118, 128
regulation 12, 19, 20, 22, 89
rehearsal, cultural; *see* cultural rehearsal
remixes 18, 133–50
        case study 145–9
        hybrid/recontextualised mimesis
            139–40
repetition 15–16
representation 17, 187, 190, 199, 201–202
residual culture 15
resource 189, 194, 203
revoicings 56
rhetoric 145, 155
rhetoric of progress 155
rhymes 2, 4, 9, 11, 14, 18; *see also*
        clapping games; singing games;
        songs
    clapping 53, 135, 158–9, 160
    counting-out 4, 57, 192
    nursery 10, 45, 57

scatological 36, 46–9, 192
Richards, Chris 4, 12, 20, 22, 24, 48, 56,
        85, 134, 136n, 150, 207, 210
Ring-a-Ring-a-Rosie 149
risk 92–4, 99, 103
Robin Hood 88, 136
Robinson, Jonathan 31
role-play 18, 25, 141
'Rosy apples, lemon & a pear' 5
Roud, Steve 13, 194, 199
rule-systems 2, 18, 19–20, 143, 213
rules 10, 19, 89–90, 91, 100, 124, 139, 143,
        208
Runescape 111, 112, 113

Sacred Seasons 111
safety 89, 90
St. Benedict's Roman Catholic Primary
        School 32
Saint, The 15, 41
salience 193
scenarios 4, 20, 85, 86, 96–8, 99, 104
schooling 11, 93, 105
schools; *see* Christopher Hatton Primary
        School; Monteney Primary School;
        playgrounds; St. Benedict's Roman
        Catholic Primary School
screaming 100, 102, 146, 148–9
Second Life 112
secrecy 101
sedimentation 14, 17
semiodic modes 163
semiotic systems 127
Sesame Street 66n
sexual play 22, 35, 46–9, 211
sexuality 10, 22, 47, 138
shared virtual environments 112
Shaw, Sandie 37, 137
Shut That Door! 37
signification 41, 144, 163
Silver Sword, The 88
Simpsons 111
Sims, The 21
singing games 32, 138, 192; *see also*
        rhymes
    'A Sailor Went to Sea, Sea, Sea' 36,
        45, 201
    'Under the Bram Bush' 42–5
Singing Street, The 8

sites for play 12
skipping games 4, 18, 38, 39, 57, 192, 200
Smith, Peter K. 90
social class 11–12
social exclusion 48, 117, 119, 120, 127
social relationships 90, 104, 113, 116, 126
socialisation 2, 10, 113
sociodramatic play 21, 46, 112, 124, 141, 148
sociographs 115–17, 120
sociology of childhood 10, 34, 36, 47, 169
songs 10, 11, 25, 31–5, 37–41, 136; *see also* clapping games; music; pop music; rhymes; singing games
   scatological 46
   variation in 4, 42–5, 63, 68–73, 76–80
Sound of Music 142
soundtracks 10
Spiderman 25
spies 139
Spina, Stephanie 104
Stallybrass, Peter 11, 48
Star Wars 20, 94, 96
Stepney Green 11, 34
storytelling 76, 155
street dance 142
street games 1, 8, 10
street play 9, 12
structures 2, 14, 15, 16, 18, 19–20, 46, 125, 139–40, 178
Super Mario 111
superheroes 18, 133, 141
Superman 88, 136
supervision 4, 99–100
surveillance 88, 90
surveys 4
Sutton-Smith, Brian 25, 40, 47, 48, 90–91, 92, 93, 96, 97–8, 101, 103, 134, 143, 144, 145, 149, 155, 173, 211
syncretism 18, 134, 135–6

Tae kwon do 98, 102
Taekwondo 137
Tag; *see* Tig
talk 55, 97, 98, 127, 212
teachers 19, 32, 90, 91, 98–9, 104
teaching 54, 58, 59, 60–68
teams 100, 101
technologies 9, 10, 25, 109, 114, 127, 155

Teenage Mutant Ninja Turtles 99
Tekken 156
television 4, 12, 18, 37, 40–41, 59, 64, 66, 97–8, 104, 111, 125, 138, 139, 141, 144, 153, 154, 155, 156, 213; *see also* specific television programs
texts 14, 134, 135, 139–40
   original 144, 145, 147
   readerly 144, 149
   writerly 144, 147, 149, 150
Thompson, John B 212
3-D visualisation of play 25, 145–9
Tig 14, 15, 18, 19, 22, 125, 127, 140, 199
time 13, 22–3, 209
Tobin, Joseph 136
tradition 8, 15, 34, 37–42, 188
transcription of games 153, 158, 160–61
transduction 163–4
transformation 56, 153, 163
transgression 11–12, 22, 31, 37–8, 47, 48
translation 163
transmission 58, 135, 153, 158, 168, 213
   offline 53, 60, 65–6, 67–8, 80
   online 60–64; *see also* YouTube
   oral 15–16, 17, 37, 43, 54
Trick-or-Treating 12
Turino, Thomas 17
TV; *see* television
twentieth century 1, 5, 9, 10, 12, 23, 24, 43, 155
twenty-first century 11, 12, 14, 20, 25, 40, 49, 112, 153, 155, 209, 213

UN Convention on the Rights of the Child 13
'Under the Bram Bush' 42–5
University of Oxford 5

variation 15–16, 54–7
   in 'Eeny Meeny Dessameeny' 68–75
   in movement patterns 73–5
   organic 14, 54
   real 54
   and social context 42–6
   in verbal text 68–73
Vicon 168
videogames 20, 104, 136, 137, 138, 140, 144, 153, 154, 155, 157; *see also* computer games; *Game Catcher, The*; specific videogames

violence 85, 88, 89n, 95, 104–105
virtual play 21, 162, 163–8, 182–3
virtual worlds 20, 110, 111, 124, 127; *see*
    also computer games; specific
    games
    children's use of 112–15
vulnerability of children 10
Vygotsky, Lev 45

war 85–6, 88, 94, 100–101, 137
weapons; *see* guns; knives
weather 165
Webb, Father Damian 5, 11, 32, 34, 36, 211
Webkinz 112
websites 110–11, 113; *see also* Internet;
    Playtimes: A Century of Children's
    Games and Rhymes; YouTube
West, American 86, 88
'When Susie Was a Baby' 15, 41
White, Allen 169
White, Allon 11, 48
Who Wants to be a Millionaire 136
Widdowson, J 15
Wii 21–22, 25, 155, 162
Wiimotes 21, 166, 168, 170

Willett, Rebekah 4, 14, 15, 18, 39, 97, 111,
    126, 133
William Tell 88
Williams, Raymond 15
Winter, Peter 113
Wiseman, Frederick 8
witches 133, 135, 139, 147
Wombles, The 40
World of Warcraft 112, 113
World War II 85–6, 88
wrestling 22, 88, 91, 101–102, 179
writerly texts 144, 147, 149, 150

X Factor, The 136, 141, 149, 183
X-Men 134

YouTube 16, 17, 23, 54, 77, 110
    clapping games on 57–60
    learning from 60–68
    teaching from 60–68

Zavaroni, Lena 10, 38, 39
Zimmerman, Eric 213
zombies 18, 19, 135, 139, 144